STATE OF NEW YORK

PROGRESS REPORT

New York, New Jersey Port and Harbor Development Commission

Appointed under Chapter 426, Laws of 1917, State of New York

Appointed under Chapter 130, Laws of 1917, State of New Jersey

WILLIAM R. WILLCOX, Chairman
EUGENE H. OUTERBRIDGE

GEORGE W. GOETHALS
Chief Consulting Engineer

JULIUS HENRY COHEN, Counsel

J. SPENCER SMITH, Vice-Chairman
DE WITT VAN BUSKIRK
FRANK R. FORD

WILLIAM LEARY, Secretary
B. F. CRESSON, Jr., Consulting Engineer
C. A. RUHLMANN, Asst. Secretary

ALBANY
J. B. LYON COMPANY, PRINTERS
1919

318

Legislative Document No. 103

STATE OF NEW YORK

PROGRESS REPORT

New York, New Jersey Port and Harbor Development Commission

Appointed under Chapter 426, Laws of 1917, State of New York
Appointed under Chapter 130, Laws of 1917, State of New Jersey

WILLIAM R. WILLCOX, Chairman
EUGENE H. OUTERBRIDGE
GEORGE W. GOETHALS
Chief Consulting Engineer
JULIUS HENRY COHEN, Counsel
J. SPENCER SMITH, Vice-Chairman
DE WITT VAN BUSKIRK
FRANK R. FORD
WILLIAM LEARY, Secretary
B. F. CRESSON, Jr., Consulting Engineer
C. A. RUHLMANN, Asst. Secretary

ALBANY
J. B. LYON COMPANY, PRINTERS
1919

STATE OF NEW YORK

EXECUTIVE CHAMBER,

APRIL 14, 1919.

To the Legislature:

I have the honor to transmit to you herewith the Progress Report of the New York, New Jersey Port and Harbor Development Commission.

ALFRED E. SMITH.

PROGRESS REPORT

NEW YORK, *April* 8, 1919.

To HON. ALFRED E. SMITH,
Governor of the State of New York;

HON. WALTER E. EDGE,
Governor of the State of New Jersey.

DEAR SIRS.— Two years ago the Legislatures and Governors of New York and New Jersey made possible a joint study of the Port of New York by the creation of the New York, New Jersey Port and Harbor Development Commission. It was recognized then that the development of the Port was the concern of all of both States, serving as it does as an outlet for so much of the trade of the two States, and supplying so many of the necessities of life. It was seen, too, that the old method of development, with each of some fifty municipalities striving to solve the problems of the Port in its own way or utterly disregarding the fact that it had any place or part in solving the problems of the Port, was failing utterly.

Blessed with the finest harbor on the Atlantic seaboard, and an abundance of trunk-line railroads, the communities have grown by leaps and bounds, and the Port of New York has long handled substantially half the foreign commerce of the country. But the trade of these communities, coming faster, almost, than it could be assimilated, has been accommodated in accordance with the immediate need, without any general direction. Haphazard facilities and methods have become institutions, as have makeshifts built around them to meet new contingencies. The result is patchwork. Obviously this has prevented the best use being made of the natural advantages of the Port.

At the same time the Port as a whole has long suffered the handicap of a differential freight rate in favor of other ports. In recent years, too, the other ports have launched a campaign to get more of New York's business. The combination of circumstances has been effective, and New York's commerce has begun to slip away. And while this slipping away is slow at present, there are unmistakable indications that the campaign of the other ports has just begun.

It is not merely a local misfortune that this condition has come about. New York has become the established gateway between the United States and foreign countries. Now of all times, when the nation has the opportunity to win a much larger share of the world's commerce, when the world has greater need than ever before for what we can give it from our boundless resources, there should be no disorganizing of established trade routes such as would follow further diversion of trade to other ports. It is to be hoped that our foreign trade will soon tax the capacity of the facilities at all of our ports. Certainly neither New York, New Jersey nor the country at large can afford to permit New York to fall behind and see her trade drawn from its natural channel.

The New York, New Jersey Port and Harbor Development Commission, created to study the needs of the Port as a whole, is deeply impressed with its responsibility — that of devising a plan that will meet the present situation and provide liberally for future trade. It has already assembled a large amount of data. The task of determining the volume, method of handling and cost thereof of all traffic coming to, originating in or passing through the Port, which is the first phase of the investigation, is 70 per cent completed, and the analysis to date seems to point to certain definite conclusions. The Commission refrains from presenting those conclusions because data yet to come may modify them, because all of the elements of the final plan and recommendations must dovetail and because with the recommendations must be proof of their economic soundness. Within a few months the Commission expects to have the complete picture and analysis of existing conditions. It can then concentrate on what it has in fact already begun, the development of the final plan, and a year from now the final report should be completed.

The Commission has felt that whatever plan is evolved there must be provision made for supervising and directing the execution of the plan. Hence the Commission prepared and urged upon Your Excellencies and the leaders of the two Legislatures early this year the adoption of a supplementary and amendatory compact between the two States creating a permanent "Port of New York District" and "Port of New York Authority." Owing to obstacles that have arisen legislative action has as you are aware been deferred until next year. The matter is reviewed at some length beginning page 39.

REVIEW OF 1918 REPORT

Facts as to the organization of the Commission are set forth in the Preliminary Joint Report, dated January 26, 1918, and transmitted to the Legislatures of New York and New Jersey February 18, 1918.

This report recites how the Commissions, of three members each, appointed in 1917 by the Governors of New York and New Jersey respectively, have organized a joint commission, the chairman being a member of the New York Commission and the vice-chairman a member of the New Jersey Commission — the purpose of the investigation, as set forth by the acts of the two Legislatures, being to make an "investigation of the Port conditions at the Port of New York and to submit a comprehensive report recommending the proper policy that shall be pursued for the best interests of the entire Port of New York, and the legislation, State and Federal, that will be necessary to make such recommendations effective."

The report of a year ago relates how the Joint Commission held meetings and conferences in 1917 with members of the Public Service Commission of New York, the Port and Terminal Facilities Committee of the Board of Estimate and Apportionment and the Commissioner of Docks of New York City, the New Jersey Board of Commerce and Navigation, the New York State Barge Canal Board, the presidents of the trunk-line railroads and various representatives of shipping, lighterage and warehouse businesses, together with engineering and legal experts of this and other ports.

It tells of inspections of the harbor, of studies of the West Side railroad terminal problem in Manhattan, of the organization at the Commission's suggestion of the War Board for the Port of New York, of other co-operation with the Federal Government.

A decision of the Interstate Commerce Commission in the New York Harbor case is referred to, wherein that body states that "historically, geographically and commercially New York and the industrial districts in the northern part of the State of New Jersey constitute a single community," and commends the creation of this Joint Commission.

The report bounds that single community by Yonkers and New Rochelle on the north, Great Neck and Far Rockaway on the east, Perth Amboy and Sandy Hook on the south, Paterson, Newark and New Brunswick on the west.

Necessity for Port Plan

Emphasis is laid in the report on the necessity for a definite Port policy and plan, with such comparison between the present methods of operation and whatever new methods may be recommended as will afford proof of the economic soundness of the plan and methods recommended.

Many studies and reports on phases of the problem have been made, as the Commission stated in its 1918 report, and the Commission promised to give them careful consideration. At the same time it pointed out that there is a great diversity of interests involved extending into two States and about fifty municipalities, that no comprehensive plan for the entire metropolitan district has ever been made, and that none of the studies and reports referred to have been supported by evidence, statistics or exact analysis of income, cost of operation and net return on the proposed investment in order to justify their economic soundness.

The Commission stated, in its 1918 report, its purpose to ascertain the volume, route, classification and time of transit of all freight movements in the metropolitan district, together with the cost of handling this freight under normal conditions and with existing facilities. This, it stated, would require detail consideration of many factors and a complete survey on the ground for an extended period of the principal lines of rail and water deliveries.

To arrive at the carrying charges of the present capital investment and of the new capital required for additional facilities, the Commission pointed out that an approximate appraisal of the value of existing facilities would be necessary. Such a valuation, it was noted, would have to be available sooner or later if the States should determine that the harbor waterfront was to be publicly owned.

In addition to the preparation of the engineering, operating and financial plans, the report contended that there must be prepared a legal plan for combining the present distributed Federal, State and local powers of administration and construction.

Extent of Investigation

Finally, the report stated that it would take two years to complete the study, at an estimated cost of $400,000. The specific recommendations of the Commission were "that the study contemplated in the legislation creating the Commission and outlined in this report be undertaken, and the report prepared, and to that end the two States of New York and New Jersey appropriate $400,000 in equal payments covering a period of two years."

The Legislatures, recognizing the importance of studying and preparing a plan and policy for the Port of New York, appropriated $100,000 each to cover half of the program. Both appropriations became available July 1, 1918.

In its pursuit of the investigation the Commission has found no reason to revise the estimate of a year ago as to the scope of the work, its probable cost and its probable duration. The problem met in the detail execution of the analysis, the difficulties to be overcome, the inevitable delays, have proved about as forecast in the 1918 report. Progress to date indicates that with the remaining $200,000 made available the Commission will have its final report and recommendations completed within the two-year period, so that it may be laid before the Legislatures a year from now.

Meanwhile the Commission has worked out a definite program for the investigation, has built up an engineering organization of about seventy persons, since funds therefor became available in July, 1918, and has already accumulated a mass of important data bearing upon the present operating conditions at the Port. The Commission does not deem it wise to make definite recommendations at this time relative to any specific problems, believing it best to have the complete picture of existing conditions so that all changes proposed may be co-ordinated. But it has recognized the urgency of some of the problems, has given them special attention, and believes it sees now where the solutions lie.

Arthur Curtiss James, one of the New York members of the Commission, resigned December 31, 1918. Up to that time he took an active part in the work of the Commission, and his fellow members take this occasion to express their sincere appreciation of his interest and co-operation, and their regret that they no longer have the benefit of his judgment in the matters that come before them. His place has not yet been filled.

ENGINEERING INVESTIGATION

On April 30, 1918, in the absence of Major-General George W. Goethals, chief consulting engineer of the Commission, the consulting engineer was placed in charge of the engineering work.

About June 1, 1918, the Commission rented the eleventh floor of the building at 12-16 John street, New York, as its working engineer office.

The engineering investigation resolved itself into three phases:

1. Study of existing conditions.
2. Analysis of the handling of commerce under existing conditions.
3. Planning of new methods and facilities.

Phases 1 and 2 are being worked out together. As previously stated, it is felt that a full knowledge of existing conditions and costs is essential to the rational planning of changes.

Investigation of existing conditions divides the problem into four major headings — railroads, steamship, lighterage, and trucking. In addition there are numerous incidental elements in the problem, some of them, such as the matter of markets and food distribution, being of the highest importance.

Organization of Work

Originally the Commission intended to employ outside engineering organizations to conduct the investigations, so as to obtain as nearly as possible a simultaneous picture of all of the operations of the Port. But it was perceived that this would require a large number of men and entail great difficulty in instructing them. To get the railroad picture alone, for example, would have taken about one thousand men. Hence the consulting engineer recommended that he be authorized to organize a force to do this work himself and his recommendation was accepted.

An experienced railroad man was obtained on leave of absence for the period of the investigation, and was put in charge of the main investigating force, with the title of railroad engineer. A force of twenty-four men was assembled quickly and divided into three squads of eight men each. On July 23, 1918, they began taking twenty-four-hour or twelve-hour observations of the railroad operations at all yards and pier stations. This force, which was subsequently increased, completed its railroad observations early this year. It was then divided up, the two sections starting the steamship and the trucking investigation simultaneously. An advantage of the continuing force was that it became increasingly familiar with the character of information needed and much time that would have been required for instructing four individual organizations was saved. The steamship field work has been virtually completed, a smaller force can complete the trucking and lighterage investigations,— the latter being covered in large measure by the railroad survey — and therefore on April 1 the field force was materially reduced.

Specialists in their line have meanwhile been employed for the incidental studies. For assembling auxiliary data, interpreting the information collected and preparing this and other reports a staff of accountants and statisticians has been assembled. There has been developed the beginning of a drafting department which will be expanded when the time arrives to work out a general plan for the Port.

On March 1 there were sixty-nine members of the engineering organization, including stenographers, clerks and other assistants. On April 1 this number was reduced to forty-seven.

Four Major Investigations

Railroads.— Twelve trunk line railroads are involved in the railroad investigation. They are the Central of New Jersey, the Lehigh Valley, the Erie, the Delaware, Lackawanna & Western, the Pennsylvania, the West Shore and the New York, Ontario & Western (the latter having traffic rights on the West Shore) on the New Jersey shore of the Hudson River, the Baltimore & Ohio on Staten Island, the New York Central on the west side of Manhattan, the New York, New Haven & Hartford in the Bronx, the Long Island in Long Island City, and the Philadelphia & Reading, which has a coal terminal at Port Reading, north of Perth Amboy.

The railroad investigation involves the analysis of the break-up and waterfront yards of each of these railroads, together with a study of the local terminals and piers for both general merchandise and special uses along most of the waterfronts of the North, East and Harlem Rivers; New York, Newark, Raritan and Jamaica Bays, and the Long Island Sound.

Steamships.— The steamship investigation entails the examination of steamship operations of all sorts along a great part of these waterfronts.

Lighterage.— The lighterage investigation involves the study of the local-waterways transportation system, more highly developed in New York Harbor than anywhere else in the world, between ship, car and local consumer or producer.

Trucking.— Trucking is employed mainly as the final or initial stage of transportation, as the case may be, for the local consumer or producer. But it is utilized also to a considerable extent in trans-shipment of goods through the Port. A visit to the district of lower Manhattan will show that here perhaps is the soundest basis for the charges of congestion made against the Port of New York, and will suggest the great importance of the trucking investigation.

Twenty-three Incidental Investigations

One of the most important of the incidental investigations, and one deeply involved in the trucking investigation, is that of public markets and food distribution. Fourteen hundred carloads each day, it is estimated, are required to feed New York and vicinity. The present system of distribution ties up a large section of lower Manhattan's most valuable waterfront, besides filling the North River with car floats and the streets of lower New York with trucks. Whether this is the best system possible or whether a different plan can be devised to benefit the public without injury to private interests called for careful study. The Commission has already gone far into this question, as is set forth elsewhere in this report, and believes it foresees what the answer will be.

Closely connected with this problem is one of the most acute problems of the Port — that of the New York Central Railroad's freight line on the West Side of Manhattan. A discussion of this also appears elsewhere in the report. A third matter treated at some length is that of an exterior belt-line railroad in New Jersey.

Criticism has often been made of the mechanical equipment of New York harbor as compared with that of some of the European cities, and New York's equipment has been as often defended on the ground that European methods are not feasible here. Thorough analysis of New York's system is necessary, and closely allied to this question are the special problems involved in the handling of building materials and grain.

The operation of private terminals and of general merchandise warehouses also have an important bearing on the situation, as do the provisions, or lack of them, for the utilization by the Port of the New York Barge Canal.

The disposal of municipal wastes, in view of the fact that the waters of the metropolitan district are near the danger point from sewage and other pollution, must be given thorough consideration in the development of any plan which will tend to impede the disposal of such wastes, or bring population and industries that will add further pollution.

All these and numerous other elements of the problem are being studied by the engineers of the Commission.

ERIE TRAFFIC COUNT

The first railroad field investigation made was that of the Erie Railroad. As the Erie is typical of the New Jersey trunk lines, a brief outline of the investigation will be of interest here.

The Erie is a double-track low-grade line between New York and Chicago, with branches to Buffalo, Dunkirk and Cleveland on Lake Erie, to the anthracite coal field of Pennsylvania and to the bituminous fields of Pennsylvania and Ohio. It taps the Great

Lakes ore traffic at Cleveland and runs through the heart of the steel district at Youngstown, Ohio. It has various other branches. In all it operates 2,400 miles of road.

Its terminal units at the Port of New York consist of a break-up and main classification yard at Croxton, on the New Jersey meadows; an auxiliary classification yard at Little Ferry; waterfront yards with pier and other facilities at Jersey City, Weehawken and Undercliff; piers on the Manhattan waterfront at Duane and Houston streets, North River, and at Coenties Slip, East River; an interior freight station between West 28th and 29th streets and 11th and 12th avenues; a station in the Wallabout Market district, Brooklyn; traffic rights at the Harlem terminal of the Delaware, Lackawanna & Western Railroad at 135th street and Harlem River; and traffic rights in common with other railroads at other private and public terminals in the harbor.

Terminal Units Examined

As a preliminary the facilities and their functions at each of these terminal units were examined and recorded. It was noted, for example, that Croxton yard has a working capacity of 4,708 cars; that nearly all inbound freight comes to it and is classified according to local destination; that in reverse order outbound freight is assembled here and classified according to destination; that facilities exist for reclassifying less than carload freight and consolidating it in other cars according to destination; that there are facilities for icing cars and for repairing crippled cars and trackage for "hold" cars and for interchange with the Delaware, Lackawanna & Western Railroad.

The yard is a gravity yard with a classification "hump" in each direction. The operation of the yard has been studied in detail — the number of tracks and the capacities of each unit, the number of classifications made and the tracks used for each, the system in effect at the transfer platform.

In like manner preliminary scrutiny showed that the Jersey City yard is in effect two yards divided by the passenger-train layout, and each yard serving certain piers and other facilities. The uses, sizes and capacities of each of these facilities were determined. Similar information regarding every one of the Erie's terminal units was obtained.

Making the Counts

Most of the traffic counts covered twenty-four-hour periods, and the men worked in three shifts of eight men each. At Croxton yard for each shift one inspector was stationed at the westerly end of the yard to count trains, engines and cars entering and leaving; a second was stationed for the same purpose at the easterly end; a third was assigned to the yardmaster's office to copy train lists; a fourth took his post at the inbound hump and a fifth at the outbound hump to keep account of classifications; a sixth and seventh were assigned respectively to the transfer platform and the icing platform, while the eighth, the squad leader, supervised the entire count and gave assistance where needed.

This count disclosed the total number of cars received inbound in a twenty-four-hour period and their destination; the number of cars received from other railroads and their destination; the number of cars forwarded to each of the waterfront terminals and to other railroads; the number of outbound cars received and their origin; the number of outbound cars forwarded and their general destination; the number of cars passed over each hump; the number of cars loaded, and a large number of incidental operations.

For the north Jersey City yards one inspector was stationed on the main classification engine, one at the yardmaster's office, one at the float bridges and one at each of the lighterage piers. Fewer cars pass through this yard, hence more detailed data were obtained. The inbound cars, for example, divided into twenty groups according to destination. The contents of cars iced were noted here as at Croxton.

The south Jersey City yard was handled in a like manner. A separate eight-hour count was made at the milk platform.

The traffic study at Duane street was made on a somewhat different basis from those at the railroad yards, inasmuch as trucking movements as well as car operations were taken into account. The census was an eleven-hour operation requiring twenty-four men divided into two shifts of twelve men each.

This is one of the typical waterfront freight stations, where the cars are brought alongside the piers on car floats and unloaded and reloaded as at the ordinary inland freight station. The system causes a piling up of trucks waiting to load and unload, and results in much loss of time to the owners. The traffic count covered not only the number of car floats and cars received and forwarded, but also the number of trucks arriving and departing and much information about where they came from and where they went.

The foregoing merely outlines the method pursued in the railroad investigation, and suggests the magnitude of the work and the mass of valuable information being obtained.

TERMINAL COSTS

Meanwhile the Commission has organized an auditing staff to go into the books of the carriers to determine the tonnages handled and the costs.

Unit costs have already been derived for terminal operations on four of the trunk line railroads. They are being determined for 1918 on the basis of the actual twenty-four-hour observations, and for 1914 on the basis of the companies' records for the month of July, 1914. It was felt that while it was desirable to know the latest costs obtainable, and the costs of operations actually observed, it was equally desirable to know the costs under the more normal conditions prior to the war. July, 1914, was selected as the most suitable month for determining pre-war costs.

CLASSIFICATION OF TONNAGES

A beginning has recently been made toward a classification of all tonnages coming to or going from the Port of New York in a typical pre-war year. As far as possible, the tonnages will be classified in three ways — by commodities, by point of origin or destination at the Port, and by general locality of origin or destination at the other end of the journey. The second classification will obviously show whether the shipment is to, from or through the Port of New York. Knowledge of what comes to and goes from the Port, whence it comes and where it goes, should help greatly in evolving the general plan.

SPECIAL INVESTIGATIONS

The special investigations have been grouped under twenty-three heads as follows:

West Side Railroad, Manhattan
Markets and Food Distribution
Exterior Belt Line, New Jersey
Mechanical Equipment of Harbor
Banking and Commercial Operations
Tariff — Charges — Rates
Stevedoring — Longshoremen — Pilotage
Disposal of Municipal Waste
Handling of Building Material
Conditions at New York Piers
Barge Canal Terminals
Canals and Waterways
Private Terminals
Warehouses
Ferries
Handling of Fuel
Handling of Ice
Handling of Grain
Express Business
Electric Power Supply
Water Supply
Trucking
Channels and Dredging

Some of these special investigations involve much more work than others, and the studies are in various stages of completion. Three of the most important of them — those covering the West Side railroad, Manhattan, the system of markets and food distribution and the exterior belt line in New Jersey — are as previously stated discussed at some length elsewhere in this report. Some of the others may be briefly outlined here.

Ice.— The handling of ice is somewhat allied to the food problem. An investigator for the Commission has made a canvass of all of the ice houses along the Hudson River from which New

York gets most of its natural ice, of the artificial ice plants which contribute to the city's supply and of the New Jersey ice sources. Data are being assembled as to the amounts of ice harvested and manufactured, the methods of distribution and the costs.

Grain.— Grain is one of the commodities handled in large quantities at the Port — a commodity that requires special facilities both for local distribution and for exporting. The handling of grain has been studied at considerable length in the light of existing facilities, the facilities at competing ports and the general volume and trend of the grain movement.

Building Materials.— The delivery of building materials — sand, gravel, stone, lime, cement, brick, steel and lumber — in New York is hampered by a shortage of open wharves, especially on the West Side of Manhattan below Forty-seventh street and the East Side below Twenty-third street. There has been no improvement in the methods of handling these materials in thirty years, and meanwhile the number of open piers available has been cut down from year to year. This has resulted in longer hauls and higher costs of delivery. An examination of the waterfront has been made to determine just what piers and bulkheads are being used now for the various materials, and what others could be advantageously put to this use.

Trucking.— While trucking constitutes one of the primary subjects for investigation, certain phases of the subject, especially the question of trucking delays and costs, were given early attention, and listed as a special investigation, because of the movement made last year to bring about store-door delivery of freight consigned to railroad pier stations in Manhattan.

The so-called Harlan plan for store-door delivery, put forth last summer by Hon. James S. Harlan, member of the Interstate Commerce Commission, followed several other plans proposed to remedy the existing evils of a multiplication of underloaded trucks on the piers, and the congestion incident to the necessity of giving consignees notice of arrival of their goods. The Commission's investigators looked up and recorded all of the plans, and their evolution into the Harlan plan.

Three of the investigators also devoted several weeks to traffic counts at certain typical points, to time studies of individual trucks and routes, and to interviews with truckmen and companies using trucks. One study of special interest was the operations for six days of a two-horse truck serving a certain drygoods store. Account was taken of loads carried, time of loading and unloading, time of transit and idle time. The result showed that the truck carried on the average only 28 per cent of a load, and that it made only 36 per cent of the distance possible, so that its efficiency, determined by the product of the two percentages, was only 10 per cent.

The investigators have also made an extensive study of the elements in the cost of trucking operations.

Stevedoring.— Stevedoring has been studied under two general heads — the equipment available at the Port and the form and execution of stevedoring contracts. Under the former head data have been recorded as to the types of machinery utilized and their form of operation; under the latter the question of stevedoring rates and costs, and the difficulties of the labor problem.

Barge Canal Terminals.— New York's new Barge Canal was put into operation last year, and it is desirable to know whether adequate provision in the way of terminals has been made to enable the Port of New York to make full use of the possibilities of this enlarged waterway. Study has been made both of such construction as has been completed and of plans not yet executed, and later on the Commission expects to be able to offer plans for additional terminals.

Canals and Waterways.— Along with the study of the possibilities of the New York Barge Canal an examination has been made of other waterways, existing or contemplated, for barges and for ships, which might be a factor in the operations of the Port. This examination embraces several existing canals for small boats to the west and southwest of the Port; the projected intracoastal ship canal system from Boston to Florida, of which the proposed New Jersey ship canal, an enlarged Chesapeake and Delaware Canal and the Cape Cod Canal would be the most important to New York; the New Jersey marginal canal (New Jersey Inland Waterway), and several projected Long Island canals.

Channels and Dredging.— An investigation is being made of the navigable depths of the various harbor waters, the controlling depths of channels, the obstructions to navigation. The dangerous reefs in the East River, the channel projects for Jamaica and Newark Bays, the desirability of deepening the Harlem River are among the matters being considered in this investigation.

Warehouses.— There are more than 600 freight warehouses and storehouses in New York and New Jersey within the metropolitan district, exclusive of a large number of houses which handle household goods only and therefore are of no interest in this investigation. A questionnaire has been sent out to the owners of all of these freight houses and in addition an investigator for the Commission has visited most of them and obtained supplementary information. Practically all of the questionnaires have been filled out and returned.

Electric Power Supply.— Electricity will undoubtedly be more and more a factor in the operation of the Port. A record has been made of every electric power plant in the district — its location, capacity, ownership, use and other characteristics. The histories and growth of the different companies have been examined, and forecasts have been made of the probable supply of and demand for power in the future.

Water Supply.— Analogous to this is the investigation of the water supply of the Port. Here again a record is being made of locations, capacities, ownership, uses and other details of watersheds, reservoirs, pumping stations, distribution systems and other elements that go to make up a waterworks system. The water supplies of the cities in New Jersey have already been covered, and the investigator is collecting similar data for the area east of the Hudson.

Disposal of Wastes.— For a long time the navigable waters of the metropolitan district have been heavily burdened with sewage and industrial wastes. Some of this overburden, under present conditions, passes out to sea quickly, while some, in the land-locked North and East rivers, surges back and forth with the tides. Elaborate plans have been promulgated to cope with the situation, and it is obvious that waterway and waterfront changes which might affect the tidal conditions and which certainly would have important bearing on any disposal scheme of the magnitude required here must take into account this whole problem. This would be true if the Port were not to continue to grow. The aim of the Commission is to devise ways and means to enhance its growth, and so it becomes doubly necessary to provide for the disposal of the wastes of future population and industries.

The question of whether harbor pollution should come under the jurisdiction of a joint port authority, if one be created, in the light of the Passaic Valley Sewerage Commission Case, is discussed in the section of this report on the proposed treaty. Irrespective of how this question should be answered, it is obvious that this Commission must co-ordinate its general plan with the sewage-disposal problem.

Of hardly less importance are the problems of the disposal of garbage and rubbish. Valuable waterfronts are used for dumps, and many scows are required to handle the Port's refuse. The methods in use have therefore been studied at some length.

Conditions at New York Piers.— Apart from the general steamship investigation is the question of the uses of New York's piers. Early last November two investigators were assigned to this work, and in about five weeks they had covered the railroad piers on the New York side of North River.

These men have visited each of these piers and noted its size, equipment and use. They have considered methods of operation in effect, and recorded practices that interfered with efficiency.

Whether reassignment of piers according to some zoning system is feasible was one of the objects of the survey. Soundings have therefore been taken alongside the piers, and a general examination has been made as to whether they could be put to other uses.

This survey is being continued along the East River and other waterfrontage of the Port.

Other Investigations.— Among the other special investigations, that of banking and commercial operations is designed to disclose the general methods of financing New York's commerce, going into such questions as credits, exchanges and discounts, and comparing them as they exist in New York with those prevalent at London and other foreign ports in order to determine what burdens are placed on New York's commerce by reason of financial operations abroad — what customs exist which interfere with New York's commerce.

The private terminal investigation covers such plants as that of the Bush Terminal Company, the New York Dock Company, the Brooklyn Eastern District Terminal Company and the Jay Street Terminal Company. The fuel investigation covers the handling of fuel both for local delivery and for the bunkering of ships. The investigation of tariffs and charges aims to determine the truth or falsity of the claim often heard of undue charges for the use of harbor facilities.

Thus are outlined some of the special investigations under way. Some of the subjects have been given little consideration in previous studies of the Port. All have important bearing if a comprehensive plan is to be evolved, and others will perhaps suggest themselves before the Commission completes its final report.

Tunnels and Other Projects

Vehicular Tunnel Under Hudson River.— A project much in the public eye at present is the proposed vehicular tunnel under the Hudson River. The recent marine workers' strikes have brought forcibly to public attention the possibility of a complete cutting off of vehicular traffic between New York and New Jersey, even though in both of these strikes the Lackawanna ferries remained in operation, and though other ferry service was resumed after three or four days.

The need for a vehicular connection between the two States, and the question of whether a bridge or a tunnel should be built, have been under study for a number of years by a special Joint Commission created for the purpose. Your Excellencies are aware of the present situation with respect to the projected tunnel, and our Commission has not deemed it necessary to make a detailed study of the tunnel project, or its economic justification. A vehicular tunnel will assuredly aid in the co-ordination of the Port, and any plan later evolved by this Commission should be able to utilize the tunnel to good advantage.

Staten Island Tunnel.— Another fact the first of the recent strikes brought out is the ease with which Staten Island can be isolated. Its only rail connection with the main land is the Baltimore & Ohio freight line to St. George. There are six ferries, from Manhattan, South Brooklyn, Bayonne, Elizabethport, Carteret and Perth Amboy respectively — only the first two, it will be perceived, giving direct connection to New York. The Manhattan ferry is the main dependence of the island, and during the first day of the strike its boats did not run. The consequent inability of thousands to reach Manhattan to fulfill their business engagements has revived the demand of the residents of the island for a tunnel connection.

There are three main possibilities for such a tunnel connection. The first is the direct tunnel under the Upper Bay to Manhattan. This is the most direct but also the most expensive. The second is a tunnel under the Narrows to Brooklyn, connecting with the transit systems in that borough. This would require a much shorter tunnel. The third involves a still shorter tunnel, under the Kill van Kull to Bayonne.

As the Commission is avoiding recommendations prior to the completion of its picture of present operating conditions, it is not ready at this time to offer a solution of the Staten Island problem.

Brooklyn Marginal Railway.— For years there has been agitation for a marginal railway in Brooklyn. Special legislation has been passed to permit the construction and operation of such a railway from the New York Dock Company's terminal near Brooklyn Bridge to the Bush Terminal in South Brooklyn. Various obstacles, however, notably the unwillingness of the trunk-line railroads while under private operation to co-operate in the undertaking, have blocked it.

Since the United States Government took over the railroads the Railroad Administration, through its budget committee, has been studying the matter further. A plan has been submitted to the Commission for a line from the Brooklyn Navy Yard up the East River and Newtown Creek to the Bushwick terminal of the Long Island Railroad, and the Commission has been over the site of the proposed line.

The Commission's ultimate findings must certainly cover the project, but the Commission is not ready as yet to make any recommendations.

CO-OPERATION WITH OTHER AGENCIES

Throughout the investigation to date the Commission has sought to co-operate with and obtain the co-operation of other agencies, and in this it has been very fortunate. As the 1918 report stated, the Commission invited and had before it at many of its 1917 meetings the presidents of the trunk-line railroads, the heads of shipping interests, the heads of terminal companies and various other interests using the harbor.

Since the Government has taken over the operation of the railroads and other industries the Commission has been in close touch with the Railroad Administration, the Port and Harbor Facilities Commission of the United States Shipping Board and the Fuel Administration.

The Commission early addressed a communication to the Secretary of War, the Secretary of the Navy, the Director General of Railroads and the chairman of the United States Shipping Board, requesting that before any construction work was done in the Port the plans be submitted to the Commission for an expression of opinion as to whether they would interfere with the carrying out of a comprehensive Port plan. The authorities in Washington readily agreed to this. There is now scarcely a week when some project is not referred to this Commission by the authorities in Washington for an expression of opinion.

As a point of contact with the Commission the regional director of railroads has appointed a committee consisting of the managers of all of the trunk lines entering New York, and the fullest co-operation has been extended in the way of permission to go upon the property of the railroads in the field and in the auditors' offices.

In like manner there has been hearty co-operation between this board and the commissioner of docks of New York City. The commissioner has readily perceived that the missions of the dock department and the Joint Commission were quite distinct — that of the former being to study and prescribe for the immediate needs of New York City, that of the latter to fit such new construction or changes in the mode of operation as are adopted into the ultimate plan, and offer objection only in case of seeming conflict with the ultimate requirements of the Port as a whole. The commissioner has therefore appeared before this Commission, submitted various plans to it and in other ways shown his desire to help the Commission in its work, and the Commission hopes it has also been of some service to him.

NEW YORK AS A PORT

New York is by far the greatest railroad, commercial and industrial center on the Atlantic seaboard.

The population of the metropolitan district of New York is four times that of Philadelphia.

The Port has the finest harbor on the Atlantic Coast, with 780 miles of waterfront.

Three times as many railroad trunk lines come to New York as come to any other city on the Atlantic tidewater.

More manufacturing industries are located in the New York district than in the combined cities of Philadelphia, Chicago, Cleveland and St. Louis, and the value of the products of the New York industries is nearly as great as the combined value of the products of those of the other four cities.

Approximately half of all the foreign commerce of the United States passes through the Port of New York.

This is one side of the picture, and it might seem that New York's position is unassailable — that as much business as the Port desires and can handle is bound to gravitate to it.

There is another side.

New York suffers a severe handicap from the differential in railroad freight rates, whereby shippers to or through the Port of New York pay more on shipments than to or through such cities as Philadelphia and Baltimore.

A determined campaign is being made to divert traffic from New York, mainly on the grounds of alleged congestion and high terminal costs at New York.

The effects of these things are already visible. The tonnage of New York's foreign commerce, mounting steadily from 1911, reached a peak in the year ended June 30, 1914, and has since fallen steadily. The 1918 figures are 26 per cent below those for 1914 and lower than those for 1911 or any succeeding year.

New York's percentage of the total foreign commerce of the United States fell from 52.67 per cent in 1916 to 44.68 per cent in 1917 and 42.36 per cent in 1918, the latter percentage being lower than in any year since 1911 inclusive.

Fewer loaded freight cars came to New York in 1918 than in any of the four preceding years. Despite the abnormal railroad traffic in 1918 in the country at large, figures compiled by the Commission's statisticians for four of the principal New Jersey trunk lines show that in the first ten months of 1918 they received 7 per cent fewer loaded cars than in the same months of the slack year 1914, and 20 per cent fewer than in those months in the heavy year 1916.

Preparing for the Future

And more important than the past is the future.

Our country is building a great merchant fleet. The opportunity of the country is here, for the nation to reach out and get its share of the world's trade. It must do so. Other ports are assuming that it will do so, and are preparing to expand their facilities to handle the increased traffic. With five times the traffic of any other Atlantic port, New York's preparations must be vastly more elaborate, in the face of vastly greater complications arising from New York's very size and rapidity of growth.

Evidently the time has passed when the needs of the Port of New York can be settled by the individual communities in the two states that constitute the Port — even by the great community of New York City. The Legislatures of New York and New Jersey have recognized this in creating this Commission.

A Broad Plan the Commission's Aim

The ultimate aim of the Commission, as has heretofore been stated, is to establish a general plan of Port operation and development that will serve as a guide for fifty years; a plan flexible to meet future conditions, but fixed as to general principles; a plan supported by detailed estimates of costs and proof of its economic soundness, and accompanied by a tentative program which will meet the most urgent needs first. If the plan is to be unassailable, the Commission must determine every factor, and the weight of every factor, that enters into the problem, and it is on this study of existing conditions that the Commission is concentrating its main efforts at the present time.

WEST SIDE RAILROAD FACILITIES, MANHATTAN

Representing the whole Port of New York, the Commission must take a broader view of the railroad problems upon the West Side of Manhattan than those who have been struggling with it for years. To them the outstanding facts are the inadequate terminals on one railroad, the running of trains at street level, the injury to Riverside Park. The Commission, considering all these things, must still remember that the problem is not for Manhattan Island alone, and so it has proceeded on the theory that the New York Central Railroad, ready to spend money to increase its ability to serve and be served by the Port, must be allowed to do so, but that this one railroad must not be permitted to bar the New Jersey railroads from rail operations along the Port's most valuable waterfront, even though the New Jersey railroads have shown no inclination thus far to spend money to bring about those rail operations. In other words, the Commission has assumed that the correct solution of the West Side problem will be a plan that will provide the New York Central with modern facilities and also provide for the necessary connections with the New Jersey railroads by tunnels or bridges.

Moving freight in New York harbor either by lighter or by car float is a costly operation. Yet all New York freight to and from the New Jersey railroads is so handled, and a large part of the New York Central's is floated in like manner from Sixtieth street south because of the inability of the rail line to handle it all. In this system the railroads occupy 30 per cent of all the North River waterfront in Manhattan from the Battery to West Thirtieth street. At the railroad pier stations trucks must enter and leave at the same point, causing constant congestion and delay.

Whether a marginal railroad is justified will depend mainly, as far as the railroads are concerned, on whether enough could be saved, taking into account the tonnage of freight handled, by an all-rail operation to pay the interest on the investment in such marginal railway, its New Jersey connections and its terminals. For the public the most easily applied test is determining how much time could be saved trucks if the waiting at piers could be eliminated.

To determine the costs of marine operations to and from lower Manhattan the Commission has made a minute analysis of the traffic of two of the New Jersey trunk lines for a period of one month, just before the war, deriving from the companies' records both the tonnages handled and the costs. These costs embrace switching costs in New Jersey, costs of water transportation, handling costs at the Manhattan piers — operation, maintenance and repairs of rail equipment, operation and maintenance of tugboats and car floats, rental, maintenance and insurance of piers. All-rail costs are being determined from the costs of all-rail operations to local terminals on the New Jersey side, modified by estimate to meet the conditions of the marginal railroad.

The tonnages handled at all of the pier stations that could be eliminated by the marginal railroad are being taken off from the records of the railroad companies, as are data relative to rentals, maintenance and other expenses of existing piers.

Estimates are being made of the costs of a marginal railroad and terminal to handle the tonnages indicated. As some advocate an elevated railroad and some a subway, estimates for both are being made. Separate computations are being made for a plan to accommodate the New York Central alone, and for the more comprehensive one with connections to the New Jersey railroads.

To make the other direct test, that of the possible saving in trucking delays, traffic counts have been made at typical railroad piers. The number of trucks there, the capacity and loading of each, the waiting, unloading and loading time of each have been recorded. From truckmen and other sources unit operating costs of trucks prevailing in 1914 are being built up. Given these unit operating costs, the number and kind of trucks required to handle the total railroad tonnage, as indicated by the traffic count, and the average delay per truck, the total cost of these delays can be closely approximated. So the cost of the smaller delays at the ideal inland terminals of the marginal railroad can be estimated, and the difference will be the interest on the expenditure justifiable from the shipper's point of view.

The Commission is attempting to make the present analysis independent of considerations that though highly important are calculable, if at all, only after more extended study. These include the release of valuable waterfront to steamship uses; reduction in the number of trucks on the streets; a possible dovetailing with plans for a better market system.

MARKETS AND FOOD DISTRIBUTION

The problem of markets and food distribution is the second of the special investigations to which the Commission has already given much attention. No problem of the Port is more important, none has a more vital bearing on the cost of living at the Port. The present market system is unquestionably uneconomical, both because of the congestion it produces and because of the wastage and loss of freshness of perishable foods through repeated handling. It is not yet known what the losses are, but whatever they are they must be carried in the prices of food and paid for by the consumer. The problem of a better system, too, is closely tied up to the West Side railroad problem, and neither can be solved independently of the other.

Every public market in New York City and most of those on the New Jersey side of the river have been visited by an investigator for the Commission, who has studied their history, the evolution of their administration, the reasons for their present locations, the character and volume of their business and their methods of operation. Reports of various food commissions have been reviewed and abstracted.

Under the present system most of New York City's food supply and a considerable part of that of New Jersey cities of the Port passes through the great primary market district on the lower West Side from Fulton street north to Canal street and from the North River to Greenwich street.

Fruits from California and Florida come to piers in this district and are sold at the piers, whence they are trucked through the streets, mainly to other markets — to Manhattan, Brooklyn or New Jersey or to the stores of the primary market near by. At the markets they are sold again and trucked again, to retail stores, or, in the case of the primary market, to other markets.

Produce brought by rail from nearer points is unloaded in Jersey City and trucked to the primary market, whence it is sold and trucked to other markets or to retail stores. In general meat and milk do not pass through the primary market, but are distributed from the railroad terminals, as are certain other commodities, such as potatoes.

Of the secondary markets there are both wholesale markets, such as the Wallabout in Brooklyn, and retail markets. The wholesale and jobbers' markets in New York, of which there are three or four, are so located as to supply retailers from a large section. The retail markets usually supply only a small area, and collectively cover only a small part of the city. Several farmers' markets are operated in connection with the wholesale markets.

In the New Jersey cities the markets are in general combination wholesale, retail and farmers' markets — wholesalers and jobbers, who truck their goods largely from the New York primary market, supplying such wares as the farmers are unable to bring.

The general system, with its large dependence on the primary market, causes congestion and confusion at the piers; a multiplication of trucks hauling food through the streets; the piling up of food on the sidewalks in the primary market district because the stores there are small and inadequate to contain the large quantities of goods brought to them; added costs and loss of freshness because of repeated handling.

Commission men and others engaged in food distribution assert that the present system is the only feasible one, and ask for still greater concentration, the giving over of all piers in the primary market district to the food industry, and the provision of better facilities at the piers. They point to several unsuccessful attempts to bypass the primary market by the delivery of cars near the other markets — attempts that have only resulted in the ultimate trucking of the goods back to the primary markets. It may be questioned, however, whether these experiments were sufficiently planned through and advertised, and of long enough duration to form a fair test. A remodeling of the market district, with the removal of activities foreign to it, would probably effect some reduction in the congestion and costs of the present system; but if any material improvement is to be brought about the Commission's studies to date indicate that it must come through a not too radical decentralization.

EXTERIOR BELT LINE, NEW JERSEY

Whether or not the New Jersey railroads are ever brought to a common terminal system in Manhattan by a bridge over or tunnel under the Hudson River, rail connection between them is necessary. Each railroad interchanges cars with every other railroad and each serves industries and steamship piers on other lines.

Under the unified government operation of the past year, furthermore, there has been much diversion of cars from congested terminals to others on other lines, and this increased the need for an adequate belt line. The Railroad Administration was compelled to depend on a combination of more or less fragmentary lines controlled by several of the trunk lines. This combination runs from Edgewater, opposite 130th street, New York, to Bayonne, along the base of the Palisades, most of the way about a mile from the waterfront, and intercepts all of the trunk lines.

This belt line, in spite of awkward location and operating difficulties, has been very effective in the past year. The limit of its capacity has been reached, however, and there is need in the estimation of many for another belt line which may be used in addition for a very different purpose — a purpose for which the existing line would be quite inadequate. This is an exterior belt line whose two main functions would be serving steamship traffic and forming an essential part of a system of unified freight terminals reaching every section of the metropolitan district. Such a line, while located in New Jersey, would be as serviceable to New York as to New Jersey, as will be developed.

The idea of union freight terminals with a belt-line collecting and distribution system is not new but has been somewhat amplified in the Commission's studies. The basic principle is consolidation of less-than-carload freight, resulting at once in better loading of cars and floats and a great reduction in trucking distances.

Under present conditions each railroad has its own freight stations, in Manhattan and elsewhere. Few of these have sufficient traffic to or from any one point to make through carload shipments possible. Each road has to maintain facilities at its break-up yard to transfer inbound freight to other cars for the various stations, and to consolidate, arranged in station order, outbound freight from the various stations. As many of these stations have insufficient business to utilize cars and boats to their full capacity, we see car floats carrying only a few cars, and cars and lighters half empty. To minimize this under-loading the railroads tend to concentrate their business at a few stations, and many of the sections of the district are almost without facilities.

From the shipper's point of view the system is highly unsatisfactory, for the reason that his truckmen, with goods on each truck for several railroads, must line up in turn at each crowded station and waste many valuable hours. Relief is afforded him by the private terminal, which receives from and delivers to all railroads; but this advantage is largely offset by the necessity imposed upon the terminal company of collecting from and distributing to several transfer stations on the New Jersey side.

To remedy this the exterior belt-line plan contemplates establishing union freight stations wherever the total available daily business is sufficient to load a car float; a collecting and distributing point for these floats at some point on the waterfront where there is adequate space for steamship piers and railroad yards; a classification yard and transfer station at that point, and a railroad, passing to the westward ot the existing break-up yards and crowded industrial area, and crossing each of the trunk lines, terminating at Piermont on the Hudson, thirty miles north of Jersey City. A Barge Canal terminal would probably be built at Piermont.

To such a line, operated independently, cars of less-than-carload freight could be delivered by the various trunk lines, and the business of breaking up for the different terminals could be concentrated at the general clearing yard at the south end of the belt line. Conversely, in one rehandling at this point, freight from all of the union terminals could be consolidated in station order in cars for the different roads.

The other primary purpose of this belt line would be to serve steamship traffic. With a terminal for freight steamships at the south end of the line, solid trains for the steamships could be made up at division points west of the belt line and diverted from the trunk lines without passing through the break-up yards; and solid west-bound trains could be made up at the steamship piers and delivered to the railroads, or to the Barge Canal, without passing through the main classification yards of the different railroads.

Thus it is seen that the exterior belt line would be of very material benefit to New York City by making it possible to establish a comprehensive system of freight stations serving all parts of the city. New Jersey, receiving less of this benefit, would derive material advantage in the possibility of attracting industries to locate along the belt line. Industries so located would be on the rails of every truck line on the New Jersey side of the harbor and have direct rail connections to shipping. The improved steamship facilities such a line would provide would help the entire Port.

It should be noted that such a belt line would be beneficial to the entire State of New York, inasmuch as four of the New Jersey trunk lines run from western New York, whose shippers would profit by the improved facilities at the New York terminal. Shippers along the Barge Canal through its entire length would derive similar benefit, as would those throughout New Jersey, every part of which is reached by the railroads the belt line would intercept.

A representative of the Commission has been over three possible routes for such a belt line, and survey parties have recently completed a preliminary study of the most favorable route. The route considered runs from Piermont north and west of Paterson and through Summit. The southern terminus has not yet been determined, nor has the cost of such a line.

MARINE WORKERS' STRIKE

An excellent opportunity to test the extent of New York's dependence on marine operations to supplement her railroad service and of her ability to do without these marine operations was afforded January 9–11, when a strike of the marine operators tied up almost every floating craft in the harbor. The strike went into effect officially the morning of January 9, although in some instances car-float and lighterage service was practically tied up during the preceding night. All operators of tugboats went out; car-float and lighterage service came to a complete standstill, and ships were unable to dock or depart except under their own power.

The ferries of the Delaware, Lackawanna & Western Railroad in the North River remained in service. During the first day of the strike the Long Island Railroad ferries in the East River were running, but service was suspended on the other two days. The Staten Island municipal ferry was not operated the first day, but after that a somewhat irregular service was maintained by the New York Police Department. A small ferry between Elizabethport and Staten Island was kept going during the strike.

The strike terminated Sunday, January 12, when most of the contending parties consented to arbitration before the National War Labor Board.

The general method of food distribution at the Port of New York has already been set forth in this report. With the declaring of the strike it is apparent that the floating of cars to the Manhattan pier stations was stopped absolutely, while trucking to Manhattan from the various New Jersey waterfront terminals could be done only via the Lackawanna ferries. The Railroad Administration at once placed general embargoes against all shipments to or through New York, but modified them to permit such shipments as could be handled otherwise than by car float or lighter. The foods brought in were trucked via the Lackawanna ferries; or hauled in cars through the Pennsylvania tunnels to Long Island or to the Harlem River terminal of the New York, New Haven & Hartford Railroad, and trucked over the East River or Harlem River bridges; or diverted to the New York Central Railroad via Albany or Poughkeepsie; or held in New Jersey until the end of the strike. Some of the food from the West was rerouted from the Erie to the New York Central at Buffalo. Staten Island was supplied by diversion to the Baltimore & Ohio Railroad, by the Elizabethport ferry and after the first day by the usual agency, the municipal ferry.

On January 10 the Commission began a study of the effect of the strike on the supply and distribution of perishable food. Inspectors were sent to various railroads with instructions to ascertain the daily receipts of perishable foods by the various railroads from January 2 to the termination of the strike and thereafter daily until further notice, in order to get data as to the normal movement of food before and after the strike; to obtain copies of all embargoes issued on account of the strike; and to learn from the various railroads the diversions and amount of perishable food made to or by them for the purpose of getting it to the inhabitants of Greater New York, and the routes and means by which such diversions were made.

A twenty-one hour census was taken of the truck traffic on the Lackawanna ferries, the census utilizing twenty-seven inspectors. One man rode on each ferry boat, with instructions to ascertain in the case of perishable foodstuffs and milk the point at which the truck was loaded, the commodity, the destination, and the times of loading, arrival in line for the ferry, arrival on boat and departure on the other side. In the case of pleasure vehicles, trucks carrying general merchandise and empty trucks, the inspector recorded the times of arrival in line for the ferry, arrival on the boat and departure from the boat, and the respective numbers of such vehicles. This information was obtained in both directions.

From data furnished by the New York Board of Health it is estimated that the city of New York normally consumes daily 1,800,000 quarts of milk, 94 carloads of refrigerated meats, 74 of livestock, 18 of live poultry, 20 of fresh fish, 127 of dairy products, 201 of vegetables and 107 of fruit. During the three days of the strike the daily milk receipts averaged 74.010 per cent of the normal daily consumption, the receipts of refrigerated meats 54.609 per cent, of livestock 108.108 per cent, of live poultry 5.555 per cent, of fresh fish 66.666 per cent, of dairy products 22.965 per cent, of vegetables 36.296 per cent, and of fruit 27.103 per cent.

In terms of the normal consumption the New York railroads, exclusive of diversions, brought 30.652 per cent and the New Jersey 43.358 per cent of the milk. For refrigerated meats the corresponding percentages were 35.106 and 19.503; for livestock 78.378 and 29.730; for live poultry 0.000 and 5.555; for fresh fish 60.000 and 6.666; for dairy products, 14.173 and 8.792; for vegetables 22.093 and 14.203; for fruit 17.757 and 9.346.

Considering now the 43.358 per cent of normal daily supply brought by the New Jersey railroads, this is divided into 25.880 per cent delivered via the rails of the New York roads and 17.478 per cent via the Lackawanna ferries. Similarly, 11.702 per cent of the normal daily consumption of refrigerated meats was delivered via the rails of the New York roads and 7.801 per cent via the Lackawanna ferries, these two figures totaling the

19.503 per cent brought in by the New Jersey roads. The corresponding percentages for the remaining items are: Live stock, 27.027 and 2.703; live poultry, 0.000 and 5.555; fresh fish, 0.000 and 6.666; dairy products, 2.887 and 5.905; vegetables, 6.811 and 7.392; fruit, 6.854 and 2.492.

For convenience in tabulation the Pennsylvania Railroad was considered a New Jersey railroad because the Pennsylvania tunnels are not ordinarily used for freight business. The West Shore Railroad was considered a New York railroad for the reason that its freight could be readily intercepted at Albany and brought down the east side of the Hudson River. An exception had to be made in the case of the New York, Ontario & Western Railway's milk business, which is a large item, and which was trucked from Weehawken via the Lackawanna ferry. The New York, New Haven & Hartford and the Long Island railroads were also considered New York roads, while the traffic of the Baltimore & Ohio was split up according to destination, as that road under normal conditions has both rail delivery to Staten Island and water delivery to other parts of New York.

In the case of almost all of the foregoing items of food, the average daily deliveries for the seven days immediately preceding the strike were far below the average normal consumption. At this season of the year the supply of most of these items is less than the demand, and the difference is made up by withdrawal from storage; hence the reduction in deliveries of foods during the strike was much less than the percentages would indicate. In the case of milk a strike of the dairymen had been in effect for a week and remained in effect after the termination of the marine strike. It reduced the milk supply materially. There was a decided falling off in the milk receipts of most of the railroads, but the Pennsylvania and the New York, New Haven & Hartford reached out into new territory as far away as Cleveland and Boston and made up a great deal of the shortage. It should be mentioned, also, that the demand for milk is less in January than in the summer months.

To effect the rail diversions from the New Jersey railroads a number of routes were utilized. A large amount of milk and a lesser amount of other perishables was hauled through the Pennsylvania tunnels to delivery stations on the Long Island Railroad or carried on via the New York Connecting Railroad to the Harlem River terminal of the New York, New Haven & Hartford.

The next nearest crossing of the Hudson River available was the Poughkeepsie bridge. This could be reached via the Lehigh & Hudson or the Lehigh & New England and the Central New England railroads. From the east end of the Poughkeepsie bridge the New York Central, New York, New Haven & Hartford and Long Island railroads could be reached. Two cars of refrigerated meat that had already reached the Jersey City terminal of the Erie were hauled back over that road to Maybrook, thence via the Poughkeepsie bridge, Beacon, Port Morris and Fresh Pond to Flatbush avenue, Brooklyn, using the Central New England, New York Central, New York Connecting and Long Island railroads.

Diversions to the New York Central crossing at Albany could be made via the Delaware & Hudson from Binghamton or at various points west of Albany. Some diversions were made from the Erie at Buffalo.

More diversions were made during the three days of the strike than are indicated by the figures, inasmuch as a number of the deliveries were not effected until some time afterward. Undoubtedly more extensive diversions would have been made if the strike had lasted longer. As far as the figures show, all diversions to the New York Central were taken care of at the distributing stations, and apparently more could have been.

The census of the Lackawanna ferries corroborates the figures for the amount of New Jersey perishable foods diverted to the ferries. The proof was found by prorating the total volume during the census to the period of the strike.

During the census no restrictions were placed upon the character of vehicles carried or upon their loading. Eastbound, 202 trucks carried food; 295 carried merchandise and 623 were empty, while at the same time 246 pleasure vehicles were hauled. Westbound, there were 86 truck loads of food, 572 of merchandise, 483 empty trucks and 220 pleasure vehicles.

Nearly half as many trucks carried food from New York by ferry as to New York. Exclusive of milk more than half as much food by weight was carried out of New York as into New York. In the case of milk for every ten quarts brought to New York from Hoboken one quart was taken back to Hoboken.

As to the effect on the markets and prices, the strike did not last long enough to give conclusive results. There seems to have been a slight increase in prices during the strike, but there was a decided drop afterward, when food temporarily held back arrived at the terminals. How much of this is attributable to the strike is questionable, inasmuch as there seems to have been a similar falling off in prices at other ports. Except as to refrigerated meats, live stock and milk, the dealers apparently were not in fear of a shortage and did not exert themselves to get supplies over from the New Jersey terminals. Offers of the railroads to reroute shipments were declined, as were offers to make Jersey City deliveries, to be trucked to New York.

In the case of live stock, the condition was complicated by the fact that abattoirs are scattered throughout the city and that many of them are reached only by water deliveries. A large part of the meat coming to New York comes on the hoof. In order to get this to the abattoirs it was found necessary to obtain special permits to drive cattle through the streets at night.

While the strike did not last long enough to permit definite conclusions, it offered much in the way of instructive information. It would be useless to attempt to compute the loss to food distributors caused by the delays to shipments and the excessive trucking necessitated. The loss must have been large, however, and a way to prevent its recurrence should be found.

A second strike of the marine workers was called March 4, as a result of their dissatisfaction with the award resulting from the arbitration at the termination of the first strike. After about four days, during which conditions were about the same as in the January strike, an agreement was reached between the workers, the Railroad Administration, the Army, the Navy and some of the private boat owners, and many of the employees returned to work, ferry, car-float and railroad lighter service being resumed. Many of the workers remained, and still remain, on strike, with no apparent prospects for an early termination of the deadlock. The Commission is watching the situation, but has found it less instructive to date than the strike in January.

COMPACT BETWEEN NEW YORK AND NEW JERSEY FOR THE CREATION OF A PORT AUTHORITY

The investigation and studies made by the Commission soon convinced the Commission that, whatever physical plan might ultimately be worked out, it was essential that the two States be brought together in an agreement or compact fixing the basis and terms of co-operation, and providing for legal machinery through which this co-operation could be made effective. The Commission, therefore, requested its counsel to make a careful and exhaustive study of all the legal phases of the problem.

Such a study was made and is now contained in the "Preliminary Report of Counsel to Accompany the Tentative Draft of Proposed Treaty Amendatory and Supplementary to the Treaty of 1834," a copy of which is submitted herewith. This study brings together the precedents bearing upon the problem and discusses at length the history of the early commercial relations between New York and New Jersey; the boundary dispute; the treaty of 1834; the purpose and meaning of that treaty; the federal power over interstate commerce and navigation; the powers of the two States, covering the title to shore-front property both in New Jersey and New York, the regulation of waterfront franchises, the various agencies — corporations, municipalities or other delegated powers — through which the States may act, the legal basis for interstate action and the treaty or compact-making power of the States; also the experiences in international law in dealing with such problems; the methods for the enforcement of an interstate treaty; State limitations upon borrowing capacity thereof, and other phases of the problem. This report is regarded by experts as the first compilation of authorities upon these phases of the problem of Port development.

The legal problem is unique. As stated by counsel, "at the threshold we face the fact of a dual political sovereignty. The Port lies in two States, each an independent sovereignty in its own land. The legal problem, therefore, can not so easily be stated or solved as it might be for New Orleans, Philadelphia, Boston or Baltimore. Again, traffic between two States across boundary waters is interstate commerce. Neither one State nor the other can wholly regulate the Port."

If it is important to overcome the physical barriers that separate the two States it is of even greater importance to overcome the legal barriers. The Commission felt that the implicit obligation of the legislation under which it was created should be reduced to the form of a compact whose terms should be explicit and definite — a compact by which the States should co-operate through a common agency in the development of Port facilities. It was convinced that there were no constitutional or legal difficulties in the way of such a compact and that it should supplement the existing compact between New York and New Jersey made in 1834, a copy of which is contained in the report of counsel to the Commission.

Acting under instructions of the Commission, accordingly, counsel for the Commission prepared a tentative draft of such a supplemental compact.

Accompanying it was the following notice:

> For the purpose of developing a legal plan for the carrying forward of such constructive recommendations as shall ultimately be approved, the Commission now presents for public discussion and consideration a proposed treaty between the two States, looking to the creation of a single Port Authority. Accompanying the tentative treaty is a report from the Commission's counsel, discussing the legal phases of the problems presented to the Commission.
>
> Criticisms and suggestions should be sent to the secretary, at the office of the Commission, 115 Broadway, New York City. A limited number of copies of the report of counsel accompanying the treaty are available for organizations or individuals desirous of making suggestions or criticism of the plan.

A copy of the draft was sent to all members of the Legislatures of both States, to the Mayor and other members of the Board of Estimate and Apportionment of New York City, to other municipal officials within the metropolitan district, to civic and commercial bodies and to the press.

The first public consideration of this draft was given at a meeting held at the New York Chamber of Commerce December 19, at which were present Hon. Charles S. Whitman, Governor of New York; Hon. Walter E. Edge, Governor of New Jersey; Hon. Charles E. Hughes; Hon. William D. Guthrie; Hon. John O. H. Pitney; Hon. Byron R. Newton, Collector of the Port; Hon. Alfred H. Smith, Regional Director of Railroads; Hon. Charles L. Craig, Controller of the City of New York; Hon. Edward Riegelmann, President, Borough of Brooklyn; Hon. Murray Hulbert, Commissioner of Docks, City of New York; the members of this Commission, its counsel and its consulting engineer.

At this time both Governor Whitman and Governor Edge took occasion to pledge their support to the proposed compact between the two States.

The main features of the proposition almost at once secured general popular approval. The New York Chamber of Commerce, Merchants' Association, City Club, Citizens' Union, Brooklyn Chamber of Commerce and Newark Board of Trade all gave their hearty support to the project. The metropolitan press was almost unanimously for it. Among the papers supporting it was the New York Times, World, Sun, Tribune, Herald, Journal of Commerce, Evening Post, Evening Mail, Evening World, Evening Sun and Globe, Newark Evening News and various other New Jersey papers.

At the request of Governor Edge the State Bar Association of New Jersey appointed Messrs. Gilbert Collins and Marshall Van Winkle of Jersey City, Edward M. Colie and Robert H. McCarter of Newark, Wayne Dumont of Paterson, William R. Wilson of Elizabeth and Adrian Lyon of Perth Amboy a special committee to consider the proposed draft. The committee approved of its legality.

Committees of the various bodies endorsing the plan made careful study of the details, and valuable suggestions and criticisms were received by the Commission and its counsel.

Public hearings were held at Newark and New York City on January 18 and 22, 1919, respectively.

At the Newark hearing the treaty was discussed by D. Grotta, president of the Newark Board of Trade; Morris R. Sherrerd, chief engineer of the Department of Streets and Public

Improvements, City of Newark; Hon. R. C. Jenkinson, vice-chairman of the New Jersey State Board of Commerce and Navigation; Peter Campbell, W. J. Bartnett, and others. The discussion was distinctly favorable to the treaty.

At the New York hearing John F. Wallace, representing the Chamber of Commerce of the State of New York; R. C. Harrison, for the City Club; F. B. DeBerard, for the Merchants' Association; William McCarroll, Charles Whiting Baker, Louis L. Tribus, representing the Staten Island Chamber of Commerce; S. Wood McClave, of the Eastern Bergen County Association of New Jersey; Hon. Byron R. Newton, Collector of the Port of New York; John W. Ward, Lindon W. Bates, and R. McL. Harding, spoke in favor of the principle of the treaty, Charles Campbell spoke in opposition.

On January 29, a conference was held at Albany between Your Excellencies, the members of the Commission and their counsel, and the following members of the Legislature of New York: Lieut.-Gov. Harry C. Walker; Hon. J. Henry Walters, president pro tem of the Senate; Hon. James A. Foley, minority leader of the Senate; Hon. Thaddeus C. Sweet, Speaker of the Assembly; Hon. Simon L. Adler, majority leader; Hon. Charles D. Donohue, minority leader, and Hon. H. E. Machold, chairman of the Ways and Means Committee of the Assembly; Hon. Murray Hulbert, Commissioner of Docks, New York City; Ed. J. McGoldrick, Assistant Corporation Counsel of New York City.

At this conference the draft of the compact was presented and discussed, and it was agreed that a legislative bi-State Commission should be appointed, which should co-operate with our Commission in the revision of the compact so that it might be presented in complementary form to the Legislatures of both States. Accordingly Gov. Alfred E. Smith; Lieut.-Gov. Harry C. Walker; Hon. J. Henry Walters, president pro tem of the Senate; Hon. Thaddeus C. Sweet, Speaker of the Assembly; Hon. Henry M. Sage, chairman of the Committee on Finance of the Senate; Hon. H. E. Machold, chairman of the Committee on Ways and Means of the Assembly; Hon. Alvah W. Burlingame, Jr., and Hon. Louis M. Martin, chairmen respectively of the Committees on Judiciary of the Senate and the Assembly; Hon. James A.

Foley, minority leader of the Senate; Hon. Simon L. Adler, majority leader of the Assembly; Hon. Charles D. Newton, Attorney-General; Hon. Frederick A. Wells and Hon. George R. Fearon, members of the Assembly; Hon. Murray Hulbert, Commissioner of Docks of New York City; Hon. William P. Burr and Edward J. McGoldrick, Corporation Counsel and Assistant Corporation Counsel of New York City, and Robert C. Cumming, legislative bill drafting commissioner, were appointed to represent New York, while Hon. Thomas F. McCran, Attorney-General; Hon. Clarence E. Case and Hon. Henry E. Ackerson, Jr., majority and minority leaders of the Senate; Hon. Arthur A. Pierson, Speaker of the Assembly; Hon. Ralph K. Kellam and Hon. Hugh C. Barret, leaders of the Assembly, and Hon. John R. Milton, corporation counsel, were appointed to represent New Jersey.

On February 15, through the courtesy of the New York Chamber of Commerce, the Commission met at the Chamber and considered the proposed compact. There were present: Your Excellencies; Lieut.-Gov. Walker, Senators Walters, Sage, Foley and Burlingame, Speaker Sweet, Assemblymen Machold, Adler, Donohue, Martin, Wells and Fearon, Attorney-General Newton for the State of New York, Corporation Counsel Burr and Assistant Corporation Counsel McGoldrick for the City of New York; Senators Runyon, Case, Ackerson, Edwards and Whitney, Assemblymen Pierson, McAcer, Kellam, Barrett and Winne, Attorney-General McCran, Comptroller N. A. K. Bugbee and State Treasurer William R. Read for the State of New Jersey; the members of this Commission and others.

The conference adjourned to March 1 after appointing to revise and redraft the proposed compact a sub-committee consisting of the Attorney-Generals of both States, the majority and minority leaders of both Houses of both States, and the corporation counsels of New York and Jersey City.

The sub-committee met on February 21 and considered all the criticisms and suggestions that had been made, and instructed counsel for the Commission to revise the draft and present it for further consideration to the sub-committee prior to the meeting of March 1.

At the adjourned meeting of the bi-State Commission held on March 1 at the Chamber of Commerce, Governor Smith, Speaker Sweet and Senator Walters requested an adjournment of the conference until the administrative officials of the City of New York might be given an opportunity to consider the proposed draft and express their views thereon. The conference, accordingly, adjourned subject to the call of the chair as soon as the New York legislative section of the conference was ready to report. Hon. J. Henry Walters, president pro tem of the Senate, addressed a communication to Mayor John F. Hylan and Hon. Robert T. Moran, President of the Board of Aldermen of New York City, a copy of which appears in Appendix A, as a part of a resolution subsequently passed by the Board of Estimate and Apportionment of New York City.

The matter having been set down by the Board of Estimate and Apportionment for a public hearing on March 26, the Commission and its counsel attended, by direction of Governor Smith, and counsel for the Commission outlined the history and purpose of the proposed compact. The hearing continued through the day, and on the following day were heard besides the Commission's counsel in support of the treaty Hon. George W. Wickersham, for the New York Chamber of Commerce; Samuel Untermyer, representing the Yonkers Waterfront Development Commission and the Merchants' Association of the City of New York; Col. Henry W. Hodge, representing the Citizens' Union; L. M. Wallstein, representing the City Club, and J. S. Davis and F. L. Cranford, representing the Brooklyn Chamber of Commerce.

There appeared in opposition Charles F. McLean, representing the New York Board of Trade and Transportation, Cyrus C. Miller, Calvin Tomkins and others.

On April 4 the Board of Estimate and Apportionment adopted the resolution herewith submitted and marked Appendix A, in which the board expressed itself as being " fully impressed with the necessity for co-operation between the two States to develop the Port of New York," and " ready to immediately consider and carefully study any comprehensive plan having that for its object "; but the board believed that the " presentation and adoption of such comprehensive plan should precede the making of the proposed treaty granting such vast power for all time to the Port Authority in the Port District to be created thereby."

The board recommended that this Commission be continued in existence so as to permit it, as a result of the studies it has already made and is still making, to present such comprehensive physical plan for examination and study, together with a comprehensive statement of the ways and means to carry such plan into effect. It is also stated that "the active and earnest co-operation of New Jersey is invited by the board in any movement tending to improve and develop the Port of New York in all its parts and to the fullest extent, including matters relative to river and harbor pollution, which now constitutes a grave menace to the harbor of New York, and the abatement of the nuisance arising from the poisonous fumes generated in the factories or plants situated on the New Jersey shore opposite Riverside Drive, which nuisance is most injurious to the health and detrimental to the property of the people residing in that locality."

Main Criticisms of Compact

The main criticisms of the form of the compact developed by the public discussion before the Board of Estimate and Apportionment, with the arguments pro and con, can now be summarized.

Constitution of Port Authority.— It seemed to be the opinion of the members of the Board of Estimate and Apportionment that the New York section of the Port Authority should be made up of the Board of Estimate and Apportionment as a whole, or that at least two of its members should be members of the Board.

In support of this proposition the argument is that since the interests of New York City are so large and extensive and the consequences to the city's development so direct and immediate, the city should have virtual control of the New York section of the Port Authority.

It is argued also that the principle of home rule applies to an agency having so much to do with the future development of the States.

Against the proposition, it is held that the future development of the Port will require a continuing body acquiring its knowledge by experience and not subject at any time to being made the football of politics; that such a continuing authority exists at all other important ports; that without it there will be no adequate consideration given to the great problems of the Port, and that the history of all administrations in the past shows that the members of the Board of Estimate and Apportionment are too busy with other matters to give time and attention necessary to Port problems. It is pointed out, furthermore, that the Port is not only a *city* matter but a *State* matter; and the State's credit may be required for its development.

The opinion of the Commission has been heretofore that the matter of selecting membership in the Port Authority was properly a subject for *legislation* and should not be embraced in the treaty. Article IV now provides that the New York members are to be chosen by the State of New York and the New Jersey members of the State of New Jersey *"in the manner and for the term fixed by the Legislatures of each State."*

Veto Power of the Governors.— It is provided that each State reserves the right hereafter to authorize the vetoing by its Governor of any action of the Port Authority. It was argued before the Board of Estimate and Apportionment that this would give either Governor power to hold up any improvement, no matter how desirable, and though concurred in by the Port Authority.

It is the opinion of the Commission that this section may well receive further consideration on the part of the Bi-State Legislative Commission.

Harbor Pollution.— It is provided that until otherwise determined by the Legislatures the term "rule or regulation for the improvement of the conduct of navigation and commerce within the district," shall not include matter relating to harbor or river pollution.

It seems to be the opinion of the members of the Board of Estimate and Apportionment that this reservation should not be made. In this connection the attention of Your Excellencies is called to the fact that there is now pending in the United States Supreme Court, a suit of the State of New York against the State of New Jersey and the Passaic Valley Sewerage Commission to restrain the construction and operation of the trunk-line sewer to be built for the purpose of conducting the discharge of sewage to a point in New York Bay. The original bill in this suit was filed October 7, 1908, and by a recent order of the United States Supreme Court the case was reopened for the purpose of taking additional testimony; and it has been stated both in New York and New Jersey that the inclusion in the proposed compact of matters of harbor pollution might embarrass the United States Supreme Court in the decision of the pending litigation. The suggestion was made by representatives of the Merchants' Association as well as by the Committee of the New Jersey Bar Association that for the time being this matter be reserved.

By chapter 539 of the Laws of 1903 the New York Legislature appointed a commission to investigate certain threatened pollution of waters in New York Bay, the commission consisting of Daniel Lewis, chairman, Olin H. Landreth, George A. Soper, Myron S. Falk and Louis L. Tribus.

This Commission made its first report on March 31, 1905, and its second report April 30, 1906. In its report of March 31, 1905, it emphasized in the following language the needs of the metropolitan district as a whole and the desirability of joint State action: "It has been suggested, therefore, that a metropolitan sewerage district should be established, to include all sections in both New York States and New Jersey which now or in future may sewer into the bay and its tributaries. This district, when authorized by joint State and Federal legislation, should be under the direction and control of a permanent interstate commission, with plenary power to control the discharge of all sewers hereafter constructed, as well as the task of evolving a comprehensive plan for ultimately rendering the present chaotic and systemless method of sewage disposal sanitary and suitable for all future requirements.

"There seems to be no possibility of a comprehensive treatment of this great question through the action of various and constantly changing local authorities, acting independently. Manhattan may continue, as at present, to follow no system whatever, simply emptying a new sewer into North or East River at any place where grades permit, even though a recreation pier or public bath may be already established at the same point. Brooklyn may, and probably will, carry its sewage into the sea, and thus ruin the bathing beaches within its limits, and pollute the great oyster beds therein, and Westchester county for forty miles from the city may contribute a large amount of sewage, while the State of New Jersey, with its constantly increasing population, will add to its present outflow from year to year.

" The necessity also exists for a central authority to not only direct, but also initiate, these great public works, upon which depend the beauty and healthfulness of the approximately 450 miles of shore within the metropolitan district.

" Immediate action should be commenced to secure such an interstate commission, for the existing conditions must steadily approach the point where the public will demand relief.

" In this country there is at present but one locality at all analogous to New York in this respect, viz., Boston, where a great metropolitan district empties its sewage into the harbor, but the difference in governing conditions is radical, as but one State is in control, while for New York harbor two great commonwealths would have to join forces.

" England permitted the pollution of the Thames for centuries, but at last was compelled to purify its waters at a cost far exceeding the expense of *preventing* such contamination had the demands of competent judges been complied with a hundred years ago.

" If New York and New Jersey should now initiate the plan above outlined the mistakes of other great municipalities could be happily avoided."

In support of the policy urged by the commission it obtained from Attorney-General John Cunneen an opinion upon the question " whether in the event this commission finds it desirable to recommend for future consideration the establishment of a metropolitan sewerage district, covering parts of the two States of New York and New Jersey, the Legislatures of the two States have authority to establish such a district and appoint a commission having adequate powers of administration," the Attorney-General answering the question as follows: " I am of the opinion that the States of New York and New Jersey may, if they see fit, construct a metropolitan sewerage district, covering parts of the territory of the two States, and giving jurisdiction thereover to the courts of one or the other of said two States, as to all matters pertaining to the proper sewerage of said district. Such concurrent acts of the States of New York and New Jersey should, however, in my judgment, be approved and ratified by an act of Congress, for the reasons hereinbefore set forth, namely, that the Federal Government has supreme control over the navigable waters of the Hudson River and New York Bay, and its approval should, therefore, be had to the joint action of the contiguous States."

Notwithstanding the very wise suggestion on the part of the New York Bay Pollution Commission, no attempt has been made since 1906 to bring the States together upon a compact which would cover this important matter and create the central authority recommended by the commission of 1903.

Your Commission was not charged primarily with the duty of considering the matter of harbor pollution, but it has no hesitancy in adopting and agreeing with the conclusion quoted from the report by the New York Bay Pollution Commission. If it were not for the pendency of the litigation in the United States Supreme Court, it would urge the wisdom of now adopting, after fourteen years' delay, the recommendations of the New York Bay Pollution Commission.

Veto Power for New York City.— At various points in the discussion before the Board of Estimate and Apportionment and in the argument made by its corporation counsel, Hon. William P. Burr, it was urged that the action of the Port Authority in the making of rules and regulations, as well as in the carrying forward of constructive plans, should always be subject to the consent of the Board of Estimate and Apportionment of New York City. Such a provision, in the judgment of the Commission, would tie the hands of the Port Authority and preclude it from going forward with its work.

The Commission realizes that there are many phases of Port development in which the assent of the authorities of the City of New York should be obtained, and that this is equally true of other municipalities in other parts of the proposed district. The Commission is of the opinion that this should be worked out in the legislation to accompany the physical plan, and should not form a part of the treaty.

Flexibility in the Comprehensive Plan.— It was urged that the provision in the proposed compact, "that no change in the plan for the comprehensive development of the Port after it has been adopted by the Legislatures of the two States shall be made except by and with the approval of the Legislatures of both States," would preclude necessary changes in the physical plan that would develop as time went on. It is only fair to state that the Commission does not aim to present a comprehensive physical plan so inflexible as to preclude any change. Such a plan, when presented, will undoubtedly distinguish between what may be called "main features" or "fixed points" and other features which will be treated as matters of detail, subject to change in accordance with provisions of the legislation accompanying the adoption of the plan.

Reversion of Property to the City.— It was explained to the members of the Board of Estimate and Apportionment that in the case of any improvement made by the Port Authority by contract with the city in which the consent of the city was essential, for the crossing or closing of streets, or in which a franchise grant from the city was essential, the city would doubtless require that the property when paid for should revert to it. Members of the Board of Estimate and Apportionment seemed to think that there should be a definite provision in the treaty to cover such a situation. Since, however, the project could not be consummated without the consent of the city, it seems reasonable to assume that any enlightened administration would make such a provision a condition of the grant or franchise.

The Commission is reluctant to insert in the treaty anything except those features absolutely essential. It would seem to be sound judgment that all matters requiring flexibility should be left to legislation following the treaty rather than be embodied in the treaty itself.

With the exception of certain minor changes that have been suggested, the foregoing present all of the subjects that have been made the basis of public discussion before the Board of Estimate and Apportionment. In the opinion of the Commission they present no insuperable difficulties or obstacles which cannot be overcome in any open-minded conference purposing to effectuate the compact.

At the hearings before the Board of Estimate and Apportionment occupying two days, March 26 and 27, it was clearly apparent that many of those present and expressing views had not carefully studied the proposals, and had no clear understanding of the elements involved in the Port problem considered as a whole and as affected by the numerous jurisdictions within the two States, and in consequence thereof of the necessity for the fullest co-operation between the two States. Some who appeared as opponents were converted by the arguments presented to being strong advocates, and your Commission is convinced that further discussion and examination of the proposed compact will lead to its better understanding and the further elimination of those elements of local pride and prejudice and natural antagonism to change which stand in the way of the consummation of the great result.

CONCLUSION

The problems of the Port of New York are more serious than is generally realized, even at the Port itself.

To the population of the Port they are serious, because if anything less than the most efficient system obtainable is in use this fact must be reflected in prices; and because if any other port can offer a more efficient system it is likely to draw trade from New York.

To all New York State and all New Jersey they are serious, because New York is the gateway to and from the interior. If there is congestion at the gateway the interior suffers. The interior trader bears his share of the extra terminal costs. He perhaps suffers a still greater loss through delays, which make his shipments undependable and put him at a disadvantage with his competitor who escapes these delays.

To the nation itself the problems are equally serious. Foreign trade has established New York as its focal point, and at this time, when we have a wonderful opportunity to serve the world and ourselves by expanding our foreign trade, it is of the utmost importance that New York be ready — ready to take half of the increase in trade as she now receives substantially half of the total trade. If large preparations are being made or planned at other ports, they must be vastly larger at New York.

The Commission, bearing all of the foregoing in mind, believes that the greatest benefit to the communities of the Port of New York, to the States of New York and New Jersey at large and to the entire country will come from a scientific development of the whole Port, and is earnestly seeking to evolve a plan for such a development. Its findings to date can be summarized as follows:

A co-ordinated plan that will be a guide for fifty years can be evolved only after the picture and analysis of present conditions have been completed.

The picture is nearly completed and the analysis is well under way.

Unquestionably the most important physical problem of the Port is that of providing for a better and more economical movement of inbound and outbound freight over the trunk lines now terminating on the New Jersey and Staten Island waterfront. Its solution can be found only when the details of the present conditions are known. Three problems that are in a way part of this general problem, but are urgent in themselves, are being given special study. They are the West Side railroad situation in Manhattan; the food distribution system of the Port, which is inseparably related to the West Side problem; and the exterior belt line in New Jersey. Another major problem which must await the complete analysis is that of providing adequate steamship terminals properly related to the railroads.

Execution of any plan will require the direction of a permanent authority with broad powers. The Commission has therefore urged the adoption of the compact discussed in the preceding section of this report. If this cannot be consummated this year the Commission confidently hopes joint action will be taken at the next sessions of the Legislatures to create a "Port of New York District" and a "Port of New York Authority."

In order that the Commission may complete its work, it recommends that the States of New York and New Jersey each appropriate $100,000, the second and final installment of the amount determined upon a year ago as necessary to cover the expenses of the investigation. Respectfully submitted,

WILLIAM R. WILLCOX,
J. SPENCER SMITH,
E. H. OUTERBRIDGE,
DEWITT VAN BUSKIRK,
FRANK R. FORD.

P. S. By direction of Governor Edge and Hon. J. Henry Walters, the bi-State conference reconvened at the call of the chairman on April 5 and the conference unanimously adopted the following resolution:

Resolved: That to the end that a compact between the two States may be submitted to the next Legislature of each State, amended in the light of suggestions made and to be made, the present conference be continued and the legislative sub-committee of each State be instructed and directed to confer with the New York, New Jersey Port and Harbor Development Commission and its counsel and present at an adjourned meeting of this conference, to be held at such time as the sub-committee is ready to report, a revision of the present revised draft of the proposed compact between the States which shall take account of all suggestions that have thus far been made or may hereafter be made; and be it further

Resolved: That it is the sense of this conference that pending the consummation of such compact and the working out of a comprehensive plan for the development of the Port, all projects for terminal facilities within the Port of New York shall be submitted to the New York, New Jersey Port and Harbor Development Commission for consideration and advice, to the end that so far as practicable all such projects shall be in harmony with such comprehensive plan when ultimately adopted; and be it further

Resolved: That the New York, New Jersey Port and Harbor Development Commission continue its work; and each State make the necessary appropriation therefor; and that the Legislatures of each State continue the present Bi-State Legislative Commission.

APPENDIX A

RESOLUTION of the Board of Estimate and Apportionment of the City of New York, adopted April 4, 1919, in relation to the Proposed Treaty between the State of New York and the State of New Jersey, submitted by the New York-New Jersey Port and Harbor Development Commission.

Whereas, the Board of Estimate and Apportionment on or about the 11th day of March, 1919, received from the Hon. J. Henry Walters, President *pro tem.* of the Senate, a communication addressed to Hon. John F. Hylan, Mayor, and to Hon. Robert L. Moran, President of the Board of Aldermen, reading as follows:

> "Chapter 426 of the Laws of 1917, State of New York, and Chapter 130, 1917, Laws of the State of New Jersey, created the New York & New Jersey Port & Harbor Development Commission to study jointly and on behalf of both States the needs of the Port of New York, and to report a comprehensive physical and legal plan of its development mutually agreeable to both States. This bi-State Commission, in order to present in both States complimentary legislation, conferred with Governor Smith of New York, and Governor Edge of New Jersey and the Leaders of both Houses in both States. Following such conference on the fifth day of February, 1919, a resolution was adopted in the Legislature authorizing the appointment of a special committee, consisting of the Governor, Lieutenant Governor, Speaker of the Assembly, the Chairman of the Committee on Finance of the Senate, the Chairman of the Committee on Ways and Means of the Assembly, the Chairman of the Committees on Judiciary of the Senate and Assembly, the Majority and Minority Leaders of the Senate and Assembly, and such others as the Governor might appoint for the purpose of consulting with a similar Committee from the State of New Jersey, and the New York and New Jersey Port and Harbor Development Commission, in relation to the proposed treaty between New York and New Jersey. Pursuant to such resolution the New York Commission was created with membership as hereinbefore indicated and in

addition Governor Smith named the following persons as members thereof, viz.; Hon. Charles D. Newton, Attorney-General; Hon. Murray Hulbert, Hon. William P. Burr, Corporation Counsel; Edward J. McGoldrick, Assistant Corporation Counsel, and Robert C. Cumming, Legislative Bill Drafting Commissioner. On behalf of New Jersey, Governor Edge designated as a conference committee to represent New Jersey the following persons: Hon. Thomas F. McCran, Attorney-General; Hon. Clarence E. Case, Majority Leader of the Senate; Hon. Henry E. Ackerson, Jr., Minority Leader of the Senate; Hon. Arthur A. Pierson, Speaker of the Assembly; Hon. Ralph K. Kellam, and Hon. Hugh C. Barret, Leaders of the Asssembly; and Hon. John K. Milton, Corporation Counsel of New Jersey.

The Legislative bi-State Commission met in New York on February fourteenth in conference with both Governors and the members of the bi-State Port Commission and their counsel. After preliminary discussion upon the subject matter of the proposed treaty a sub-committee was appointed consisting of the Attorneys General of both States and the Majority and Minority Leaders of both Houses of both States, and the Corporation Counsel of New York City and Jersey City, for the purpose of drafting a proposed compact or treaty which might be agreeable to the representatives of both States, with instructions to report back the results of its deliberations to the general conference of the bi-State Commissions. Such bi-State sub-committee, after several sessions and after prolonged discussion and deliberation, submitted on March first, to the general conference a proposed compact or treaty for its consideration. In the submission of such proposed compact or treaty the representatives of each State reserved the right to further criticize or amend such proposal.

During the deliberations of the sub-committee as to the context of the articles of the proposed compact or treaty, Mr. Burr, Corporation Counsel of New York, on behalf of the State of New York, suggested that the approval of the City of New York be first obtained before the treaty should become binding and effective.

The importance of the subject matter to the City of New York, its future development, its harbor development, its prestige as a leading commercial port in this country and in order that the interests of the great metropolis might be fully safe-guarded in every respect, the New York State Committee requested the bi-State Commission to suspend further consideration of the report of the sub-committee until after a compact or treaty had been submitted to the officials of New York City; the members of the New York State Commission expressly reserving decision as to its final action until an examination and investigation, and a report of comment, criticism, suggestion, amendment, approval or disapproval thereof was made upon the part of the City of New York.

The representatives of New Jersey acquiesced and granted the request, and accordingly the conference adjourned to await the call of the Chairman, dependent wholly upon the action and attitude of the City of New York.

As Chairman of the New York Legislative Commission, and as Leader of the Senate, I have now the honor to transmit to you copies of the proposed compact, treaty or agreement and to request you officially to advise us whether or not the proposed instrument meets with your approval and whether or not there are any criticisms, suggestions or amendments which you wish to offer in furtherance of and to safeguard the city's interest.

The comprehensive scheme proposed by the bi-State Port and Harbor Development Commission involves the waiving of very material power and authority now lodged in the City of New York over the conduct and supervision of its water fronts and appurtenances. It comprehends the delegation of regulatory powers to such commission. On the other hand it is suggested that broad powers be granted to such Commission by the respective States so as to protect the City of New York and the Port of New York and to encourage and make attractive the investment of millions of dollars for the development of a great port beneficial to both States under a comprehensive plan which would unify and harmonize operation of a great port. Because of the objections and suggestions made on behalf of the City of New York and called to the attention of the New York State Commission, the members of the Legislature of this State are unwilling to proceed with the proceedings involving the entry into such compact or treaty, or to create such Port Authority as proposed with or without power until the City of New York, through its elected officials, has made its position in relation to the same definitely known. The responsibility of the acceptance or rejection of the proposed comprehensive scheme must now rest with the City of New York.

The New York and New Jersey Port and Harbor Development Commission will contemporaneously herewith submit to you copies of its report to the Legislature.

The New York State Commission desires to urge you to give the matter your immediate attention and serious consideration and beg you to report back with all convenient speed.

Respectfully submitted,

J. HENRY WALTERS."

and

WHEREAS, accompanying said communication, the proposed Treaty or Agreement between the State of New York and the State of New Jersey, submitted by the New York-New Jersey Port and Harbor Development Commission, was transmitted, which proposed Treaty reads as follows:

"WHEREAS, In the year 1834 the States of New York and New Jersey did enter into an agreement fixing and determining the rights and obligations of the two States in and about the waters between the two States, especially in and about the bay of New York and the Hudson River; and

WHEREAS, Since that time the commerce of the port of New York has greatly developed and increased and the territory in and around the port has become commercially one center or district; and

WHEREAS, It is confidently believed that a better co-ordination of the terminal, transportation and other facilities of commerce in, about and through the Port of New York, will result in great economies, benefiting the Nation, as well as the two States of New York and New Jersey; and

WHEREAS, The future development of such terminal, transportation and other facilities of commerce, will require the expenditure of large sums of money, and the cordial co-operation of the States of New York and New Jersey in the encouragement of the investment of capital, and in the formulation and execution of the necessary physical plans; and

WHEREAS, Such result can best be accomplished through the co-operation of the two States by and through a joint or common agency.

NOW, THEREFORE, The said States of New Jersey and New York do supplement and amend the existing agreement of 1934 in the following respects:

ARTICLE I. They agree to and pledge, each to the other, faithful co-operation in the future planning and development of the Port of New York, holding in high trust for the benefit of the Nation the special blessings and natural advantages thereof.

ARTICLE II. To that end the two States do agree that there shall be created and they do hereby create a district to be known as the 'Port of New York District' (for brevity hereinafter referred to as 'The District') which shall embrace the territory bounded and described as follows: (Note: This territory is to be the territory substantially as indicated in the map presented by the New York, New Jersey Port and Harbor Development Commission, accompanying this report, the description and boundary lines in such map are approved generally and are to be worked out in detail and inserted herein by the Commission.) The boundaries of said district may be changed from time to time by the action of the Legislature of either State concurred in by the Legislature of the other.

ARTICLE III. There is hereby created 'The Port of New York Authority,' (for brevity hereinafter referred to as the 'Port Authority'), which shall be a body corporate and politic, having the powers and jurisdiction hereinafter enumerated, and such other and additional powers as shall be conferred upon it by the Legislature of either State concurred in by the Legislature of the other or by Act or Acts of Congress, as hereinafter provided.

ARTICLE IV. The Port Authority shall consist of six commissioners — three resident voters from the State of New York, two of whom shall be resident voters of the City of New York, and three resident voters from the State of New Jersey, two of whom shall be resident voters within the New Jersey portion of the district, the New York members to be chosen by the State of New York and the New Jersey members by the State of New Jersey, in the manner and for the terms fixed and determined by the Legislature of each State respectively.

Each commissioner may be removed from office as provided by the Law of the State for which he shall be appointed.

ARTICLE V. The Commissioners shall, for the purpose of doing business, constitute a board and may adopt suitable by-laws for its management.

ARTICLE VI. The Port of Authority shall constitute a body, both corporate and politic, with full power and authority to purchase, construct, lease and/or operate any terminal or transportation facility within said district; and to make charges for the use thereof; and for any of such purposes to own, hold, lease and/or operate real or personal property, to borrow money and secure the same by bonds or by mortgages upon any property held or to be held by it. No property now or hereafter vested in or held by either State, or by any county, city, borough, village, township or other municipality shall be taken by the Port Authority, without the authority or consent of such State, county, city, borough, village, township or other municipality, nor shall anything herein impair or invalidate in any way any bonded indebtedness of such State, county, city, borough, village, township or other municipality, nor impair the provisions of law regulating the payment into sinking funds of revenues derived from municipal property, or dedicating the revenues derived from any municipal property to a specific purpose.

The powers granted in this article shall not be exercised by the Port Authority until the Legislatures of both States shall have approved of a comprehensive plan for the development of the Port as hereinafter provided; provided, however, that the Legislature of either State with the approval of the Legislature of the other State may from time to time authorize the Port Authority to proceed with specific matters.

ARTICLE VII. The Port Authority shall have such additional powers and duties as shall hereafter be delegated to or imposed upon it from time to time by the action of the Legislature of either State concurred in by the other. Unless and until otherwise provided, it shall make an annual report to the Legislature of both States setting forth in detail the operations and transactions conducted by it pursuant to this agreement and any legislation thereunder. The Port Authority shall not pledge the credit of either State except by and with the authority of the Legislature thereof.

ARTICLE VIII. Unless and until otherwise provided, all laws now or hereafter vesting jurisdiction or control in the Public Service Commission, or the Public Utilities Commission, or like body, within each State respectively, shall apply to railroads and to any transportation, terminal or other facility owned, leased, operated or constructed by the Port Authority, with the same force and effect as if such railroad, or other transportation, terminal or other facility were owned, leased, operated or constructed by a private corporation.

ARTICLE IX. The Legislatures of the two States, prior to the signing of this agreement, or thereafter as soon as may be practicable, will adopt a plan or plans for the comprehensive development of the Port of New York. Thereafter, no change in such plans shall be made except by and with the approval of the Legislature of both States.

ARTICLE X. The Port Authority shall from time to time make plans for the further development of said district, supplementary to or amendatory of any plan theretofore adopted and when such plans are duly approved by the Legislatures of the two States, they shall be binding upon both States with the same force and effect as if incorporated in this agreement.

ARTICLE XI. The Port Authority may from time to time make recommendations to the Legislatures of the two States or to the Congress of the United States, based upon study and analysis, for the better conduct of the commerce passing in and through the Port of New York, the increase and improvement of transportation and terminal facilities therein and the more economical and expeditious handling of such commerce.

ARTICLE XII. The Port Authority may petition any Interstate Commerce Commission (or like body), Public Service Commission, Public Utilities Commission (or like body), or any other federal, municipal, State or local authority, administrative, judicial or legislative, having jurisdiction in the premises, after the adoption of the comprehensive plan as provided for in Article IX for the adoption and execution of any physical improvement, change in method, rate of transportation, system of handling freight, warehousing, docking, lightering or transfer of freight, which, in the opinion of the Port Authority, may be designed to improve or better the handling of commerce in and through said district, or improve terminal and transportation facilities therein. It may intervene in any proceeding affecting the commerce of the Port.

ARTICLE XIII. The Port Authority shall elect from its number a Chairman, Vice-Chairman and may appoint such officers and employees as it may require for the performance of its duties and shall fix and determine their qualifications and duties.

ARTICLE XIV. Unless and until the revenues from operations conducted by the Port Authority are adequate to meet all expenditures, the Legislatures of the two States shall appropriate, annually, for the salaries, office and other administrative expenses, in equal amounts, such sum or sums as shall be recommended by the Port Authority and approved by the Governors of the two States, not exceeding for each State the sum of $100,000.

ARTICLE XV. Unless and until otherwise determined by the action of the Legislatures of the two States, no action of the Port Authority shall be binding unless taken at a meeting at which at least two members from each State are present and unless four votes are cast therefor, two from each State. [Each State reserves the right hereafter to provide by law for the exercise of a veto power by the Governor thereof over any action of the Port Authority.]

ARTICLE XVI. Unless and until otherwise determined by the action of the Legislatures of the two States, the Port Authority shall not incur any obligations for salaries, office or other administrative expenss, within the provisions of Article XIV prior to the making of appropriations adequate to meet the same.

ARTICLE XVII. The Port Authority is hereby authorized to make suitable rules and regulations not inconsistent with the Constitution of the United States or of either State, and subject to the exercise of the power of Congress for the improvement of the conduct of navigation and commerce, which when concurred in by the Legislatures of both States, shall be binding and effective upon all persons and corporations affected thereby.

ARTICLE XVIII. The two States shall provide penalties for violations of any order, rule or regulation of the Port Authority, and for the manner of enforcing the same.

ARTICLE XIX. The territorial or boundary lines established by the agreement of 1834, or the jurisdiction of the two States established thereby shall not be changed except as herein specifically modified.

ARTICLE XX. Definitions.— The following words as herein used shall have the following meaning: "*Transportation facility*" shall include railroads, steam or electric, motor truck or other street or highway vehicles, tunnels, bridges, boats, ferries, car-floats, lighters, tugs, floating elevators, barges, scows or harbor craft of any kind, air craft suitable for harbor service, and every kind of transportation facility now in use or hereafter designed for use for the transportation or carriage of persons or property. "*Terminal facility*" shall include wharves, piers, slips, ferries, docks, dry docks, bulkheads, dock-walls, basins, car-floats, float-bridges, grain or other storage elevators, warehouses, cold storage, tracks, yards, sheds, switches, connections, overhead appliances, and every kind of terminal or storage facilty now in use or hereafter designed for use for the handling, storage, loading or unloading of freight at steamship, railroad or freight terminals. "*Railroads*" shall include railways, extensions thereof, tunnels, subways, bridges, elevated structures, tracks, poles, wires, conduits, power houses, substations, lines for the transmission of power, car-barns, shops, yards, sidings, turn-outs, switches, stations and approaches thereto, cars and motive equipment. "*Facility*" shall include all works, buildings, structures, appliances and appurtenances necessary and convenient for the proper construction, equipment, maintenance and operation of such facility or facilities or any one or more of them. "*Real Property*" shall include land under water, as well as uplands, and all property either now commonly or legally defined as real property or which may hereafter be so defined. "*Personal Property*" shall include choses in action and all other property now commonly or legally defined as personal property or which may hereafter be so defined. "*To lease*" shall include to rent or to hire. "*Rule or regulation,*" until and unless otherwise determined by the Legislatures of both States, shall mean any rule or regulation not inconsistent with the Constitution of the United States or of either State, and, subject to the exercise of the power of Congress, for the improvement of the conduct of navigation and commerce within the district, and shall include charges, rates, rentals or tolls fixed or established by the Port Authority; and until otherwise determined as aforesaid, shall not include matters relating to harbor or river pollution. Wherever action by the Legislature of either State is herein referred to, it shall mean an act of the Legislature duly adopted in accordance with the provisions of the Constitution of the State.

Respectfully submitted,"

In addition thereto "A Preliminary Report of Counsel to Accompany the Tentative Draft of Proposed Treaty" was also furnished to the Board. This Report, after an exhaustive presentation of the legal and economic bases on which the Proposed Treaty is claimed to rest, concludes as follows (p. 139):

"CONCLUSIONS

"From all of which it would appear that the States of New Jersey and New York may join in the consummation either of an original treaty, or, preferably, one amendatory of and supplementary to the Treaty of 1834, preserving in full the sovereignty of each State, but pledging each to the other perpetual co-operation in the development of the port which is common to both. For the purpose of carrying out the comprehensive development of the port, they may create an agency vested with as little or as great power as it shall please the States to grant. *Included in this power is the power to take and hold real estate, to construct, maintain and operate every conceivable kind of terminal facility, and to regulate, within the limitations arising from the paramount power of Congress, and to govern the operation of such facilities. Such a body may be authorized to borrow money upon the credit of the States, to the extent that each State is willing to pledge its credit or to borrow upon its own credit. Upon its acquisition of property, it may itself hold and operate it or lease it to private enterprise upon satisfactory terms.* It can receive grants of the power of eminent domain which each State possesses. It can receive power from Congress to the extent that it pleases Congress to grant power, and like the United States toward the Panama Canal, the two States may declare that they create and hold all of these powers and properties under *a sacred trust — for the benefit of the Nation as a whole.*"

and

WHEREAS, public hearings were had before this Board on the 26th and 27th days of March, 1919, at which public hearings those in favor of the Proposed Treaty or Agreement and those opposed thereto were fully heard and the Board having given careful consideration to the arguments presented pro and con and to all the facts produced, it is hereby

Resolved, That while the Board of Estimate and Apportionment is impressed with the necessity for co-operation between the two States of New York and New Jersey to develop the Port of New York, and to that end is ready to immediately consider and carefully study any comprehensive plan having that for its object, the Board is fully convinced that the presentation and adoption of such comprehensive plan should precede the making of the Proposed Treaty granting such vast powers for all time to the Port Authority in the Port District to be created thereby, and recommends that the present existing New York-New Jersey Port and Harbor Development Commission appointed under Chapter 426, Laws of 1917, State of New York, and Chapter 130, Laws of 1917, State of New Jersey, be continued in existence so as to permit the said Commission, as a result of the studies it has already made and is still making, to present such comprehensive physical plan for examination and study, together with a comprehensive statement of the ways and means to carry such plan into effect.

The said New York-New Jersey Port and Harbor Development Commission was appointed

> "to negotiate or agree upon a joint report, recommending a policy to be pursued by the State of New York, the State of New Jersey and the United States by legislative enactment or treaty or otherwise, to the end that the said port shall be efficiently and constructively organized and furnished with modern methods of piers, rail and water and freight facilities and adequately protected in the event of war. Before making such report, such commission shall make a thorough investigation of port conditions in this country and shall take and employ such engineering, legal or other professional skill and assistance as it may need for the effective working out of a comprehensive and adequate interstate and federal port policy, to meet commercial needs in times of peace and the protection of the harbor and adjacent localities in times of war."

The Board of Estimate and Apportionment will give its most earnest thought and consideration to devising methods by which such comprehensive plan, if approved, may be successfully carried into operation, either through the Proposed Treaty or such other legal procedure as may be deemed necessary or advisable. As matter of fact, the Treaty proposed defers the exercise of any real power by the Port Authority until the adoption of the comprehensive plan (Article VI). Therefore, no harmful delay can result from the change in procedure now recommended by this Board.

The City of New York has for many years been engaged in the development of the Port through its Dock Department and Sinking Fund Commission, and has made great progress since 1871 in carrying out such port and harbor development and improvements.

In the New York Harbor case, recently decided by the Interstate Commerce Commission, December 17, 1917, Commissioner Harlan said:

LACK OF CENTRAL ADMINISTRATIVE CONTROL IN NEW JERSEY

"The inactivity of the municipalities and of the State authorities in New Jersey with respect to the improvement and development of the west side of the harbor is noticeable. The contrast between the notable progress of the city of New York, on the one hand, and the inaction of New Jersey on the other is striking.

This difference in policy is attributable primarily to a difference in conditions. For more than forty years, as previously explained, New York's whole harbor policy has been in the hands of a single department, which now has jurisdiction not only in Manhattan but in the Bronx, in Brooklyn, and in Staten Island, all of which are a part of the greater city. The results of this concentration of authority in a single body have been most beneficial. The whole Port, or such part of it as lies in the State of New York, can be developed as a unit, with dûe regard to the advantage and disadvantage of each part. If all the large steamers can not be accommodated on the west side of Manhattan they may be accommodated in South Brooklyn; if a railroad applicant for pier space on the east side of Manhattan can not be accommodated there, it may be conveniently located in Wallabout Bay; if the ferry service between Manhattan Island and Staten Island is unsatisfactory, the city of New York constructs and operates municipal ferryboats to afford the desired service; and if the ferries operating across the East River are not adequate to carry the rapidly increasing number of passengers traveling between Manhattan Island and Long Island, tunnels are constructed under the river and subway trains operated through them. The advantages which the city derives from the concentration of Port Authority in a single administrative body are numerous and obvious.

In New Jersey the opposite conditions prevail. In that portion of the State which is commonly regarded as being within 'the metropolitan district,' embracing all or parts of the counties of Hudson, Bergen, Passaic, Essex, Union and Middlesex, there are scores of cities, towns and villages, each of which has separate control of its own municipal affairs. Opposite Manhattan Island, on the west side of the Hudson River, are the towns of Edgewater, Guttenburg and Weehawken and the cities of Hoboken and Jersey City, and farther to the south is the city of Bayonne. Each of these municipalities has a separate corporate existence, and each has the power, independently of the others, to take such action as it pleases with reference to the development of its own water front, or to take no action at all.

In 1910, the then Governor of New Jersey appointed a commission of three members to study the problem of port development, and especially to find some method of accommodating large vessels in the harbor without extending the piers farther into the river. That commission worked in co-operation with a similar body representing the State of New York. In 1911, following the report of the New Jersey Commission to the Legislature of that State, the New Jersey Harbor Commission was created, consisting of five members. In 1915 this commission was merged, together with several others, into the New Jersey Board of Commerce and Navigation. Investigations conducted by this board led it to the conclusion that the present adjustment of freight rates results in injustice to New Jersey, and it therefore recommended to the Governor of that State that he appoint a special committee to discover ways and means of procuring a more equitable rate adjustment. That committee, which is known as 'the Committee on Ways and Means to Prosecute the Case of Alleged Rate and Service Discrimination at the Port of New York,' was duly appointed, and it has joined with the New Jersey Board of Commerce and Navigation, with the cities of Newark, Hoboken, Jersey City and Elizabeth, in instituting the present proceeding.

There is no department or board in New Jersey, either State or municipal, whose powers are analogous to those possessed by the Dock Department of the City of New York. The New Jersey Board of Commerce and Navigation has power to lease or sell riparian lands belonging to the State; to inspect power vessels on inbound waterways; to aid in the movement for the construction of a ship canal across the State; to aid the municipalities in developing their water fronts; and generally to supervise the development of port facilities. The board has no power to construct docks or bulkheads, to dig channels, or to provide the funds which are needed for the proper development of the harbor. It can accomplish those things, if at all, only indirectly, by using its influence with the several municipalities and urging them to co-operate. Even the Legislature of the State of New Jersey is forbidden, by a constitutional provision, to incur a debt of more than $100,000 without the consent of the people of the State.

* * * * * * * * *

The result of the division of authority in New Jersey and of the lack of foresight on the part of individual municipalities is strikingly evidenced at Jersey City. Located almost in the heart of one of the best harbors in the world, with more than five miles of frontage on the lower Hudson River and upper New York Bay, and served by five of the country's great trunk lines of railroad; in short, possessing all the qualifications which a seaport of the first rank should have Jersey City has been content to see her valuable water front 'turned into a huge railroad yard.' Of her five miles of shore line more than 90 per cent is owned by the carriers. Of the 133 long piers on the New Jersey side of the harbor only one is publicly owned. An engineer employed by the municipal authorities of Jersey City in 1915 to study the general conditions of the water front and to report on the opportunities for developing it, discovered that of the total harbor frontage of 26,454 feet the city owned but 125 feet; and he could only report that Jersey City, 'intended by nature to be a great seaport,' had 'failed lamentably in the realization of this manifest destiny' and that she had 'entirely neglected to take advantage of these natural and artificial opportunities for greatness in maritime affairs.'

* * * * * * * * *

Since the very earliest days of transportation through the Erie Canal it has been customary to apply the same rates by boat from Manhattan and Brooklyn as from Jersey City and Hoboken, and the same policy will be followed when the new Barge Canal is completed."

This Board invites and will welcome the active and earnest co-operation of New Jersey in any movement tending to improve and develop the Port of New York in all its parts and to the fullest extent, including matters relating to river and harbor pollution, which now constitutes a grave menace to the harbor of New York, and the abatement of the nuisance arising from the poisonous fumes generated in the factories or plants situated on the New Jersey shore opposite Riverside Drive, which nuisance is most injurious to the health and detrimental to the property of the people residing in that locality.

A true copy of resolution adopted by the Board of Estimate and Apportionment, April 4, 1919.

JOSEPH HAAG,
Secretary.

APPENDIX B

PRELIMINARY REPORT OF COUNSEL TO ACCOMPANY THE TENTATIVE DRAFT OF PROPOSED TREATY AMENDATORY AND SUPPLEMENTARY TO THE NEW YORK-NEW JERSEY TREATY OF 1834.

Introduction

The need for enlarging the port and terminal facilities of our country, including those of New York, is no longer the subject of debate. In a public announcement by the United States Shipping Board, made August 4th last, that body says:

"A doubling, and perhaps trebling, of docks, piers, marine railways, and terminal facilities in general of Atlantic, Gulf, and Pacific ports will probably be called for by the swiftly increasing American merchant marine. To provide for the fullest possible service of the ships, once they are released from traffic, even new ports may become necessary.

"The survey of port facilities undertaken shows them taxed to capacity by the present shipping — in many instances overtaxed, and in nearly all instances, unless they are speedily expanded, facing serious congestion. *This is especially true of the facilities of New York Harbor, the greatest problem of port development in the world to-day.*"

United States Interstate Commerce Commissioner James S. Harlan, in a report to the Director General of Railroads (March 30, 1918), says, referring to the Port of New York: "*Wholly aside from the extraordinary volume of the traffic, to and through the port, of the allied and of our own military and naval establishments at this time, new and enlarged terminal facilities must be provided, apparently on a liberal scale and on both sides of the river, if the port of New York is to hold its commanding place in our domestic and foreign commerce.*"

"The Iron Age" for June 20th last reports that there has already been established a "red-flag zone" covering an area comprising the New England States, eastern and southern New York, eastern Pennsylvania, New Jersey, Delaware, and eastern Maryland, exclusive of Baltimore, making a line roughly bounded by Albany, Altoona, Shippensburg, Rutherford Yards, Baltimore and the balance of Maryland, and the Atlantic Ocean, into which zone, by the action of the War Industries Board and the Fuel and Railroad Administrations no new factories may be established until further notice " because it is already so congested with steel-works, munition plants, factories of all kinds, and shipyards that it is practically impossible to secure adequate supplies of labor, coal, and satisfactory transportation facilities for existing concerns."

In the Joint Report made to the Legislature of the State of New York, January 3, 1917, by the Governor's Market Commission, the Food Supply Committee appointed by the Mayor of the city, and the Wicks Legislative Committee, approved also by the Food and Market Committee of the New York State Mayors' Conference, it is stated: " The improvement and enlargement of existing terminal facilities and the addition, where necessary, of further terminal market facilities, at points convenient for distribution, would reduce the cost of handling foodstuffs. * * * Improved terminal facilities would not only reduce the ultimate cost of food to the consumer but would permit dealers to do business more economically and would provide them with facilities for doing a much larger business."

Governor Whitman, in transmitting the Preliminary Report of the New York, New Jersey Port and Harbor Development Commission under date of February 18, 1918, said: " The time has come to look forward and to plan in advance for the future demands that will be made upon the port. Haphazard, piecemeal attempts to solve the terminal problem at the port will hinder, not hasten, the desired solution. * * * This [work of planning] cannot be done by any commission representing either state alone. *The task must be a joint task.*" Indeed, the New York, New Jersey Port and Harbor Development Commission itself represents the registered will and purpose of the two states to engage in this joint and common undertaking.

The problem presented to the Commission has many facets. The engineering, economical, commercial and financial phases of the problem are being thoroughly studied and are to be treated in a separate report. In the Preliminary Report of the Commission (January 26, 1918) it was stated that in addition to the engineering and commercial phases of the problem, there must be worked out " a sound and practicable legal plan." This report deals with the legal phases of the problem only and with the tentative solution to be offered for public discussion. For this purpose it is assumed that the Commission will conclude from its study that *comprehensive development of the port facilities must come about through the co-operation of the two states,* joining, where necessary, with the federal and municipal authorities, acting through some form of agency which shall be vested with broad legal powers to build, maintain and operate port facilities, to improve commerce and navigation at the port, to borrow money for such purposes, and vested with adequate power to deal with all phases of the matter whether such facilities be under public or private ownership or operation, or both.

At the threshold; we face the fact of dual political sovereignty. The port lies in two states, each an independent sovereignty in its own land. The legal problem, therefore, cannot so easily be stated or solved as it might be for New Orleans, Philadelphia, Boston or Baltimore. Again, traffic between two states across boundary waters is *interstate commerce.* Neither one state nor the other can wholly regulate the port. Yet in its recent decision in the New York Harbor Case, No. 8994, the Interstate Commerce Commission held (p. 713) that " Historically, commercially and industrially the cities of northern New Jersey within the metropolitan district constitute a part of New York," and that this fact is true is shown by the most casual inspection of the charts annexed to the opinion, indicating the growth in population and assessed valuation, in the number of persons engaged in manufacturing, in the capital invested in manufacture and the value of manufactured products in the northern counties of New Jersey, as well as in greater and lesser New York. These show that the progress of the northern counties of New Jersey parallels the progress of the communities on the corresponding New York side of the port. The progress is interrelated and the progress of each part reacts upon the other.

The Federal Census Bureau issues a compilation of what is called " The New York City Metropolitan District." It takes in not only Greater New York City (comprising Bronx, Kings, New York, Queens and Richmond counties), but the whole of Westchester county (with such cities as New Rochelle, Mount Vernon and Yonkers) besides Bergen, Essex, Hudson, Middlesex, Passaic and Union counties in New Jersey (including such cities as Jersey City, Hoboken, Harrison, Elizabeth, Rahway, Newark, Orange, Montclair, Paterson, etc.). This district embraces 616,928 acres of territory, of which but 183,555 acres constitute the area of New York, and 433,373 acres constitute the area of the outlying territory. The estimated population of the city in 1914 was 5,333,539, and that of the outlying territory but 1,936,568, the total for the district being 7,270,107. As defined in the census of 1910, the "New York City Metropolitan District" includes, in addition to the central city, fifteen cities, forty-one boroughs, two villages, seventeen towns and seventeen townships.

The Interstate Commerce Commission refers to the great and valuable results that may be expected to follow from the creation of the New York, New Jersey Commission.

The problem presented to the Port Commission is, how shall this interstate relationship — now politically divided — be effectively united to promote the welfare of the two states and the nation? No constructive solution, in our opinion, can be found which fails to take full account of the historical factors and the legal questions involved.

The Early Commercial Relations Between New York and New Jersey

In 1798, Robert Livingston secured from the state of New York a monopoly for the operation of steamboats upon the waters of the state. With Livingston's support and on the basis of the state monopoly, Robert Fulton built the "Clermont." On the 7th of August, 1807, she traversed the one hundred and fifty miles between New York and Albany in thirty-two hours and thereby won for her owners "the sole right to use steam on the lakes and rivers of New York State for twenty years to come." (McMaster's History of the People of the United States, Vol. 3, pp. 490–491).

In 1808, John Cox Stevens at Hoboken built the "Phoenix," intended to ply as a passenger boat between New Brunswick and

New York, but the monopoly held by Fulton and Livingston prevented that vessel from entering the waters subject to the jurisdiction of New York State. Accordingly Stevens sent her by sea to the Delaware and ran her between Philadelphia and Trenton. A year later Fulton built another boat called the "Raritan." The "Raritan" made three trips a week between New Brunswick and New York. McMaster tells us: "The route between the two chief cities of the country was thus partly by land and partly by water, and was strongly recommended to such as wished to avoid dust, mosquitoes, and a dangerous ferry. The traveller could leave Philadelphia at seven o'clock on any Monday, Wednesday, or Friday morning by the Phoenix, enjoy a cool and pleasant sail up the Delaware, breakfast and dine on board, and reach Bordentown at one. From Bordentown he went by stage to New Brunswick, where he must spend the night. At six the next morning the steamboat Raritan carried him to New York." By 1810 the "Raritan" and the "Phoenix" ran in connection with each other as parts of one route. It was then possible at a cost of $5.00 in money and twenty-six hours in time to cover the ninety miles which separated Philadelphia from New York, three times a week. The profits of the "Raritan" trade, twelve shillings for each passenger, went to the Fulton and Livingston Company. This provoked the wrath of the people of New Jersey and in the legislature the monopoly of Fulton and Livingston was boldly attacked. New Jersey demanded that if its citizens could not build a steamboat and send it across the Hudson to New York without the permission of Fulton and Livingston, then no boat having the Fulton and Livingston license should enter the waters of New Jersey. In consequence of this demand, New Jersey passed an act which (says McMaster) "greatly enraged the monopolists." In the New York statute it was provided that if anyone should navigate a steamboat within the jurisdiction of the state of New York without a license, the party aggrieved might "seize the boat, engine, tackle, and apparel." New Jersey, referring to this New York law, passed a statute which provided that if anyone did seize such a boat belonging to a citizen of New Jersey and lying on the waters between the two states, the owners might seize in return any boat belonging to any citizen of New York found in any waters of New

Jersey. The New York company thereupon threatened to withdraw their boat, place it on the Sound, grant no licenses to run steamboats to New Jersey, stop the ferry at Paulus Hook and ruin New Brunswick. This unhappy controversy, however, was settled by the courts. A rival of the New York company sprang up and a boat called the "Hope" was soon running between New York and Albany without a license. Fulton and Livingston applied for an injunction which the New York Court of Appeals sustained but which the United States Supreme Court reversed. Thereby was established the great authority of *Gibbons v. Ogden,* 9 Wheat. 1; 6 L. ed. 23 (see also *Gibbons v. Ogden,* 17 Johns. (N. Y.) 488), holding that the legislature of the state of New York *had no power to grant a monopoly upon navigable waters and that since traffic between the two states constituted interstate commerce the power to regulate such commerce lay with Congress.*

The Boundary Dispute

The history of the boundary dispute between the two states has been well told by two judges — by Judge Garrison in the case of *Central Railroad of New Jersey v. Jersey City,* 70 N. J. L., 41 Vroom 81, and Judge Lucius Q. C. Elmer in *State v. Babcock,* 30 N. J. L. 29. (Judge Elmer was in fact one of the Commissioners representing New Jersey in the negotiations that finally brought into existence the treaty of 1833-4.)

The lands and territory now constituting the states of New York and New Jersey, including the Hudson River, were originally granted by Charles II in 1664 to James, Duke of York, who became vested by reason of this grant with both governmental and proprietary rights on each side of the waters that separated the two colonies. The Duke granted to Lord Berkeley and Sir George Carteret the territory now known as the State of New Jersey, describing it as

"All that tract of land adjacent to New England and lying and being to the west of Long Island and Manhitas Island, and bounded on the east by the main sea, and part of Hudson's river, and hath upon the west the Delaware Bay and to the northward as far as the northernmost branch of said bay or the river of Delaware, which is forty-one degrees and forty minutes of latitude, and crosses over thence in a straight line to Hudson's river in forty-one degrees of latitude."

Between the date of this grant and the Revolutionary War, the charters of New York City and the proceedings of the New York authorities indicate that it had always been claimed by New York that the whole of the Hudson River, up to the low water mark on the westerly shore, belonged to that state. The war of the Revolution resulted in New York and New Jersey emerging as free and sovereign states. After the Revolution, when it appeared that if New York's claim were acquiesced in, all the wharves and improvements on the Jersey shore would be subject to the control of New York, New Jersey claimed that by conquest from the Crown the right of New Jersey was extended to the middle of the river. Thus, in 1806 New Jersey passed a statute in which it recited that it had become "invested with full right and lawful authority to exercise jurisdiction in and over the Hudson river and the main sea and all the ports, harbors and havens lying adacent to and along the Jersey shore and coast in such manner as belongs to a sovereign and independent state to use and exercise."

Judge Washington decided, however, that the grant to New Jersey limited its territory to the eastern shore of the Delaware River and Bay, a decision acknowledged by the courts of New Jersey to be correct, (see *State v. Davis,* 1 Dutcher 386) and, what was still more adverse to the claim of New Jersey in reference to the Hudson, the Supreme Court of the United States laid down the doctrine that "When a great river is the boundary between two nations or states, if the original property is in neither, and there be no convention respecting it, each holds to the middle of the stream;" "when, as in this case," said the court, "one state is the original proprietor, and grants the territory on one side only, it retains the river within its own domain, and the newly created state extends to the river only;" and upon this principle the United States Supreme Court held that the Ohio River was exclusively within the territorial limits of Kentucky, and that Indiana had no jurisdiction over or right to the river. *Handly's Lessee v. Anthony,* 5 Wheat 374.

This controversy over the boundaries was a sore spot in the relations between the two states, which the statesmen on both sides of the Hudson tried to remove. In 1806, New Jersey appointed a commission to meet with a similar commission appointed by New York to make an agreement to settle and determine this boundary dispute. Such a commission met in 1807 but reached no agreement. In 1826, the Deputy Sheriff of Richmond County of New York was arrested and indicted by the New Jersey authorities for serving process within the jurisdiction of New Jersey. In 1828, Governor Williamson of New Jersey addressed the Legislative Council and General Assembly, summarizing the history of the boundary dispute, pointing out that both in 1806 and in 1818, New Jersey had made attempts to put an end to the dispute and that nothing had been accomplished. In 1829, the states having still failed to agree, New Jersey filed a bill against New York in the Supreme Court of the United States, a summary of which is to be found in 108 U. S. 406-410. No appearance in this suit was ever entered by the State of New York, although various attempts were made to compel her to appear. 3 Pet. 461; 5 Id. 283; 6 Id. 323. (The bill was finally dismissed on February 15th, 1836, two years after the confirmation by each state of the treaty of 1834, see below.)

In 1833, Governor Marcy of New York wrote to Governor Southard of New Jersey, expressing great regret over this unfortunate boundary controversy and suggesting that another effort be made toward an amicable adjustment. Accordingly, in 1833 an act was passed by each state giving each of the Governors power to appoint three commissioners to confer. These commissioners were to meet, and if possible, to adjust the controversy between the two states. The names of the New Jersey commissioners were:

Hon. Theodore Frelinghuysen
James Parker
Lucius Q. C. Elmer

and the New York Commissioners were:

Benjamin F. Butler
Peter A. Jay
Henry Seymour.

They were entirely successful and the result of their discussion was the adoption of the New York-New Jersey Treaty of 1833-4.

(Ch. 8, Laws of New York, 1834; Laws of New Jersey, 1833-34, p. 118.) The two acts were confirmed by the Congress of the United States, June 28, 1834. (U. S. 23 Cong. 1 sess. Sen. doc. No. 239.) This treaty is very brief It is as follows:

The New York-New Jersey Treaty of 1834

Article 1. The boundary line between the two states of New York and New Jersey, from a point in the middle of Hudson River, opposite the point on the west shore thereof, in the forty-first degree of north latitude, as heretofore ascertained and marked, to the main sea, shall be the middle of the said river, of the bay of New York, of the waters between Staten Island and New Jersey, and of Raritan Bay, to the main sea, except as hereinafter otherwise particularly mentioned.

Article II. The state of New York shall retain its present jurisdiction of and over Bedlow's and Ellis' Islands, and shall also retain exclusive jurisdiction of and over the other islands lying in the waters above mentioned, and now under the jurisdiction of that state.

Article III. The state of New York shall have and enjoy exclusive jurisdiction of and over all the waters of the Bay of New York, and of and over all the waters of Hudson River, lying west of Manhattan Island, and to the south of the mouth of Spuyten Duyvel Creek, and of and over the lands covered by the said waters to the low water mark on the westerly or New Jersey side thereof; subject to the following rights of property and of jurisdiction of the State of New Jersey, that is to say:

1. The state of New Jersey shall have the exclusive right of property in and to the land under water, lying west of the middle of the bay of New York and west of the middle of that part of the Hudson River, which lies between Manhattan Island and New Jersey.

2. The state of New Jersey shall have the exclusive jurisdiction of and over the wharves, docks and improvements made and to be made on the shore of the said state, and of and over all vessels aground on said shore, or fastened to any such wharf or dock; except that the said vessels shall be subject to the quarantine or health laws, and laws in relation to passengers, of the state of New York, which now exist or which may hereafter be passed.

3. The state of New Jersey shall have the exclusive right of regulating the fisheries on the westerly side of the middle of the said waters; *Provided,* that the navigation be not obstructed or hindered.

ARTICLE IV. The state of New York shall have exclusive jurisdiction of and over the waters of the Kill Van Kull, between Staten Island and New Jersey, to the westernmost end of Shooter's Island, in respect to such quarantine laws and laws relating to passengers as now exist or may hereafter be passed under the authority of that state, and for executing the same; and the said state shall also have exclusive jurisdiction, for the like purposes, of and over the waters of the Sound, from the westernmost end of Shooter's Island to Woodbridge Creek, as to all vessels bound to any port in the said state of New York.

ARTICLE V. The state of New Jersey shall have and enjoy exclusive jurisdiction of and over all the waters of the Sound between Staten Island and New Jersey, lying south of Woodbridge Creek and of and over all the water of Raritan Bay, lying westward of a line drawn from the lighthouse at Prince's Bay, to the mouth of Mattavan Creek, subject to the following rights of property and of jurisdiction of the State of New York:

1. The state of New York shall have the exclusive right of property in and to the land under water, lying between the middle of the said waters and Staten Island.

2. The state of New York shall have the exclusive jurisdiction of and over the wharves, docks and improvements made and to be made, on the shore of Staten Island; and of and over all vessels aground on said shore, or fastened to any such wharf or dock, except that the said vessels shall be subject to the quarantine or health laws, and laws in relation to passengers of the state of New Jersey, which now exist or which may hereafter be passed.

3. The state of New York shall have the exclusive right of regulating the fisheries between the shore of Staten Island and the middle of the said waters, provided that the navigation of the said waters be not obstructed or hindered.

ARTICLE VI. Criminal process issued under the authority of the state of New Jersey, against any person accused of an offense committed within the state, or committe.. on board of any vessel being under the exclusive jurisdiction of that state as aforesaid, or committed against the regulations made, or to be made, by that state in relation to the fisheries mentioned in the third article; and also civil process issued under the authority of the state of New Jersey, against any person domiciled in that state, or against property taken out of that state to evade the laws thereof; may be served upon any of the said waters within the exclusive jurisdiction of the state of New York, unless such person or property shall be on board a vessel aground upon, or fastened to the shore of the state of New York, or fastened to a wharf adjoining thereto; or unless such person shall be under arrest, or such property shall be under seizure, by virtue of process or authority of the state of New York.

ARTICLE VII. Criminal process issued under the authority of the state of New York, against any person accused of an offense committed within that state, or committed on board of any vessel being under the exclusive jurisdiction of that state as aforesaid; or committed against the regulations made or to be made by that state, in relation to the fisheries mentioned in the fifth article; and also civil process issued under the authority of the state of New York, against any person domiciled in that state, or against property taken out of that state to evade the laws thereof; may be served upon any of the said waters within the exclusive jurisdiction of the state of New Jersey, unless such person or property shall be on board a vessel aground upon, or fastened to, the shore of the state of New Jersey, or fastened to a wharf adjoining thereto, or unless such person shall be under arrest, or such property shall be under seizure, by virtue of process or authority of the state of New Jersey.

ARTICLE VIII. This agreement shall become binding on the two states when confirmed by the legislatures thereof respectively, and when approved by the Congress of the United States.

The Purpose and Meaning of the Treaty

The treaty has been frequently passed upon by the courts both of New York and New Jersey. In *State v. Babcock,* 1 Vroom 29, the New Jersey Court held that an indictment for a nuisance by placing wrecks in the Hudson River below low water mark on the

New Jersey shore would not lie in the state of New Jersey, upon the ground that by the compact of 1834 exclusive jurisdiction over offences in or upon the water or lands under them resided in the state of New York. In *Central Railroad of New Jersey v. Jersey City*, 41 Vroom 81, Judge Garrison quotes with approval (p. 96) the statement of Judge Andrews of the New York Court of Appeals as follows: "The purpose of vesting exclusive jurisdiction over these waters in the state of New York was to promote the interests of commerce and navigation, which would, as supposed, be best subserved by giving to this state the exclusive control and regulation of the waters of the bay and harbor of New York." Judge Garrison held that what was granted over these waters was not "sovereignty" but jurisdiction as "distinct from sovereignty" and that in consequence the power to tax the property under water still remained with New Jersey. On appeal to the United States Supreme Court (209 U. S. 472), decided April 27th, 1908, Justice Holmes delivered the opinion, saying: (p. 479) "But we agree with the state courts that have been called on to construe that part of the agreement, that the purpose was to promote the interests of commerce and navigation, not to take back the sovereignty that otherwise was the consequence of article 1. This is the view of the New York as well as of the New Jersey court of errors and appeals, and it would be a strange result if this court should be driven to a different conclusion from that reached by both the parties concerned."

Judge Elmer, reviewing the history resulting in the Treaty of 1834, says in *State v. Babcock*, 1 Vroom 29, pp. 33 and 34:

"When the commissioners of New Jersey and New York again met, in 1833, and it was found that those of the latter state appeared to be desirous of arranging the dispute upon fair and liberal terms, but deemed it indispensable that their great commercial emporium should have the exclusive control of the police on the surrounding waters, and full power to establish such quarantine regulations as should be found necessary, the commissioners of this state deemed it wise to secure the exclusive property in the soil to the middle of the river, and exclusive jurisdiction over the wharves, docks, and other improvements made or to be made on the Jersey shore, and of the vessels fastened thereto, and the right to regulate the adjacent fisheries, leaving to New York, which was thought to be quite as much a burthen as a privilege, the exclusive jurisdiction over offences in or upon the waters or the land covered by the water outside of the low water mark. As it was thought possible that the time might come when Perth Amboy should be an important city, like exclusive jurisdiction over the adjacent waters to low water mark on Staten Island was secured to this state. Nothing has since occurred to make the propriety of this arrangement doubtful; on the contrary, there is every reason to believe that it has secured important rights to this state, which otherwise might have been lost.

"In further elucidation of this subject, it is to be noticed that the river Delaware was never within the jurisdiction either of this state or of Pennsylvania until, by the Revolution, the rights of the crown were extinguished, and each state then held to the middle. Under these circumstances, the agreement between the two states, adopted in 1783, *Nix. Dig.* 824, provided that the two states should have concurrent jurisdiction in and upon the water of that river. Of so little importance, however, was this regulation, that it was not until so lately as 1856 that any law of this state was passed providing for the punishment of offenses committed on the river."

In *People v. Central Railroad of New Jersey,* 42 N. Y. 283, at p. 295, June, 1870, Judge Smith said: "It is quite apparent, I think, that they [the Commissioners] well and wisely considered that the necessities of the case, the welfare of these states, the exigencies of commerce, and the interests of the city and port of New York in particular, in whose prosperity, as the commercial metropolis of the country, New Jersey had, in a large degree, a common interest, required that there should be a unity of control over said waters, and a single and exclusive jurisdiction exercised over them by one of the said states."

In the same case Judge Earl said:

"At the date of this agreement [1833], certain docks and wharves had already been made on the New Jersey side, and it was foreseen that others might thereafter be needed and be made. New Jersey had but little commerce and no important city or seaport upon these waters. New York City then controlled by far the largest share of the commerce of this country, and these waters were mainly important as her seaport. It was important that this port should be subject to but one state jurisdiction, and that its jurisdiction should be of the state possessing the city of New York, and having by far the largest interest in regulating, protecting and governing the port. It was clearly the intention of the commissioners, as gathered from the whole agreement, to place that port under the exclusive jurisdiction of the state of New York, so that she could control and regulate it in the interest of her great commerce and her great commercial city.

"At the time this agreement was made, New York was a large and flourishing commercial city, with the finest port, and destined to be one of the largest commercial emporiums in the world, while New Jersey had no commerce, no commercial port, and no brilliant commercial prospects."

Under an act passed in 1886, a suit was brought in the courts of New York against one Ross to recover a penalty for depositing dredgings from a slip in the city of New York into the waters of the North River. Ross and his associate, in December, 1887, dumped a scow-load of material which they dredged from a slip in the city of New York into the river opposite New York City, but on the Jersey side at a point about one-quarter of a mile from the New Jersey shore. It was claimed that since the deposit had been made within the territorial limits of New Jersey, the state of New York had no jurisdiction to enact a law subjecting persons to liability for an act done within the territory of that state. The Court of Appeals held that the compact of 1834 settled the matter and gave to New York jurisdiction over such matters to low water mark on the Jersey side, Judge Andrews saying:

"The purpose of vesting exclusive jurisdiction over these waters, in the state of New York, was to promote the interests of commerce and navigation, which would, as supposed, be best subserved by giving to this state the exclusive control and regulation of the waters of the bay and harbor of New York. * * *

" The 8th section of the act of 1886 was manifestly enacted for the protection of the harbor of New York in the interest of commerce and navigation. The citizens of New York City may possibly have a greater stake in the matter than citizens in other localities, but the destruction or serious impairment of the harbor of New York would directly affect the prosperity of the state. It would impair its revenues, imperil its system of river, canal and railroad transportation, and it is not too much to say that every industrial interest, agricultural or mechanical, would feel its blighting influence." (June, 1891. *Ferguson v. Ross,* 126 N. Y. 459, at p. 463 and p. 465.)

Our Commission has concluded — tentatively — that the structure of a Port Authority for the Port of New York should be built upon the firm foundation of the New York-New Jersey treaty of 1834. It has concluded, further, that in such an amendment of the treaty account should be taken of what is now known as the "Metropolitan District" and that commercially, as well as historically, the district is in fact, if not in law, one district. The difficulties that arise in the erection of such an authority at once suggest themselves: To what extent *can* power be vested in such an authority? To what extent *should* such power be vested? What power shall such a port authority possess over municipalities and communities embraced within the territory? How shall it deal with property, title to which is now vested in such localities? What shall become of the bonded indebtednesses of these various communities and of their constitutional debt limitations, especially in the case of New York City? On the one side are all the municipalities and townships now embraced in Greater New York, organized into one large single political unit; on the other are various small units still unorganized. How, if at all, shall these units be represented and how shall their authority be balanced? These questions are not entirely legal questions. They do, however, present legal phases. They are in the main *political* questions. They must take account of the habits of thinking and feeling of all of these communities, as well as of the legal principles involved.

Interstate Commerce and Navigation — The Federal Power

"Commerce * * * ," said Chief Justice Marshall in *Gibbons v. Ogden,* 9 Wheat. 189, "is intercourse." The power to regulate commerce extends to the regulation of navigation.

In *Gilman v. Philadelphia,* 3 Wall. 713, Mr. Justice Swayne, speaking for the Court, said: "Commerce includes navigation.

The power to regulate commerce comprehends the control for that purpose, and to the extent necessary, of all the navigable waters of the United States which are accessible from a state other than those in which they lie. For this purpose they are the public property of the nation, and subject to all the requisite legislation by Congress. This necessarily includes the power to keep them open and free from any obstruction to their navigation, interposed by the states or otherwise; to remove such obstructions when they exist; and to provide, by such sanctions as they may deem proper, against the occurrence of the evil and the punishment of offenders.

"It is for Congress to determine when its full power shall be brought into activity, and as to the regulations and sanctions which shall be provided."

Congress has vested the Secretary of War with power to determine when bridges constitute obstructions to navigation. The Secretary of War may go so far that if at any time he find a bridge constructed over any of the navigable waters of the United States to be an unreasonable obstruction to the free navigation of such waters either on account of insufficient height, width of span, or otherwise, he may direct the removal or alteration of the bridge so as to render navigation through or under it free, easy, and unobstructed. This same power may be applied to other structures on, over or under navigable waters. The United States Supreme Court has repeatedly held that this is not an unconstitutional delegation of legislative or judicial power to the Secretary. Only recently has it been held by the United States Supreme Court, Judge Pitney writing the opinion, that even though a bridge span be constructed at great expense pursuant to a franchise granted by Congress, neverthless the Secretary of War may decide that the bridge was of insufficient horizontal clearance of the channel span and order the alteration of the bridge (as occurred in the case of the Ohio Falls bridge, a bridge built across the Ohio River, at Louisville, Ky., under the authority of an Act of Congress approved in 1865). Judge Pitney said:

"It is true that Congress must have contemplated that a large investment of private capital would be necessary, and that the bridge when once constructed could not be abandoned or materially changed without a total or partial loss of value. [It was claimed that it would cost over $400,000 to comply with the order of the Secretary of War.] This is a very grave consideration, and we have not at all overlooked it; but we cannot deem it controlling of the question presented." *Louisville Bridge Co. v. United States,* 242 U. S. 409, 61 L. ed. 395, 37 Sup. Ct. Rep. 158.

Accordingly, the court held that the authority of Congress to compel changes was precisely the same as if the bridge had been constructed under state legislation without license from Congress, as in *Union Bridge Co. v. United States,* 204 U. S. 364, 388, 400, 51 L. ed. 523, 534, 539, 17 Sup. Ct. Rep. 367; *Monongahela Bridge Co. v. United States,* 216 U. S. 177, 193, 54 L. ed. 435, 442, 30 Sup. Ct. Rep. 356; or had been constructed under Congressional consent or authorization, coupled with an express reservation of the right of revocation or amendment, as in *Newport & C. Bridge Co. v. United States,* 105 U. S. 470, 481, 26 L. ed. 1143, 1147; *Hannibal Bridge Co. v. United States,* 221 U. S. 194, 207, 55 L. ed. 699, 704, 31 Sup. Ct. Rep. 603.

The paramount power of Congress is illustrated by the decision in *Stockton v. Baltimore & N. Y. R. Co.,* 32 Fed. Rep. 9. In this case the Staten Island Railroad Company was organized under the laws of the state of New York to operate a railroad in Staten Island. It procured from Congress the supplementary power to build a bridge across the Arthur Kill, between Staten Island and New Jersey, and proceeded to lay the foundation of the bridge upon the shore and land under waters of the Kill within the state of New Jersey. By the Act of April 6, 1886, New Jersey had prohibited any person or corporation from erecting any bridge, etc., over or in any part of the navigable waters where the tide ebbs and flows, and separating that state from other states, without permission from the legislature of that state. The Attorney General of New Jersey sought to restrain the railroad company from building its bridge across the Kill. Judge Bradley held that the statute of New Jersey was unconstitutional in that it was in conflict with the paramount power of Congress to deal with commerce and navigation. Judge Bradley afterwards, as is well known, became a judge of the United States Supreme Court. This opinion of his has been frequently cited with approval, especially in the United States Supreme Court. See *Scranton v.*

Wheeler, 179 U. S. 141, at p. 159 and p. 186; *Illinois Central R. Co. v. People of the State of Illinois,* 146 U. S. 387; *Luxton v. North River Bridge Co.,* 153 U. S. 525.

Judge Bradley said concerning the paramount powers of Congress: "It matters little whether the United States had or has not the theoretical ownership and dominion in the waters, or the land under them; it has, what is more, the regulation and control of them for the purposes of commerce. So wide and extensive is the operation of this power that no state can place any obstruction in or upon any navigable waters against the will of Congress, and Congress may summarily remove such obstructions at its pleasure. And all this power is derived from the power to 'regulate commerce.' Is this power stayed when it comes to the question of erecting a bridge for the purposes of commerce across a navigable stream? We think not. We think that the power to regulate commerce between the states extends, not only to the control of the navigable waters of the country, and the lands under them, for the purposes of navigation, but for the purpose of erecting piers, bridges, and all other instrumentalities of commerce which, in the judgment of Congress, may be necessary or expedient." (pp. 20, 21.)

Further, as a part of the decision, Judge Bradley held that the power which Congress thus possesses may be delegated to a New York railroad corporation. Thus the land under water of New Jersey which, as it happened in the Stockton case, was leased for oyster culture, from which the State of New Jersey derived a revenue, was taken for the construction of the bridge without compensation to the state or to the private owners.

The same question came up before the Circuit Court for the Southern District of New York before the late Judge Wallace (*Decker v. Baltimore & N. Y. R. Co.,* 30 Fed. Rep. 723). Judge Wallace held as did Judge Bradley, in the course of his opinion saying:

"Whether the waters are wholly within the boundaries of a state, or, as here, lie between two states, is not material. They are navigable waters of the United States, if they form by themselves, or by uniting with others, a continuous highway for commerce with other states or countries. *The Daniel Ball,* 10 Wall.

557; *Escanaba Co. v. Chicago,* 107 U. S. 682, 2 Sup. Ct. Rep. 185.

" The power of control over such waters necessarily includes the power of deciding what structures are impediments to commerce; and, by an unbroken line of decisions, it is settled that the paramount authority regulating bridges that affect the navigation of the navigable waters of the United States is in Congress.

" So long as this authority lies dormant, the states may authorize the erection of bridges over navigable waters within their limits, which may to some extent obstruct navigation, or, by concurrent action, may bridge the waters lying between them; but, so soon as Congress intervenes and exercises its power of regulation, what has been done by state authority must give way to the paramount authority of Congress. The power of the state ends where that of the nation begins. * * *

" The lands under the water on the New Jersey side of Arthur Kill belong to the state of New Jersey, or to those who have derived title from the state. The shores of navigable waters, and the soil under them, were not granted by the constitution to the United States, but were reserved to the states respectively. *Pollard v. Hagan,* 3 How. 212. The right of eminent domain over such lands, for all municipal purposes, resides in the state within the boundaries of which they lie, and within the legitimate limitations of this right the power of the state to appropriate the shores of navigable waters, and the lands under them, is absolute. *Ormerod v. New York, W. S. & B. R. Co.,* 21 Blatchf. 106, 13 Fed. Rep. 370."

In *People v. Rensselaer & S. R. Co.,* 15 Wend. 113, Chief Justice Savage, after asserting that the power to erect bridges over such waters existed in the state legislature before the adoption of the federal constitution, says:

" It is not pretended that such power has been delegated to the general government as is conveyed under the power to regulate commerce and navigation. It remains, then, in the state legislature, or it exists nowhere. It does exist because it has not been surrendered any further than such surrender may be qualifiedly implied; that is, the power to erect bridges over navigable streams must be considered so far surrendered as may be necessary for a free navigation upon those streams."

Judge Wallace in the Decker case says further:

"The argument that the rights of the state of New Jersey are ignored or invaded by permitting such a bridge to be built without her consent is purely a sentimental one. She has no control of the water-way for the purposes of navigation which is not subordinate to the will of Congress. She can make no use of it against the will of Congress. The act of Congress does not attempt to appropriate any of the property of her citizens, or to interfere with her power of eminent domain.

"If the constitutional power of Congress over the navigable waters of the United States is confined to a mere negation of state authority over them, if Congress can only ratify and prohibit what the state proposes, if it has no faculty of independent action, and no vigor to originate, then, instead of being paramount, the power is practically subordinate to the power of the state. Yet it has never been doubted that, within the scope of its powers, the government of the United States is supreme, or that its authority, when asserted, is, to the extent asserted, of necessity exclusive." (pp. 724, 725, 727, 728.)

More recently, in the state of New York (*People v. Hudson River Connecting Railroad Corporation,* 104 Misc. 19), the same federal authorities have been applied by Mr. Justice Chester in the Supreme Court of Albany County (June, 1918) in a suit brought by the state to restrain the Hudson River Connecting Railroad Corporation from constructing a bridge across the Hudson River between a point near Castleton in Columbia County and a point near Selkirk in Albany County. This is to be the "federal cut-off." By an Act of Congress approved by the President on March 13, 1914, the railroad was granted power "to construct, maintain and operate a bridge, together with the necessary approaches thereto, across the Hudson River, at a point suitable to the interests of navigation, between Castleton and Schodack Landing . . ." and by subsequent Act of Congress (August 9, 1916) the time for the commencement of the construction of the bridge was extended to March 30, 1918, as to commencement, and to March 30, 1920, as to the completion. Under various Acts of Congress vesting the Secretary of War with power, plans for the bridge were submitted to and approved by him, and on May 2, 1917, he made and filed his certificate, approving the revised plan and permitting the building of the bridge under regulations and conditions specified in the certificate. By Chapter 166 of the Laws of New York of 1918 (approved by the Governor on April 9th of that year), the proposed bridge was forbidden and the Attorney-General was authorized to bring proceedings to enjoin its construction and also to forfeit the charter of the defendant. Judge Chester holds that Congress, under the constitutional power to regulate commerce, " has the paramount right to regulate such commerce over highways, railroads and bridges as well as upon navigable waters," and that "the Hudson River in part forms the boundary line between two states, and with the enlarged Erie Canal forms a navigable waterway for commerce to Canada and to several western states," and the bridge in question is " a connecting link from the east to the west which will carry commerce from and to foreign countries and between the states." Although the sentiment behind the passage of the law in the state of New York was unusually strong, Judge Chester says " there is but one answer which can be given to this question, and this answer should not be given by yielding to public sentiment or to the desires of influential public bodies who have spoken on the subject, but must be responsive to the controlling power of the supreme law of the land.

" It has been settled by a long line of authorities from the time of the decision of the Supreme Court of the United States in the early and leading case of Gibbons v. Ogden (9 Wheaton 1) *to the present day, that under the clause of the Federal Constitution which vests in Congress power ' to regulate commerce with foreign nations and among the several states ' (U. S. Const. Art.* 1, *Sec.* 8, *Clause* 3), *Congress has paramount authority under such clause over all navigable waters of the United States."*

In *Erie Railroad Company v. People of the State of New York,* 233 U. S. 671, at p. 681, it is said: " The relative supremacy of the state and national power over interstate commerce need not be commented upon. Where there is conflict, the state legislation must give way. Indeed, when Congress acts in such a way as to manifest its purpose to exercise its constitutional authority, the regulating power of the state ceases to exist."

In the Hudson River Connecting Railroad Corporation case, as in the Stockton case, the state owned the land under water on which it was proposed to erect the ends of the defendant's bridge. Judge Chester follows Judge Bradley's decision.

The Powers of the State

Notwithstanding these declarations, there is a broad field in which the states may still exercise power. In the first place, as Chief Justice Marshall in *Gibbons v. Ogden* said: "The completely internal commerce of a state . . . may be considered as reserved for the state itself." This language, quoted by Mr. Justice Hughes, speaking for the United States Supreme Court in the Minnesota Rate Case (230 U. S. 352 (1912) at p. 398), is the basis for holding that in the absence of federal action effect may not be denied to the laws of the state enacted in the field which it is entitled to occupy *till its authority is limited through the exertion by Congress of its paramount constitutional power.* (p. 400.) "But within these limitations," says Mr. Justice Hughes, "there necessarily remains to the states until Congress acts, a wide range for the permissible exercise of power appropriate to their territorial jurisdiction, although interstate commerce may be affected. It extends to those matters of a local nature as to which it is impossible to derive from the constitutional grant an intention that they should go uncontrolled pending federal intervention. Thus, there are certain subjects having the most obvious and direct relation to interstate commerce, which nevertheless, with the acquiescence of Congress, have been controlled by state legislation from the foundation of the government because of the necessity that they should not remain unregulated, and that their regulation should be adapted to varying local exigencies; hence, the absence of regulation by Congress in such matters has not imported that there should be no restriction, but rather that the states should continue to supply the needed rules until Congress should decide to supersede them. *Further, it is competent for a state to govern its internal commerce, to provide local improvements, to create and regulate local facilities, to adopt protective measures of a reasonable character in the interest of the health, safety, morals, and welfare of its people, although interstate commerce may incidentally or indirectly be involved.*

Our system of government is a practical adjustment by which the national authority as conferred by the Constitution is maintained in its full scope without unnecessary loss of local efficiency. Where the subject is peculiarly one of local concern, and from its nature belongs to the class with which the state appropriately deals in making reasonable provisions for local needs, it cannot be regarded as left to the unrestrained will of individuals because Congress has not acted, although it may have such a relation to interstate commerce as to be within the reach of the federal power."

The United States Supreme Court held in the Minnesota Rate Case, 230 U. S. 352, at p. 403, that "A state is entitled to protect its coasts, to improve its harbors, bays, and streams, and to construct dams and bridges across navigable rivers within its limits, unless there is conflict with some act of Congress. Plainly, in the case of dams and bridges, interference with the accustomed right of navigation may result. But this exercise of the important power to provide local improvements has not been regarded as constituting such a direct burden upon intercourse or interchange of traffic as to be repugnant to the federal authority in its dormant state."

In the most recent utterance of the United States Supreme Court on the matter of the power of Congress over interstate commerce (*Hammer v. Dagenhart,* — U. S. 660, Advance Sheets No. 15, July 1, 1918, Child Labor Law), Mr. Justice Day, writing the prevailing opinion of the Court, repeats Chief Justice Marshall's reference in *Gibbons v. Ogden*, 9 Wheat. 1, 6 L. ed. 23, to "that immense mass of legislation which embraces everything within the territory of a state, not surrendered to the general government,— all of which can be most advantageously exercised by the states themselves. Inpection laws, quarantine laws, health laws of every description, as well as laws for regulating the internal commerce of a state, and those which respect turnpike roads, ferries, etc., are component parts of this mass." Mr. Justice Day quotes also from the same great judge's decision in the Dartmouth College case (4 Wheat. 518, 629): "That the framers of the Constitution did not intend to restrain the states in the regulation of their civil institutions, adopted for internal government, and that the instrument they have given us is not to be so construed, may be admitted." Judge Day reminds us that "In interpreting the Constitution it must never be forgotten that the nation is made up of states, to which are intrusted the powers of local government. And to them and to the people the powers not expressly delegated to the national government are reserved."

In dealing with matters affecting navigation and interstate commerce, the United States Supreme Court has had opportunity many times to mark the line of delimitation between state and federal power. Thus, in the prevailing opinion in the recent case of *Southern Pacific Co. v. Jensen*, 244 U. S. 205, it is said: "'Where the subject is national in its character, and admits and requires *uniformity of regulation, affecting alike all the states,* such as transportation between the states, including the importation of goods from one state to another, Congress can alone act upon it and provide the needed regulations. The absence of any law of Congress on the subject is equivalent to its declaration that commerce in that matter shall be free.'" But whether or not the subject "is national in its character, and admits and requires uniformity of regulation, affecting alike all the states," of course depends upon the particular statute in question. Thus, in the *Passenger Cases*, 7 How. 283, the United States Supreme Court held unconstitutional a New York statute which authorized the Health Commissioner of the state to demand, and, if not paid, to sue for and to recover from the master arriving in the Port of New York from a foreign port $1.50 for each cabin passenger and $1.00 for each steerage passenger, mate, sailor or mariner, etc., which moneys were to be appropriated to the support of the marine hospital on Staten Island. Following this decision of the United States Supreme Court, the State of New York modified this statute so as to require the master or owner, etc., to make a report, and upon this report the Mayor was required to endorse a demand upon the master or owner that he give a bond for every passenger landed in the city in the penal sum of $300, conditioned to indemnify the Commissioners of Immigration and every county, city and town in the state against any expense for the relief or support of the person named in the bond for four years thereafter; but the owner or consignee might compute for such bond and be relieved from giving it by paying, within 24 hours after landing of the passengers, the sum of $1.50 for each passenger. It was held, however, in *Henderson v. Mayor of New York*, 92 U. S. 259 (1876) that while the state could require the master or owner of every vessel landing passengers from a foreign port to make a report in writing, under oath, within 24 hours after arriving, to the mayor of the city of the name, date of birth, last legal settlement, age and occupation of every passenger brought from any country out of the United States, etc., nevertheless, the imposition of the dollar and a half for each passenger was unconstitutional and void, as being one of the subjects which " are in their nature national, or admit of one uniform system or plan of regulation." " The laws which govern the right to land passengers in the United States from other countries ought to be the same in New York, Boston, New Orleans and San Francisco."

Nevertheless, the United States Supreme Court has repeatedly sustained those state laws which provide for improvements of rivers, bays and harbors of states. The act of February 16, 1867, of the State of Alabama was an act to provide for the improvement of the river, bay and harbor of Mobile. A commission was created for this purpose, with power to issue bonds up to one million dollars and to apply the proceeds to the cleaning out, deepening and widening of the river, harbor and bay of Mobile, or the construction of an artificial harbor in addition to such improvement. Pursuant to this power, it arranged to cut a channel in the harbor of Mobile. Mr. Justice Field, writing for the Court in *County of Mobile v. Kimball*, 102 U. S. 691, said: " Of the class of subjects local in their nature, or intended as mere aids to commerce, which are best provided for by special regulations, may be mentioned harbor pilotage, buoys and beacons to guide mariners to the proper channel in which to direct their vessels.

" The rules to govern harbor pilotage must depend in a great degree upon the peculiarities of the ports where they are to be enforced." It is quite obvious that the improvement of harbor facilities and the making of local regulations facilitating commerce and navigation do not fall within that group of cases over which Congress exercises exclusive control. " The improvement of harbors, bays and navigable rivers within the states," says Mr. Justice

Field, "falls within this last category of cases. The control of Congress over them is to insure freedom in their navigation, so far as that is essential to the exercise of its commercial power. *Such freedom is not encroached upon by the removal of obstructions to their navigability or by other legitimate improvement. The states have as full control over their purely internal commerce as Congress has over commerce among the several states and with foreign nations; and to promote the growth of that internal commerce and insure its safety they have an undoubted right to remove obstructions from their harbors and rivers, deepen their channels and improve them generally, if they do not impair their free navigation as permitted under the laws of the United States, or defeat any system for the improvement of their navigation provided by the general government.* Legislation of the states for the purposes and within the limits mentioned do not infringe upon the commercial power of Congress . . ." Mr. Justice Field gives us the key to an understanding of "some of the divergence of views upon this question among former judges." He says they "have arisen from not always bearing in mind the distinction *between commerce as strictly defined, and its local aids or instruments, or measures taken for its improvement.* Commerce with foreign countries and among the states, strictly considered, consists in intercourse and traffic, including in these terms navigation and the transportation and transit of persons and property, as well as the purchase, sale and exchange of commodities. For the regulation of commerce as thus defined, there can be only one system of rules applicable alike to the whole country; and the authority which can act for the whole country can alone adopt such a system. Action upon it by separate states is not, therefore, permissible. Language affirming the exclusiveness of the grant of power over commerce as thus defined may not be inaccurate, when it would be so if applied to legislation upon subjects which are merely auxiliary to commerce."

Thus the same judge, writing the opinion in *Hamilton v. Vicksburg, Shreveport and Pacific R. R. Co.,* 119 U. S. 280, held that the grant of authority to the Vicksburg, Shreveport and Texas Railroad Company by the Louisiana legislature to construct a railroad in the State of Louisiana and to build all the necessary bridges for the crossing of navigable streams was valid. "Until Congress intervenes in such cases," says he, "and exercises its authority, the power of the state is plenary. When the state provides for the form and character of the structure, its directions will control, except as against the action of Congress, whether the bridge be with or without draws, and irrespective of its effect upon navigation." The same principle has been applied by the United States Supreme Court to the building of dams across interior streams. See *Manigault v. Springs,* 199 U. S. 473. The right of states or municipalities to build improved terminal facilities and to charge for their use has been repeatedly established by the United States Supreme Court. In *Packet Co. v. St. Louis,* 100 U. S. 423, it is held that a municipal corporation, owning improved wharves which it maintained at its own cost, although engaged in commerce upon the navigable waters of the United States, is not prohibited by the Constitution of the United States from charging and collecting from parties using its wharves and facilities such reasonable fees as will fairly remunerate it for the use of its property. Of course, this is subject to the limitation that there must not be any discrimination. Thus, in *Guy v. Baltimore,* 100 U. S. 434, an ordinance of Baltimore, while requiring vessels laden with the products of other states to pay for the use of public wharves of that city, relieved all vessels containing the products of Maryland from the payment of any fee. The United States Supreme Court held that the City of Baltimore could, if it chose, permit the public wharves which it owned to be used without charge. Under the authority of the state, it might also exact wharfage fees equally "from all who use its improved wharves, *provided such charges do not exceed what is fair remuneration for the use of its property. But it cannot employ the property it thus holds for public use so as to hinder, obstruct, or burden interstate commerce in the interest of commerce wholly internal to that state.*" Exactions of this sort "in the name of wharfage, must be regarded as taxation upon interstate commerce." Again, state laws regulating pilotage, although regulations of commerce, fall within that class of powers which may be exercised by the states until Congress has seen fit to act upon the subject. *Olsen v. Smith,* 195 U. S. 332. See also *Cooley v. Board of Wardens of Port of Philadelphia,* 12 How. 299. In the absence of legislation by Congress, a state may authorize a navigable stream within its limits to be obstructed by a bridge or highway. *Cardwell v. American River Bridge Co.,* 113 U. S. 205. The cases cited in the opinion, says Mr. Justice Field, "recognize the full power of the states to regulate within their limits *matters of internal police, which embraces, among other things, the construction, repair and maintenance of roads and bridges, and the establishment of ferries.*" The reason for distinguishing between local regulations and national regulations is given by Mr. Justice Field at page 208. "The states," he says, "are more likely to appreciate the importance of these means of internal communication and to provide for their proper management, than a government at a distance."

In the recent case of *Arkansas v. Tennessee,* decided March 4, 1918, 246 U. S. 158, 62 L. ed., Judge Pitney, writing for the Court, says: "How the land that emerges on either side of an interstate boundary stream shall be disposed of as between public and private ownership is a matter to be determined according to the law of each state, under the familiar doctrine that it is for the states to establish for themselves such rules of property as they deem expedient with respect to the navigable waters within their borders and the riparian lands adjacent to them." Thus, in the case before him, he holds that Arkansas may, by its law, limit riparian ownership by the ordinary high water mark, and Tennessee, while extending riparian ownership upon navigable streams to ordinary low water mark and reserving as public the lands constituting the bed below that mark, may nevertheless, in the case of an avulsion, followed by a drying up of the old channel of the river, recognize the right of former riparian owners to be restored to that which they had lost by gradual erosion in times preceding the avulsion.

(In the final report of the National Waterways Commission, 1912, (62d Congress, 2nd Session, Sen. Doc. 469) there is a very carefully prepared brief on the law of waters by G. W. Mooney, wherein it will be found that the common law rule of riparian rights is modified and in many cases to a greater or less extent superseded by local common law, constitutional and statutory provisions.)

The railroad bridges across the Passaic River at Newark, New Jersey, and the plank road bridges across the same river, constructed under the authority of the State of New Jersey, were held to be within the powers of the state and not in violation of the federal constitution, notwithstanding the fact that Congress had made Newark a port of entry. (See *Passaic Bridge Cases*, 3 Wall. 782, 793, September, 1857), Mr. Justice Grier saying: "Congress, by conferring the privilege of a port of entry upon a town or city, does not come in conflict with the police power of a State exercised in bridging her own rivers below such port. If the power to make a town a port of entry includes the right to regulate the means by which its commerce is carried on, why does it not extend to its turnpikes, railroads, and canals,— to land as well as water?"

Thus, too, in dealing with the Chicago River (*Escanaba Co. v. Chicago,* 107 U. S. 678), although the United States Supreme Court held that the Chicago River and its branches are navigable waters of the United States over which Congress may exercise control to the extent necessary to protect and improve their free navigation, until that body acts the state of Illinois has plenary powers over bridges across them within the limits of the state, and may vest in Chicago jurisdiction over the construction, repair and use of these bridges within the city, Mr. Justice Field saying: (683) "But the states have full power to regulate within their limits matters of internal police, including in that general designation whatever will promote the peace, comfort, convenience and prosperity of their people. This power embraces the construction of roads, canals and bridges, and the establishment of ferries, and it can generally be exercised more wisely by the states than by a distant authority. *They are the first to see the importance of such means of internal communication, and are more deeply concerned than others in their wise management* . . . When its power [the state's] is exercised so as to unnecessarily obstruct the navigation of the river or its branches, Congress may interfere and remove the obstruction. If the power of the state and that of the federal government come in conflict, the latter must control and the former yield . . . *But until Congress acts on the subject, the power of the state over bridges across its navigable streams is plenary.*"

(p. 687) "The doctrine declared in these several decisions [after reviewing many cases] is in accordance with the more general doctrine now firmly established, that the commercial power of Congress is exclusive of state authority only when the subjects upon which it is exercised are national in their character and admit and require uniformity of regulation affecting alike all the states. Upon such subjects only that authority can act which can speak for the whole country. Its non-action is, therefore, a declaration that they shall remain free from all regulation." (Citing *Welton v. Missouri,* 91 U. S. 275; *Henderson v. Mayor of New York,* 92 Id. 259; *Mobile Co. v. Kimball,* 102 Id. 691.)

"The uniformity of commercial regulations, which the grant to Congress was designed to secure against conflicting state provisions," says Mr. Justice Field, speaking for the Court in the *County of Mobile v. Kimball,* 102 U. S. 691, 698, "was necessarily intended only for cases where such uniformity is practicable. Where, from its nature or the sphere of its operation, the subject is local and limited, special regulations adapted to the immediate locality could only have been contemplated. State action upon such subjects can constitute no interference with the commercial power of Congress, for when that acts the state authority is superseded. Inaction of Congress upon these subjects of a local nature or operation, unlike its inaction upon matters affecting all the states and requiring uniformity of regulation, is not to be taken as a declaration that nothing shall be done with respect to them, but is rather to be deemed a declaration that for the time being, and until it sees fit to act, they may be regulated by state authority."

Mr. Justice Swayne, in *Ex parte McNiel,* 13 Wall. 236, 240, passing upon the New York statute providing for pilotage of the channel of the East River (Hell Gate), gave a very clear definition of the division of power in this field of legislation:

"In the complex system of polity which prevails in this country the powers of government may be divided into four classes. Those which belong exclusively to the States. Those which belong exclusively to the National government. Those which may be exercised concurrently and independently by both. Those which may be exercised by the States, but only until Congress shall see fit to act upon the subject. The authority of the State then retires and lies in abeyance until the occasion for its exercise shall recur. The commercial power lodged by the Constitution in Congress is, in part, of this character. Some of the rules prescribed in the exercise of that power must, from the nature of things, be uniform throughout the country. To that extent the power itself must, necessarily, be exclusive; as much so as if it had been so declared to be, by the organic law, in express terms. Others may well vary with the varying circumstances of different localities. In the latter contingency the States may prescribe the rules to be observed until Congress shall supersede them; the Constitution and laws of the United States in such case, as in all others to which they apply, being the supreme law of the land."

In *Huse v. Glover,* 119 U. S. 543 (1886), the State of Illinois adopted measures for improving the navigation of the Illinois River, including the construction of a lock and dam at Henry and at Copperas Creek on the river. She created a Board of Canal Commissioners and invested it with authority to supervise the construction of the locks and dams, and to control and manage them after their construction, and to prescribe reasonable rates of tolls for vessels. The works were constructed at an expense of several hundred thousand dollars, principally borne by the state. The United States Supreme Court refused to sustain the contention that the charging of tolls was in violation of the constitutional and federal statutes, distinguishing *Gibbons v. Ogden* (where, as we have seen, the U. S. Supreme Court held unconstitutional the action of the state of New York conferring upon Livingston and Fulton the exclusive right to navigate on waters within its jurisdiction vessels operated by steam) and said: "The exaction of tolls for passage through the locks is as compensation for the use of artificial facilities constructed, not as an impost upon the navigation of the stream. The provision of the clause that the navigable streams should be highways without any tax, impost or duty, has reference to their navigation in their natural state. *It did not contemplate that such navigation might not be improved by artificial means, by the removal of obstructions, or by the making of dams for deepening the waters, or by turning into the rivers waters from other streams to increase their depth. For outlays caused by such works the state may exact reasonable tolls. They are like charges for the use of wharves and docks constructed to facilitate the landing of persons and freight, and the taking them on board, or for the repair of vessels."* In other words, *the State of New York and the State of New Jersey, each within its own territory, may build and construct improved warehouses, docks, piers, wharves and every known agency for the improvement of commerce, and so long as the charges therefore are reasonable, may make charges for the use thereof.* As Mr. Justice Field said in *Huse v. Glover,* at p. 548: "The state is interested in the domestic as well as in the interstate and foreign commerce conducted on the Illinois River [Port of New York], and to increase its facilities and thus augment its growth, it has full power. It is only when, in the judgment of Congress, its action is deemed to encroach upon the navigation of the river as a means of interstate and foreign commerce, that that body may interfere and control or supersede it." To improve a port, of course, is not to impede its navigation. "If, in the opinion of the state, greater benefit would result to her commerce by the improvements made than by leaving the river in its natural state — and on that point the state must necessarily determine for itself — it may authorize them, although increased inconvenience and expense may thereby result to the business of individuals. The private inconvenience must yield to the public good. The opening of a new highway, or the improvement of an old one, the building of a railroad and many other works in which the public is interested, may materially diminish business in certain quarters and increase it in others; yet, for the loss resulting, the sufferers have no legal ground of complaint."

See *Transportation Co. v. Parkersburg,* 107 U. S. 691, 696, 698, distinguishing between a charge of wharfage according to the tonnage of a vessel and a duty of tonnage prohibited by the Constitution, the Court saying: "They are not the same thing; a duty of tonnage is a charge for the privilege of entering or trading or lying in a port or harbor; wharfage is a charge for the use of a wharf."

In *Packet Co. v. Keokuk,* 95 U. S. 80 (1877), the Legislature of Ohio granted a charter to the City of Keokuk, under which it was given power to establish and regulate wharves and fix rates of wharfage for the use of wharves. The constitutionality of this act was sustained, Mr. Justice Strong saying: ". . . a charge for services rendered or for conveniences provided is in no sense a tax or a duty. It is not a hindrance or impediment to free navigation. The prohibition to the State against the imposition of a duty of tonnage was designed to guard against local hindrances to trade and carriage by vessels, not to relieve them from liability to claims for assistance rendered and facilities furnished for trade and commerce. It is a tax or a duty that is prohibited; something imposed by virtue of sovereignty, not claimed in right of proprietorship. Wharfage is of the latter character. Providing a wharf to which vessels may make fast, or at which they may conveniently load or unload, is rendering them a service. The character of the service is the same whether the wharf is built and offered for use by a State, a municipal corporation or a private individual; and when compensation is demanded for the use of the wharf, the demand is an assertion, not of sovereignty, but of a right of property."

In *Sands v. Manistee River Improvement Co.,* 123 U. S. 288 (1887) under a Michigan statute a corporation was authorized to improve the Manistee River, a stream wholly within that State. The improvements consisted in the removal of obstacles to the floating of logs and lumber down the stream, principally by cutting new channels at different points and by confining the waters at other points by embankments. It was held that the exaction of tolls for the use of the improvement of the natural waterway was not within the prohibition of the Constitution, Mr. Justice Field saying: "The internal commerce of a State — that is, the commerce which is wholly confined within its limits — is as much under its control as foreign or interstate commerce is under the control of the General Government; and, to encourage the growth of this commerce and render it safe, the States may provide for the removal of obstructions from their rivers and harbors, and deepen their channels, and improve them in other ways, if, as is said in *Mobile County v. Kimball,* the free navigation of those waters, as permitted under the Laws of the United States, is not impaired, or any system for the improvement of their navigation provided by the General Government is not defeated."

The principles which we have here been discussing have been

extended to cover ferries operating between two States. In the Port Richmond Ferry Case (234 U. S. 317), it appeared that the Port Richmond & Bergen Point Ferry Company was incorporated in 1848 by Chapter 306 of the Laws of the State of New York for the purpose of maintaining a ferry across the Kill van Kull from Port Richmond, Staten Island, to Bergen Point, Hudson County, New Jersey. The United States Supreme Court held, Mr. Justice Hughes speaking for the court, after a careful review of all the authorities, that both New York and New Jersey had the right to fix tolls for this ferry and the fact that rates were fixed by New York did not preclude New Jersey from establishing reasonable rates with respect to the ferry establishment maintained on its side. The possibility of conflict between the two states is clearly recognized by Mr. Justice Hughes in this opinion (pp. 332-3. "If the state," says he, "may exercise this power, it necessarily follows that it may not, in its exercise, derogate from the similar authority of another state. The state power can extend only to the transactions within its own territory and the ferriage from its own shore. It follows that the fact that rates were fixed by New York did not preclude New Jersey from establishing reasonable rates with respect to the ferry establishment maintained on its side." But the important fact in the Port Richmond Ferry Case is, as stated by Mr. Justice Hughes at page 320 of the opinion, that "The ferry is not operated in connection with any railroad. Where the ferry is operated in connection with a railroad, a different question is presented. This latter question has received most careful study on the part of the New Jersey judges and finally by the United States Supreme Court. It was involved in the consideration of the validity of the ordinance of New Jersey regulating the rates of ferriage for foot passengers on the Weehawken Ferry connected with the West Shore Railroad. The New Jersey Supreme Court (*New York Central Case,* 74 N. J. L. 367), Mr. Justice Swayze writing the opinion, held that since the ferries were used in connection with railroads, the ordinance was unconstitutional. The Court of Errors and Appeals (76 N. J. L. 664) held that the ordinance was valid in so far as it related to the operation of the ferry between New York and New Jersey and did not relate to the transportation of freight. The United States

Supreme Court, however, in 227 U. S. 248, Chief Justice White writing the opinion, said: (p. 263) "to dispose of the case we are called upon only . . . to determine the single and simple question *whether there has been such action by Congress as to destroy the presumption as to the existence in the state of vicarious and revocable authority over the subject.*" This "*vicarious and revocable authority*" Judge White finds to have been taken away by Congress in the enactment of the Interstate Commerce Commission Act (Act of February 4, 1887, Chapter 104, 24 Stat. at L. 379), in which it is declared that "the term 'railroad,' as used in this act, shall include all bridges and ferries used or operated in connection with any railroad, and also all the road in use by any corporation operating a railroad, whether owned or operated under a contract, agreement or lease . . . ."

It must be apparent from a study of these cases that to steer safely through the legally established channels for such a course as our Commission proposes to follow, we shall need to take careful soundings as we go, lest we break upon the rocks or get caught upon the shoals where navigation is not yet free. We must bear in mind that the exercise of federal power *under war authority* is a different matter than the exercise of federal power under the interstate commerce clause of the Constitution. The places at which the states still continue to exercise "*vicarious and revocable authority*" are exceedingly numerous. They already cover, as we see, pilotage regulations, construction of wharves, piers, bridges, dams, tunnels, operation of ferries (not connected with interstate railroads), quarantine and policing regulations. The political philosophy underlying the distinction between the exercise of state and federal power in these questions has nowhere been caught or defined more effectively than it was in the address by ex-Justice Charles E. Hughes before the New York State Bar Association in January, 1916, made while he was still a justice of the United States Supreme Court. Speaking to the subject "Our Dual System," he said: "Our recent reports abundantly show that questions of utmost nicety are constantly being presented in the application of new statutes, and evidence the extreme difficulty of the work of carrying out the will of Congress over the activities within its control while at the same time avoiding encroachment upon the State field . . . .

"But in the face of the difficulties already upon us, and destined to increase in number and gravity, *we remain convinced of the necessity of autonomous local governments. An over-centralized government would break down of its own weight.* It is almost impossible even now for Congress in well-nigh continuous session to keep up with its duties, and we can readily imagine what the future may have in store in legislative concerns. *If there were centered in Washington a single source of authority from which proceeded all the governmental forces of the country — created and subject to change at its will — upon whose permission all legislative and administrative action depended throughout the length and breadth of the land, I think we should swiftly demand and set up a different system. If we did not have states we should speedily have to create them.*"

In the *Minnesota Rate Case* (230 U. S. 352) Mr. Justice Hughes had to consider to what extent state public service or public utility commissions might act in the fixing of in*tra*state rates upon railroads engaged in in*ter*state commerce. In his opinion are many illustrations of the field in which the states may act until Congress has acted. "In the intimacy of commercial relations," said he, "much that is done in the superintendence of local matters may have an indirect bearing upon interstate commerce. *The development of local resources and the extension of local facilities may have a very important effect upon communities less favored, and to an appreciable degree alter the course of trade. The freedom of local trade may stimulate interstate commerce, while restrictive measures within the police power of the state, enacted exclusively with respect to internal business, as distinguished from interstate traffic, may in their reflex or indirect influence diminish the latter and reduce the volume of articles transported into or out of the state.*" (pp. 410, 411.)

Again: "The interblending of operations in the conduct of interstate and local business by interstate carriers is strongly pressed upon our attention. It is urged that the same right of way, terminals, rails, bridges, and stations are provided for both classes of traffic; that the proportion of each sort of business varies from year to year, and, indeed, from day to day; that no division of the plant, no apportionment of it between interstate and local traffic, can be made today, which will hold tomorrow;

that terminals, facilities, and connections in one state aid the carrier's entire business, and are an element of value with respect to the whole property and the business in other states; that securities are issued against the entire line of the carrier and cannot be divided by states; that tariffs should be made with a view to all the traffic of the road, and should be fair as between through and short-haul business; and that, in substance, no regulation of rates can be just which does not take into consideration the whole field of the carrier's operations, irrespective of state lines. The force of these contentions is emphasized in these cases, and in others of like nature, by the extreme difficulty and intricacy of the calculations which must be made in the effort to establish a segregation of intrastate business for the purpose of determining the return to which the carrier is properly entitled therefrom." (p. 432.)

Notwithstanding these considerations, the United States Supreme Court sustained the power of the states to regulate intrastate traffic on railroads doing an interstate business.

In the recent case of *Wilmington Transportation Co. v. Railroad Commission of California,* 236 U. S. 151 (1914), it is held, ex-Justice Hughes writing the opinion, that Congress may regulate interstate transportation by ferry as well as other interstate commercial intercourse, but until it does do so a state may prevent an unreasonable charge for ferriage from a point of departure within its borders. In this case the limitations of the power of the Interstate Commerce Commission over ferries was developed, and it was apparent that the subject presented was "of a local nature, admitting of diversity of treatment according to local necessities, and it could not be supposed that it was the intention to deny to the states the exercise of their protective power, in the absence of Federal action. . . . The rule which the plaintiff in error invokes is not an arbitrary rule, with arbitrary exceptions, but it is one that has its basis in a rational construction of the commerce clause. As repeatedly stated, it denies authority to the state in all cases where the subject is of such nature as to demand that, if regulated at all, its regulation should be through a general or national system, and that it should be free from restraint or direct burdens save as it is constitutionally governed by Congress; and on the other hand, as to those matters which are distinctively local in character, although embraced within the Federal authority, the rule recognizes the propriety of the reasonable exercise of the power of the states, in order to meet the needs of suitable local protection, until Congress intervenes." (pp. 154, 155.) In the case under discussion, the transportation by ferry was between San Pedro on the mainland and Avalon on Santa Catalina Island, both places being within the County of Los Angeles in the State of California. The Court "assumed upon this record that the state claims the right to exercise its authority only as to transportation between the mainland and the island, and solely with respect to such shipments over this route as are local to the state, both as to the beginning and the end of the transportation. There is no passage through the territory of another state; the transportation, in its entire course, is subject to a single authority,— either that of Congress or that of the state,— and the latter would yield to the exercise of the former." (p. 156.)

Thus, clearly as to ferries operated wholly within the State of New York, in the absence of Congressional regulation the State of New York can act, and similarly, as to ferries operated wholly within the State of New Jersey, the State of New Jersey can act. As we have seen, this applies also to bridges. It is important to keep in mind, however, that in the matter of lighterage and car floatage between the two states, the Interstate Commerce Commission has jurisdiction. In United States v. Baltimore & Ohio Railroad Co., 231 U. S. 274, at pages 288 and 289: "'The mere fact that the physical rails stop at Jersey City does not mean that the railroad transportation there ends. It continues over to Brooklyn by means of car floats, upon which further rails are laid and on which empty and loaded freight cars stand and are transported, so that the rails upon the car floats are brought into contact with the rail ends at Jersey City, and the continuation thereof at Brooklyn, and in this way the transportation by railroad is carried on without interruption from the western points directly to Brooklyn.'" That this phase of transportation is one over which the Interstate Commerce Commission has jurisdiction appears clearly from the briefs and decision in the *New York Harbor Case,* I. C. C. No. 8994. In the case of *Sault Ste. Marie v. International Transit Co.,* 234 U. S. 333 (1913), it was held that a ferry that ran between the

City of Sault Ste. Marie, Michigan and Canada was subject to the protection of Congress and that the State of Michigan could not pass a law requiring a Canadian corporation operating ferryboats to one of its own wharves at Sault Ste. Marie to obtain a license.

In *St. Clair County v. Interstate Sand & Car Transfer Co.*, 192 U. S. 454, it was held that the business of transporting railroad cars was not a ferry business in the proper sense, and that an ordinance passed by a county of Illinois requiring a ferry license for the transporting of cars across the Mississippi between points in Illinois and Missouri was invalid, the Court holding that the requirements of the ordinance made it a direct burden on interstate commerce.

It is by virtue of powers still remaining in the States that the Public Service Commission of New York and the Public Utility Commission of New Jersey are acting with reference to the regulation of public utilities within the two States respectively. It is quite obvious that an agency of both States which can appear before the Commissions of both States upon occasions when the circumstances justify, and present such considerations as are common to the interests of both States, can bring about a harmony of action tending ultimately to the benefit of the port as a whole. As ex-Justice Hughes said in the address to which we have referred: "It would seem to be clear that bodies of intelligent men dealing as experts, for example, with the interstate and intrastate phases of traffic situations, should be in practical accord, or that at least such differences as may appear to exist should be put to the test of mutual statement, analysis and consultation under plans more definitely designed to prevent unnecessary divergencies. . . . I should think that many of our difficulties might be solved by perfecting the machinery of administration with the direct purpose of promoting harmony of action in dealing with those activities which are conducted in the world of affairs as parts of the same enterprises. It should not be deemed impracticable to secure the protective purposes of state and Nation without injury or needless embarrassment to the honest undertakings upon which both depend."

In the dissenting opinion of Mr. Justice Pitney in *Southern Pacific Co. v. Jensen,* 244 U. S. 205, at page 244, and in the dissenting opinion of Mr. Justice Brandeis in *New York Central Railroad Co. v. Winfield,* 244 U. S. 147, at p. 156, will be found a long series of cases in which the exercise of state power has been sustained where Congress has acted only generally. The following quotation from Gould on the Law of Waters, 3rd Edition, Section 35, is a good summary of the legal situation:

"Under the Constitution of the United States a state has the right, if its legislation does not conflict with the action of Congress upon the same subject, to authorize bridges and dams across the navigable waters within its limits; to license wharves, piers and docks intruding upon such waters; to establish harbor lines to which wharves may be extended; to prescribe the places and manner in which vessels may lie in a harbor; what lights they are to carry at night, or what course they shall pursue in navigating a river; to pass reasonable quarantine and inspection laws, and pilotage, or port regulations; to regulate harbor beacons, buoys, salvage, and similar matters of a local and limited nature; to improve the navigability of its waters, and to authorize the collection of tolls in consideration of such improvements."

See also the recent case of *People v. International Bridge Co.,* 223 N. Y. 137.

The Title to Shore Front Property Upon Navigable Rivers

In *Lewis Blue Point Oyster Cultivation Co. v. Briggs,* 198 N. Y. 287, affirmed by the United States Supreme Court in 229 U. S. 82, 57 L. ed. 1083, the rights of private owners as against the State and the Nation of land under navigable waters was very carefully considered by both the New York Court of Appeals and the United States Supreme Court. The Lewis Blue Point Oyster Cultivation Co. held a grant under Colonial patents from the King of England, under which it cultivated oyster beds in the waters of the Great South Bay. A contractor employed by the United States Government proceeded to dredge a channel over the land in question for the purpose of increasing the depth of the water in aid of commerce and navigation, and his work, if successful, would have destroyed the oyster beds planted by the lessees. The latter sought to enjoin the contractor from doing the work. The New York courts held (and were later sustained by the United States Supreme Court): The shores of navigable rivers and streams and the lands under the waters thereof belong to the state within whose territorial limits they lie and the state may authorize the construction of bridges, piers, wharves or other obstructions in navigable waters, and when such obstructions are not obnoxious to the regulation of Congress and do not come in conflict with the paramount authority of the United States, they are not nuisances even though they cut the access of riparian owners to the channels of substreams or bodies of water. While a non-navigable stream is the private property of riparian owners and cannot be invaded without compensation, a non-navigable stream being a stream incapable, continuously or at periodic intervals, "in its natural state and its ordinary volume of water, of transporting, in a condition fit for market, the products of the forests or mines, or of the tillage of the soil upon its banks" (*Morgan v. King,* 35 N. Y. 454, 459), no such rule applies to navigable streams; and "In patents from sovereign to subject the rule of construction which controls deeds between individuals is reversed and the terms are taken most strongly against the grantee, because the public interest is involved." (198 N. Y. 287, at p. 292.) And "For the same reason it is held that from grants of water land there is impliedly reserved the right of navigation, and, as a necessary part of so important a subject, the right to improve navigation for the benefit of commerce." (Idem) ". . . in every grant of lands bounded by navigable waters where the tide ebbs and flows, made by the crown or the state as trustee for the public, there is reserved by implication the right to so improve the water front as to aid navigation for the benefit of the general public, without compensation to the riparian owner. The implication springs from the title to the tideway, the nature of the subject of the grant and its relation to navigable tidewater, which has been aptly called the highway of the world. The common law recognizes navigation as an interest of paramount importance to the public." Consequently, if the grant from the king be silent upon the subject, nevertheless, "when any public authority conveys lands bounded by tidewater, it is impliedly subject to those paramount uses to which government, as trustee for the public, may be called upon to apply the water front for the promotion of commerce and the general welfare.

. . . We think . . . that the conveyance of the uplands in question to a subject should, from public considerations of the highest importance, be held to have been made with the implied reservation of the right to freely improve the navigation of the great seaport, within the general limits of which said uplands were situated." (*Sage v. Mayor, etc. of N. Y.*, 154 N. Y. 61, 79; quoted in Lewis Blue Point Oyster Co. case, 198 N. Y., 287, 293, 294.) Accordingly, Judge Vann, writing the opinion in the Oyster Co. case, says concerning the oyster cultivation company: "It ran the risk when it planted its oysters that the crop might be interfered with whenever Congress decided to dig a channel, or otherwise improve navigation in Great South Bay for the benefit of commerce. Its loss may be severe, but Congress is not apt to deal ungenerously with those who have good grounds for relief." In the United States Supreme Court (Judge Lurton writing the opinion), the decision is rendered almost simultaneously with the decision of *United States v. Chandler-Dunbar Water Power Company,* 229 U. S. 53, 57 L. ed. 1063. The Chandler-Dunbar Co. claimed compensation by virtue of its control of the water power capacity of the rapids and falls of the St. Marys River, upon whose foreshore it operated. Congress, by the Act of March 3, 1909, provided that the entire St. Marys River between the American bank and the international line, as well as all of the upland north of the present ship canal, was necessary and should be taken. Judge Lurton says:

"This title of the owner of fast land upon the shore of a navigable river to the bed of the river is, at best, a qualified one. It is a title which inheres in the ownership of the shore; and, unless reserved or excluded by implication, passed with it as a shadow follows a substance, although capable of distinct ownership. It is subordinate to the public right of navigation, and however helpful in protecting the owner against the acts of third parties, is of no avail against the exercise of the great and absolute power of Congress over the improvement of navigable rivers. That power of use and control comes from the power to regulate commerce between the states and with foreign nations. It includes navigation and subjects every navigable river to the control of Congress. All means having some positive relation to the end in view which are not forbidden by some other provision of the Constitution are admissible. If, in the judgment of Congress, the use of the bottom of the river is proper for the purpose of placing therein structures in aid of navigation, it is not thereby taking private property for a public use, for the owner's title was in its very nature subject to that use in the interest of public navigation. If its judgment be that structures placed in the river and upon such submerged land are an obstruction or hindrance to the proper use of the river for purposes of navigation, it may require their removal and forbid the use of the bed of the river by the owner in any way which, in its judgment, is injurious to the dominant right of navigation. So, also, it may permit the construction and maintenance of tunnels under or bridges over the river, and may require the removal of every such structure placed there with or without its license, the element of contract out of the way, which it shall require to be removed or altered as an obstruction to navigation."

It must not be assumed, however, from the foregoing statement that either Congress or the two states, in their respective territories or combined, are wholly free to deal with the waterfront in and about the Port of New York. The principle is subject to qualifications requiring careful statement. In this respect, it is important to bear in mind that the United States Supreme Court, in dealing with the rights of riparian owners upon a navigable stream, is governed by the law of the State in which the stream is situated (see *Weems Steamboat Co. v. People's Steamboat Co.*, 214 U. S. 345, and *St. Anthony Falls Water Power Co. v. St. Paul Water Commissioners,* 168 U. S. 349), and that the extent of the authority conferred upon a city by its charter, the construction of the charter, and the validity, scope and effect of ordinances and proceedings thereunder and rights of parties thereto under state law, are regarded by the United States Supreme Court as *matters of state law* as to which the decisions of the state courts are controlling. *St. Louis & Kansas City Land Co. v. Kansas City,* 241 U. S. 419.

A: New Jersey

Chancellor Zabriskie, in the leading New Jersey case of *Stevens v. P. & N. R. R. Co.,* at page 554, 34 N. J. L. 532 (1870), says: "The question [of the rights of private riparian owners] is an important one, and its consequences of great moment. On the one hand, every owner of lands on such waters who has purchased and held them in the belief that this adjacency to the water added to their value, and was an incident that could not be taken from him, must lose this supposed right without compensation. And the owner of docks and wharves built by permission of the state, and only valuable for purposes of commerce, may have their value destroyed by a grant to a stranger of ten feet under water adjacent to them. On the other hand, the state will be entitled to the profits and advantages of a sale of all the fisheries the water fronts in its bounds, which, in front of the lands on the Hudson river and bay of New York, and especially of the docks and wharves erected there, will be of immense value and contribute greatly to the financial prosperity of the state, to the advantage of all the inhabitants, and inflict injury on no one except those who have purchased rights, and built wharves, piers, or docks, with indiscreet confidence in the opinions of lawyers and judges, the declarations of legislators as to the rights of the riparian owner, the legislation of the state seemingly conferring certain rights, and in the apparent current of public opinion."

One of the leading cases in New Jersey is *Gough v. Bell,* 22 N. J. L. (2 Zab.) 441. "The ancient rule of the common law," said Green, C. J., "is, that the title of owners of land bounded by the sea, or by navigable rivers where the tide ebbs and flows, extends to ordinary high water mark only. The title to the *shore* between ordinary high and low water mark, as well as the title to the soil under the water, belongs *prima facie,* to the sovereign." This title, which by the common law of England is vested in the king, upon the Revolution, became vested in the people of the state of New Jersey. "In such lands," says Depue in *American Dock and Improvement Co. v. Trustees of Public Schools,* 39 N. J. Eq. (12 Stew.) 409, 411, 412, "the king had a double right — a right of jurisdiction for the purposes of government, and a right of property and ownership — the former as part of the prerogatives of the king as sovereign, the latter as part of the *jura regalia* of the crown." In the province of East Jersey the rights in lands under tidewaters were granted by Charles II to the Duke of York by the charters of 1664 and 1674, and thereby the land or soil under such waters became vested in the Duke of York and were held by him in the same manner as title to the soil under the navigable waters of England was held by the crown. All these rights, including the right of property in the land under tidal waters as the right of sovereignty, were transferred by the Duke of York to the proprietors of East Jersey, and by the surrender of 1702 were restored to the crown. When the people of New Jersey took possession of the government and assumed the powers of sovereignty, the prerogatives and *jura regalia* which had previously belonged to the Crown or to Parliament thereupon became immediately vested in the State. Accordingly, among the rights to which the State succeeded was the right formerly vested in the Crown, of property in the soil under tidal waters, "and the title of the state in such lands," says Depue, idem, "is proprietary in its fullest sense, including the power to grant and convey them to individuals, to be held in private ownership."

In *Stevens v. P. & N. R. R. Co.*, supra, Beasley, C. J., carefully reviewed the history of these water rights and came to the position "that all navigable waters within the territorial limits of the state, and the soil under such waters, belong in actual propriety to the public; that the riparian owner, by the common law, has no peculiar rights in this public domain as incidents of his estate." Nevertheless, in *Gough v. Bell* it was decided, after extensive examination of the law of the state of New Jersey, that there existed in New Jersey a modification of the common law. This modification is the right or license to "wharf out," by which right, "when the land was reclaimed, or the wharf erected by the tacit or express consent of the legislature, it became private property, and divested of its public character. And the owner has the same absolute domain over it, the same exclusive right of enjoyment in it, that he has in and over other private property." (See *O'Neill v. Annett,* 27 N. J. L. (3 Dutch.) 290, 293, 294, per Chief Justice Green.)

In *Marcus Sayre Co. v. Newark,* 60 N. J. Eq. (15 Dick. Ch. 361; 13 Dick. Ch. Rep. 136), Judge Depue says: "Property in a wharf or dock on a navigable stream consists in the ability of the owner to use the structure in connection with the navigable water." (p. 375.) "But this right of acquiring property in lands under tidal waters by improvement or reclamation was restrained within the limit of the ordinary low-water mark," per

Depue in *American Dock and Improvement Co. v. Trustees of Public Schools,* 39 N. J. Eq. 409, 412. This right to wharf out is "a mere license, revocable at the will of the legislature," *which becomes irrevocable only when the license has been executed and the riparian owner has effected the reclamation.* Before the reclamation is actually made, the state may convey its lands to any one, either for public or private use, without making compensation to the riparian owner in front of whose lands the conveyance is made. (p. 413.) *Stevens v. P. & N. R. R. Co.,* 5 Vr. 532, 34 N. J. L. 532. The history of the evolution of the law of New Jersey upon this subject is succinctly stated by Judge Depue in the *American Dock and Improvement Co.* case. In New Jersey, accordingly, the common law is modified to the extent of the existence of this license to "wharf out," which, when exercised, takes the form of a grant from the state irrevocable in its nature. Nothing short of a complete survey of all the grants of lands on the waterfront of New Jersey, therefore, will establish to what extent the control of the waterfront has passed from the state into the hands of private owners. Thus in *New York, Lake Erie & Western R. R. Co. v. Yard,* 43 N. J. L. 632, the Court of Errors and Appeals of New Jersey considered the rights of the railroad to land under water at Weehawken, title to which was derived through the "Weehawken Docks," a corporation which was created by an act of the legislature of New Jersey passed March 22, 1867. Passing upon all of the statutes and grants through which the railroad company claimed title to the waterfront, New Jersey's highest court held: "Neither of the incorporating acts referred to contains any grant of lands the title to which was in the state. They operated only as grants of corporate franchises; and such grants, by the settled law of this state, will not be construed to give by implication, any title to lands of the state below the high-water line." (p. 636.) "As riparian owners," says the Court, "these corporations respectively would have annexed to their title to the upland a privilege, incident to the ownership of lands on tide water, of reclamation, and the acquisition thereby of title to the lands reclaimed. Power to erect and construct the works necessary to the execution of this privilege is enumerated among the franchises granted by their charters.

But the inchoate right which the owner of the upland has to acquire an exclusive title to lands under water by wharfing out or otherwise improving the same, gives him no property in the land before it is reclaimed; he has a mere license, revocable by the legislature at any time before it shall be executed." (Idem) So, too, in *Stevens v. P. & N. R. R. Co.,* (supra) the license had not been executed. On the other hand, in *Hoboken Land and Improvement Co. v. Mayor of Hoboken,* 36 N. J. L. (7 Vroom) 540, the Court held that the land had been reclaimed and that the license was, therefore, executed and title to the company was good. In *Marcus Sayre v. Newark,* 60 N. J. Eq. 361 (1900), the Court clearly holds: " The legislature had the power to grant lands in a navigable river below high-water mark, without regard to the owner of the adjacent upland ". The Court quotes Chief Justice Beasley in the *Stevens v. P. & N. R. R. Co.* case: " ' that all navigable waters within the territorial limits of the state, and the soil under such waters, belong in actual propriety to the public; that the riparian owner, by the common law, has no peculiar rights in this public domain, as incidents of his estate; . . . that, as a general rule, the public domain is subject altogether to the control of the legislature; . . . that, unless in certain particulars protected by the federal constitution, the public rights in navigable rivers can, to any extent, be modified or absolutely destroyed by statute; . . . that the dominion of the legislature over the *jura publica* appears to be unlimited. By this power they can be regulated, abridged or vacated.' " " These explicit declarations of the judgment of this court," says Dixon, J. (p. 366-367), " seem to place beyond question the power of the legislature to authorize the municipalities of the state to use the tidal navigable streams within our borders for sewerage purposes. *The federal constitution interposes no obstacle to the exercise of such a power, provided the availability of the stream for interstate and foreign commerce be not impaired; and as no private property exists in such waters, there remain only the jura publica, over which, in the words of the chief-justice, the dominion of the legislature appears to be unlimited.*" On the other hand, by the local common law of this state, " the owner of riparian lands acquires a property in his reclamations by wharfing out or otherwise improving, and the state cannot appropriate the shore so recovered to public use without adequate compensation. Consequently, for any invasion of his property or use of it without lawful authority such owner is entitled to the same remedies as the owner of property is entitled to under the general law of the state. Among the rights of a riparian owner who has made his improvements between high and low-water mark is the right to the use of his wharf and of access to the navigable waters." (p. 372). Thus in the late case (1900) of *Palen v. Ocean City,* 64 N. J. L. (35 Vroom) 669, the Court of Errors and Appeals, per Collins, J., says at p. 673: "It is lastly urged by the defendant that . . . the nonsuit was right because the title of the land on which the wharf stands is not in the plaintiff, but in the State of New Jersey. This contention ignores the local usage declared in *Gough v. Bell,* 2 Zab. 441, and upheld in this court in *Stevens v. Paterson and Newark Railroad Co.,* 5 Vroom 532, that the shore owner has a license, irrevocable after execution, to build wharves, or reclaim, in front of his lands down to low water mark. This right is confirmed by the Wharf act of 1851. *Gen. Stat.,* p. 3753. *A wharf so built becomes private property.*"

In *Morris Canal and Banking Co. v. Central Railroad Co.,* 16 N. J. Eq. 419, the claim of the Associates of the Jersey Company was not sustained, but it appeared that their charter merely gave them a privilege to build wharves, docks and piers and when so built to appropriate them to their own use, and conferred upon them no power to transfer or convey the privilege to any other corporation. In this case the Master said, at p. 431: "When we take into consideration the extent and value of those lands under water, their situation in relation to our own state and to the city of New York, with its extensive and valuable trade and commerce, and forming, as those waters do, an important part of the harbor of New York, the best, not only in this country but upon this continent, it is most reasonable to conclude that, if the legislature intended to grant and convey the fee in said lands, or such right over them as is contended for by the complainants, that their intention would be made plainly to appear, and that the grant itself would be made in clear, direct, and explicit terms." See also *Newark Aqueduct Board v. Passaic,* 45 N. J. Eq. (18 Stew.) 393.

B: New York

A similar, though not identical, legal situation is presented with reference to the shore front property on the New York side. In the recent case of *First Construction Co. v. State of New York*, 221 N. Y. 295, Judge Hiscock writing the opinion, the Court considered and interpreted grants from the state, including rights to "wharf out." The Referee in this case, Ex-Judge Haight, reported (See Vol. 106, 1916, Court of Appeals Cases, Bar Association Cases on Appeal, p. 98 et seq.): "Under the Common Law of England the title of lands under tide waters vested in the King, who could grant and convey the same; but the dominion and control of the waters in the interests of commerce and navigation was exercised by Parliament for the benefit of all the subjects of the Kingdom. After the Revolution and the separation of the Colonies from the Kingdom, the title of lands under tide waters, in and surrounding this State, under the constitution adopted, vested in the people, who, through their Executive and Legislature, exercised the powers that were formerly vested in the crown and Parliament, in trust, however, for the benefit of the public. The Legislature of the State have, therefore, from time to time enacted laws creating a land board of commissioners of the sinking fund empowered to grant lands under water to the upland owners; and in addition thereto the Legislature has from time time by special acts made grants to individuals designed to be in aid of commerce and not inconsistent with public rights. These grants, however, were all subject to the consent of Congress, who, under the Commerce Clause of the Federal Constitution, is empowered to regulate interstate commerce. This power is now exercised by the Secretary of War under the provisions of an act of Congress approved March 3, 1899.

"The owners of uplands abutting upon tideways are entitled to privileges or easements in excess of those possessed by the public. Such owners are not only riparian proprietors who may pass to and from their own uplands across the tideway to the navigable waters, thus having access to all of their frontage, but in addition thereto they may load and unload boats, receive and ship goods, and thus engage in the commerce of the country. Such upland owners may, with the consent of the Legislature and the approval of the Secretary of War, erect wharves, piers and bulkheads and fill in the lowlands so as to afford ways and means for the shipping and landing of articles of commerce and thus facilitate navigation. When such improvements have been so made and the filling and structures, to the extent made, become a part of the realty and vests in the riparian owners a right of use in the nature of a grant, thus creating a right of property of which they cannot be deprived without consent *except by due process of law or under the powers of eminent domain.*" The grant in this case contained the following: "that it shall be lawful for William Beard and others, owners of real estate fronting upon the waters of the bay, their heirs, and assigns, to erect, construct, build and maintain a sea-wall or breakwater pier, docks, wharves, bulkheads, piers and warehouses and a basin for commercial purposes on the lands under water in front of their premises and to fill in the same." This, the Court of Appeals said, "is not a grant of a fee to such land; but is a permit by which, in so far as such owners of uplands have under the authority of the statute entered upon and improved the same by filling in, or the construction of piers, docks, wharves, bulkheads, etc." The state of New York sought to take the property for the construction of the Barge Canal without compensation for this particular property. Judge Hiscock, writing for the Court of Appeals, held that the statutory grant constituted a privilege to fill in and erect wharves and piers. Differing with the courts of New Jersey, Judge Hiscock said that it was not "a mere license, revocable by the state at will and without payment of compensation"; but "the privilege amounts to more than this and . . . an act granting the right to fill in lands under water, and thereby acquire title to the same, gives an inchoate, vested interest in the lands described which is a property right and of which, unless forfeited or lost in some way, the grantee cannot be deprived without compensation." (p. 316). He says further (317, 318): Grants like the one under consideration are not nude pacts, but rest upon obligations expressly or implicitly assumed to carry on the undertaking to which they relate . . . They are made and received with the understanding that the recipient is protected by a contractual right from the moment the grant is accepted and during the course of performance as contemplated, as well as after that performance." And that, being in their nature franchises, under the principles established by the United States Supreme Court in *New York Electric Lines Co. v. Empire City Subway Co.*, 235 U. S. 179, 193, they cannot be revoked. In *Town of Brookhaven v. Smith,* 188 N. Y. 74, it was held that the Town of Brookhaven could not deprive a riparian owner whose land is bounded by navigable water from access thereto from the front of his lot. Judge Gray carefully reviews the English common law and refuses to accept its doctrine, saying: "Different political and geographical conditions may justify modifications and whether common-law rules will be followed strictly by our courts will, necessarily, where no vested rights are actually concerned, depend upon the extent to which they are reasonable and in accord with our public policy and sentiment." "It is a matter of general observation," said Judge Gray, "of which judicial notice may wisely be taken, that riparian owners everywhere upon the numerous navigable bodies of waters within the territorial limits of this state have made their easement, or right of access, practical and available by the construction of docks, piers or wharfs, and have done so without interference by the state, where superior public rights have not been obstructed. These interests must be very large and if we shall hold with the English common-law doctrine, that they are purprestures, or unlawful encroachments upon the proprietary rights of the state, as would follow, if we affirm this judgment, and that they are removable at pleasure, it would result in causing a very grave loss. Such a decision would be to ignore what has been believed to be a common right, within numerous adjudications of our courts."

"The right of access is conceded to be a valuable one and, unless the foreshore has been appropriated by the general government to some superior, and lawful, public use, as for example, by grant to a municipality, or for navigation purposes, it is entitled to the protection of the law. It has recognition in the statutory provisions which confer upon the owner of the upland the primary right to a grant of the land under water. It is not objected that these defendants have erected a nuisance, in itself, or in some obstruction to public navigation. If it were that, the exercise of the right would be unreasonable; for such ownership is qualified and is subordinate to the public right of navigation, and must be subject to such rules as the legislature may impose for the protection of the public rights in the navigable waters. The courts of this state have been careful, in all cases, while sustaining the rights of the riparian owner, to declare them subordinate to the exercise of the power of the legislature, or of the Congress, for the improvement of navigation, or for the regulation of commerce. They must yield to the demands of public commercial necessities. This structure is conceded to be proper enough for the purpose intended by the defendants and it is no appropriation of the land under water; other than as the soil is used to hold the piles. The defendants have, simply, made their right of access practical. It is a general rule that when the use of a thing is granted, everything is granted by which the grantee may enjoy such use. By analogy, we may reason that the riparian owner's right of access to the navigable waters in front of his upland comprehends, necessarily and justly, whatever is needed for the complete and innocent enjoyment of that right."

On the other hand, at p. 317 of his opinion in *First Construction Co. v. State of New York*, 221 N. Y. 295, Judge Hiscock points out that it is an implied condition of all the grants, like the implied condition of the grant of a franchise to a railroad, that for failure to exercise it or to comply with its conditions, it can be forfeited by the state. "Although the franchise is property, 'it is subject to defeasance or forfeiture by failure to exercise it, or by subsequent abandonment after it has been exercised.' If 'no time is prescribed, the franchise must be exercised within a reasonable time.'" (Quoted by Judge Hiscock at p. 319, from *New York Electric Lines Co. v. Empire City Subway Co.*, 235 U. S. 179, 194, 195.) Following this decision, the Attorney-General procured an amendment to the Public Lands Law of the state (§77, Chapter 308, Laws of 1917), which imposes the duty upon the Secretary of State and the State Engineer and Surveyor to search out defaults of compliance with such grants, and imposes upon the Attorney-General the duty to bring appropriate action to annul such grants in which there is default.

Accordingly, as in the case of New Jersey, a most careful survey of the titles to the waterfront property vested in private individuals is necessary before we can determine the extent to which the state may take over waterfront property without making compensation. The particularity with which such an examination must be made is illustrated in the very excellent report made by Harold G. Aron, Special Counsel to the Public Service Commission, examining the titles of the New York Central Railroad to waterfront property along the west side of Manhattan.

C: The City of New York

Under the Dongan charter, in 1686, the Crown of England granted to the city of New York so much of the land around the Island of Manhattan as lay between high and low water mark, with jurisdiction over the same, coupled with power " to take in, fill, and make up and lay out all and singular the lands and grounds in and about said city and island Manhattan, and the same to build upon or make use of in any other manner or way as to them shall seem fit, as far into the rivers thereof and that encompass the same as low-water mark aforesaid." In 1730, the city received a further grant by the Montgomerie charter. This strip, four hundred feet in width, lies immediately outside of low water mark and extends from Corlear's Hook, on the East River, around the southern extremity of the island to Bestaver's rivulet, excepting, however, the space in front of the Battery, with full authority at any time thereafter " to fill, make up, wharf, and lay out all and every part thereof." In 1798, the Common Council presented a petition to the Legislature in which they represented " that as well for the ornament and improvement of the city, as for the enlargement of the trade and commerce of the state, and the safety of the shipping at the wharves of the city, they had lately ' directed a permanent street, seventy feet wide, to be laid out and completed at and on the extremity of their grants already made, and hereafter to be made, to individuals on the East River, called South street, and on the North River, called West street, south and west of which streets, no buildings of any description ' were to be permitted to be erected; that by reason of the curving, and otherwise irregular state of the shore at low-water mark in the two rivers, at the time of the making of the grants by their predecessors, a general map of which, if ever made, could not then be found, such grants were deemed to extend to unequal distances into both rivers, which occasioned difficulties in making the two permanent streets regular; that in many instances, although they were willing gratuitously to give the soil under water, on which the two streets, seventy feet wide, were to be made, yet doubts were entertained whether they could compel any of the proprietors of the lots fronting on such streets and who might be willing, to make those streets for public use in any given reasonable time to be appointed by the common council; that part of their plan was to extend piers at right angles from those 'permanent streets' into the rivers, but that doubts had also arisen whether they could compel the individual proprietors of the wharves to sink and lay out such piers, or, if they should refuse, whether they would be authorized to sink and build the piers at the expense of the city, and receive the wharfage, without incurring a breach of the conditions and covenants contained in their grants to individuals; that some adequate remedy was essentially necessary in the premises, as well to secure the health of the citizens as to effect ornament and regularity in the fronts of the city, and convenience and safety to the trade and commerce thereof; and they prayed that the legislature would confer such power and authority upon them as would be proper to remove the difficulties and doubts stated, or make such provision as to the legislature should seem meet." In compliance with this petition, in the same year the legislature passed an act under which West street was laid out, and by §2, provision was made for the erection of wharves adjoining the streets, and by §5, for the erection of piers. By Chapter 126 of the Laws of 1806, the legislature further confirmed the rights of those who had erected piers by the direction of the city. In April, 1807, by Chapter 115 of the laws of that year, the commissioners of the land office were authorized to grant by letters-patent to the city of New York all the right and title of the people of the state to the lands covered with water along the easterly shore of the North River, as described in the grant, and also along the westerly shore of the East River, and in December, 1807, the commissioners of the land office by letters-patent granted to the city all the right and title of the people of the state of New York to the lands covered by water along the North and East Rivers.

John Jacob Astor, as the owner of certain uplands, pursuant to a grant from the city under the foregoing statutes, built wharves and streets and claimed to have acquired access to piers at the foot of King street. The right of his grantees came before the Court of Appeals in *Langdon v. Mayor*, 93 N. Y. 129, in which, after reviewing the foregoing history, Earl, J., writing the opinion for the Court, held: ". . . taking the language of the charters and grants, the course of legislation, and all the statutes in *pari materia,* the situation of the lands granted and the use to which many portions of them had, with the knowledge and consent of the legislature, been from time to time devoted, it is very clear that the lands under water around the city were conveyed to it in fee, to enable it to fill them up as the interest of the city might require, and to regulate and control the wharves and wharfage." Thus, having the power and the title, the city could transfer and convey it to individuals. "Having the power to extend the *ripa* around the city, and thus make dry land, it could authorize any individual to do it. Whatever wharves and docks it could build, it could authorize individuals to build, and whatever wharfage it could take, it could authorize individuals to take." Accordingly, it was held that Astor's grantees could not be deprived of their rights, even when the property was needed for a public use, except under the right of eminent domain, and upon making compensation; that the legislature could not authorize a destruction or impairment of these property rights without compensation. In the course of the opinion, Judge Earl said that the common law rule requiring both that "all grants by the sovereign of exclusive privileges and franchises, and all gratuitous grants of land should be strictly construed against the grantee . . . should not be applied to grants of land made for a valuable and adequate consideration paid or agreed to be paid by the grantee." He said: "The Federal government annually makes numerous grants of lands for value paid, and so do some of the states and cities, and it would be quite absurd and perhaps alarming to apply to such grants, usually made by intelligent public officers, with deliberation, in language carefully chosen, under the advice of counsel, the strict rule of construction which at common law was applied to the grants of the English sovereigns." In discussing the power of the city, Judge Earl said:

"It is, however, further contended by the appellants that the city did not have the power to grant the permanent easement claimed by the plaintiff; that the legislature had not conferred upon it the power, by creating an easement over land yet covered by water, forever to preclude either the city or state from exercising that public dominion over navigable waters which was necessary to enable it to discharge the trust of furnishing to the commerce of a great seaport those accommodations which, in the judgment of the city or the state, such commerce may, from time to time, require; that even if the state could delegate the power to the city to grant such an easement, applying the strict rule of interpretation which they invoke for the construction of public grants, there is no language in the act of April 3, 1807, from which any power to create such an easement can be inferred; that the control over the waterfront of the city is a public right pertaining to the sovereignty of the state, and that any surrender of it, even to a subordinate governmental agency, such as municipal corporation, can be proved only by the most indubitable evidence; and that the corporate authorities of the city at any particular time could not bind their successors and prevent a further extension of the water-front in the future.

"These views have at least in part been answered by what has already been written. As we think we have shown, the state could have made the grant to Astor as broad as the plaintiff claims it to be. It could make the same grant to the city, and it could authorize it to make the grant to an individual. Under its old charters and the acts of 1798 and 1807, the city had the right to build wharves along its water fronts, and to take the wharfage accruing therefrom. The land under water with the rights of wharfage was property belonging to it as proprietor, which it is believed, the state could not take without making compensation. (Dill on Mun. Corp. [2d ed.] §40; Cooley's Const. Lim. [4th ed.] 292). It is property which it could lease and sell to individuals, and which it has always been accustomed to lease and sell, and its right to do so is provided for or recognized in various acts of the legislature."

Judge Earl said further: "The views we have expressed leave the city and the state with ample power to improve the harbor of the city in the interest of commerce. The right of eminent domain is not impaired and has not been surrendered. The legislature cannot surrender it, and it may be exercised whenever the public exigencies call for its exercise. It would doubtless be less expensive for the city arbitrarily to take this easement and thus appropriate the wharfage to its own use. But a constitutional barrier stands in the way. It, however, imposes no burden upon the city, in requiring it to make compensation for what it takes, as it gets a dollar of value for every dollar it is obliged to pay."

The same subject received consideration by the Court of Appeals in *Williams v. Mayor,* 105 N. Y. 419, where Judge Finch wrote the opinion. He again reviews the grants under the Dongan and Montgomerie charters and the statutes by which the city was authorized to erect piers, wharves and bulkheads, and reaches the conclusion "that the state did by its earlier acts and their recognition in 1857, permit solid filling on its lands under water within the bulkhead lines, and by that process part with its title and transfer it to him who lawfully made the new land as an approach to the docks. And this view is further strengthened by the two facts that the State has seen this process going on for about half a century without once interfering or asserting a hostile right, but, on the contrary, has given to the city, whenever requested, formal conveyances of its lands so occupied." The following observations of Judge Finch seem pertinent: "It seems only necessary to add that we do not view the grant by the State to the city as without consideration, and purely and simply a gift. *The state owned but a single seaport open to commerce and touched by tide water, and that one a harbor of remarkable size and convenience. Its interest to concentrate there ships and cargoes from all parts of the world, by protecting the harbor and lining it with docks and piers, was very great, and took on the character of a duty due to the prosperity of the commonwealth. It early imposed that duty upon the city and the citizens by whom it has been steadily performed, at very great cost, and one in the future to be largely increased. Every grant the state made was in aid of the expenditure involved in the performance by the city of that duty, and in consideration of that performance. Little enough of its own duty has been borne by the state, and to call that little a pure gratuity amounts almost to a sarcasm.*"

Again, in the *Matter of Mayor, etc., of New York,* 182 N. Y. 361, where the question arose concerning property abutting upon Riverside Drive between 72nd and 129th streets, Judge Haight writes the opinion for the Court:

"The rights of the sovereign, whether crown or state, to land under water in navigable streams and arms of the sea are doubtless twofold, proprietary and governmental. As proprietor, the sovereign may sell or convey to others, but as to the power to govern, the sovereign holds as trustee for the use of the public, under such laws, rules and regulations as may from time to time be adopted and which shall be deemed to best serve the interests of commerce and the state. These powers may be transferred by the sovereign to local subordinate governments which have been established, constituting such governments the trustees of the public and the guardians of the rights and privileges of the people. The king of England, therefore, during our colonial period had the power to grant a charter to the mayor, aldermen and commonalty of the city of New York, constituting it a body corporate and politic with powers of local government, and to convey to it the lands under water surrounding Manhattan island, on which the city is located. This power the king exercised through his colonial governors, who from time to time have enlarged the powers and jurisdiction of the city. While the king had the power to convey the tideway on the shores of the high seas and navigable rivers, he will not be presumed to have done so by merely bounding the conveyance upon the sea or the river; such conveyance will carry title only to high-water mark. Other words must be employed in the conveyance which would clearly indicate his purpose and intent to convey the lands under water in order to pass the title thereto. (*Trustees of Brookhaven v. Strong,* 60 N. Y. 56; *Sage v. Mayor, etc. of N. Y.,* 154 N. Y. 61; *Mayor, etc. of N. Y. v. Hart,* 95 N. Y. 443.) At page 366, Judge Haight reviews the grant of powers in the Dongan charter of 1686, italicizing the words "dockage or wharfage" in the phrase which granted "their rights and appurtenances, together with all the profits, benefits and advantages which shall or may accrue and arise at all times hereafter, for *dockage or wharfage* . . . ." and says: (pp. 368-9)

"It is quite apparent from a reading of the charter that a local subordinate municipal government was here established, to which the sovereign delegated the powers of local government, not inconsistent with the laws of England or of the province of New York, and to which he conveyed the tideway surrounding the island. While we have no express provision of the charter delegating to the municipality the sovereign power to hold the tideway as trustee for the use of the public and for commerce, and to make laws, rules and regulations with reference thereto, we think this power was intended to be delegated to the municipality, and that such intent is clearly inferable from the provisions of the charter growing out of the general powers given to its common council to make laws, ordinances and constitutions, and to amend the same from time to time as may be deemed necessary, and from the fact that he conveyed to the city the land between high and low-water mark. The conveyance of the tideway to the city interposed a barrier between the body of the river and the uplands which would prevent the sovereign from erecting docks, piers or wharves thereon for the accommodation of commerce, and is inconsistent with the purpose of the sovereign to longer retain jurisdiction, control and management thereof for the interest of the public. We, therefore, are of the opinion that it was the intention of the sovereign to delegate to the municipality the power to hold and control the tideway in the interest of commerce and of the public; and that this is apparent from the fact that the charter not only conveyed to the city the tideway, but also granted to it the bridge, docks and piers already constructed, with the right to collect wharfage therefrom. If we are right in this conclusion, it follows that the officers of the city, in conveying to De Kay in 1701, did so as the representatives of the sovereign power delegated to it as a municipal government; and it is deemed, therefore, to have intended only to have included in the conveyance the uplands to high-water mark, retaining the tideway and lands under water as trustee of the public domain in the interests of commerce and of the state."

On the other hand in *Sage v. Mayor,* 154 N. Y. 61, the plaintiff traced his title back to a grant to Governor Nichols in 1667, whereby the inhabitants and freeholders of the village of New Harlaem acquired certain lands bounded on one side by the Harlem River, together with " all the soils, creeks . . ." etc. Under a plan adopted in 1887 for the improvement of the Harlem River between 94th and 95th streets, the city began building a sea-wall behind which it was filling in. This improvement was made pursuant to prior legislation for the improvement of the waterfront of the city of New York, and was in accordance with plans adopted by the Dock Department. The outer portion of the improvement consisted of bulkheads, docks and piers, traversed by a marginal street 125 feet wide, running parallel with the river and situate below the old low-water mark. The plaintiff claimed that his grant ran to low-water mark and covered the lands under water to the bulkhead line established by the Harbor Commission, and sought to restrain the defendants from continuing with the improvement. The opinion of Judge Vann in this case is cited with approval by the United States Supreme Court in *Scranton v. Wheeler,* 179 U. S. 161, 45 L. ed. 137, 21 Sup. Ct. Rep. 48. "As against the general public," says Judge Vann, " as organized and represented by government, they [riparian owners] have no rights that do not yield to commercial necessities, *except the right of pre-emption,* when conferred by statute, and *the right to wharfage,* when protected by a grant and covenant on the part of the state, as in the *Langdon* and *Williams* cases."

The right of riparian owners bordering on the old city of Brooklyn, however, rests upon a different set of facts, as appears from *Steers v. City of Brooklyn,* 101 N. Y. 51, which the Court distinguished in *Sage v. Mayor* at p. 83. In *Bedlow v. N. Y. Floating Dry Dock Co.,* 112 N. Y. 263, 273, the Court of Appeals said that certain grants made to the city of New York of land under water " were obviously made to extend municipal control over said lands, and enable the city to regulate the erection of necessary structures upon the land under water around the island, with a view of promoting facilities for the growing commerce and trade of the port of New York and to regulate and preserve the rights of riparian owners in such lands, and the navigable waters covering them."

The origin of the rights of the old city of New York to *ferry* charters is told by Earl, J., in writing the opinion for the Court of Appeals in *Mayor v. Starin,* 106 N. Y. 1. In this case it was held that the city of New York had the exclusive right to maintain and operate ferries between New York and Staten Island, and that having that right, it could lease to the Staten Island Ferry Co.; that the grant by the Montfomerie charter to the city of New York of ferry franchises from the "Island Manhattan's to any of the opposite shores all around the same island" was intended to secure to the city all the ferry franchises to and from it. . Judge Earl said: "The sovereign was competent to grant and the city to receive these ferry franchises. Such a franchise is property, and the sovereign power is just as able to make an irrevocable grant of it as of any other property. If it can grant a ferry franchise for a term of years, it can do so forever. By so doing, it does not part with any political or governmental function. It still may regulate the conduct of the ferry for the public good and control the tolls to be charged; and it can resume the proprietary right in the franchise only by exercising the right of eminent domain or by forfeiture enforced through regular judicial proceedings. By this grant the city did not merely receive the political right to establish and regulate ferries, but it received the property in the ferry franchises as it received the other property granted to it by its various charters; and we do not find any evidence in the record that what it so received it has ever lost or been deprived of."

The New York Court of Appeals, therefore, has treated the grants of wharf and ferry rights to the city of New York, and, through the city to private individuals, as in their nature *franchises,* and has applied the same principle as it has applied in the grant of street railway franchises by the city of New York.

"The title to streets in New York," said Ruger, Chief Justice, in *People v. O'Brien,* 111 N. Y. 1, at p. 38, "is vested in the city in trust for the people of the state, but under the Constitution and statutes it had authority to convey such title as was necessary for the purpose, to corporations desiring to acquire the same for use as a street railroad. The city had authority to limit the estate granted either as to the extent of its use or the time of its enjoyment, and also had power to grant an interest in its streets for a public use in perpetuity, which should be irrevocable."

In the most recent utterance upon this subject, the New York Court of Appeals has said: (April, 1918 — *Matter of Quinby v. Public Service Commission,* 223 N. Y. 244, at pages 261, 262, Pound, J.): " . . . *our Constitution, by requiring the con-*

sent of the local authorities, recognizes that our municipalities are pro tanto independent of legislative control, exercising some fragment of power, otherwise legislative in character, which has been thus irrevocably transferred by the fundamental law from the legislature to the locality. The grant by the municipality of authority to use the streets is not a mere privilege or gratuity. Once accepted, it becomes a contract which neither the state nor its agencies can impair."

While recognizing fully, therefore, the limitations in private grants of waterfront property (as the Court did in the *Sage* case and the *Blue Point Oyster* case), and recognizing fully the reserved federal and state power to regulate commerce and navigation, it still remains true that by "the right to wharf out" in New Jersey, by express grants from the states, and by grants from the city of New York, rights in the nature of franchises are outstanding, irrevocable in their nature and to be acquired only by the exercise of the power of eminent domain. In the case of the city of New York there are at present outstanding bonds for dock improvements amounting to $122,872,036, the proceeds of which as issued were applied to dock and ferry improvements. The waterfront property which the city owns forms part of the assets pledged to secure these bond issues. By the Constitution of the state of New York, Article VIII, §10, the city is forbidden to borrow more than ten per cent of the assessed valuation of the real estate within its city limits, but in the computation of the indebtedness, property which is self supporting, that is, pays the interest and sufficient to create a sinking fund to amortize the principal of the debt, is excepted. It would seem, therefore, as though the city's dock and ferry property involved not merely the rights of the city itself, but also the rights of those holders of municipal securities which have been issued upon the basis of the ownership of the docks and ferries by the city.

We shall presently consider the power of the state to alter or destroy municipal corporations; but in *Graham v. Folsom* (1905), 200 U. S. 248, recognizing this power of the state to change municipal boundaries, the United States Supreme Court held, nevertheless, that, so far as the impairment of the obligation clause of the Federal Constitution is concerned, the power of the state

5

to alter or destroy its municipal corporation is not greater than the power to repeal its legislation, and the alteration or destruction of subordinate governmental divisions is not the proper exercise of legislative power when it impairs the obligations of contracts previously entered into. In that case a municipal corporation had incurred substantial indebtedness. The legislation by which its organization was destroyed and its territory added to other municipalities was held to be unconstitutional. Likewise, in *Mount Pleasant v. Beckwith,* 100 U. S. 514, and *Mobile v. Watson,* 116 U. S. 289, where, similarly, municipal corporations had incurred indebtedness and state legislators later sought to destroy the municipal corporation and to add their territory to other municipalities, the legislation by which this was sought to be accomplished was held to be in impairment of the obligation clause of the Federal Constitution. In *Graham v. Folsom,* at pages 253, 254, Mr. Justice McKenna, speaking for the Court, said: "It was argued in those cases, as it is argued in this, that such alteration or destruction of the subordinate governmental divisions was a proper exercise of legislative power, to which creditors had to submit. The argument did not prevail. It was answered, as we now answer it, that such power, extensive though it is, is met and overcome by the provision of the Constitution of the United States which forbids a state from passing any law impairing the obligation of contracts. See also *Shapleigh v. San Angelo,* 167 U. S. 646, 42 L. ed. 310, 17 Sup. Ct. Rep. 957. And this is not a limitation, as plaintiffs in error seem to think it is, of the legislative power over subordinate municipalities, either over their change or destruction. It only prevents the exercise of that power being used to defeat contracts previously entered into."

"The repeal of a law may be more readily undertaken than the abolition of townships, or the change of their boundaries or the boundaries of counties. The latter may put on the form of a different purpose than the violation of a contract. But courts cannot permit themselves to be deceived. They will not inquire too closely into the motives of the state, but they will not ignore the effect of its action." (p. 253).

"The city," says Judge O'Brien, speaking for the Court of Appeals in *People ex rel. Rodgers,* 166 N. Y. 1, at p. 11, "is a corporation possessing all the powers of corporations generally and cannot be deprived of its property without its consent or due process of law any more than a private corporation can, and since its revenues must be used for municipal purposes, it is difficult to see how the legislature can make contracts for it which involve the expenditure of these revenues without its consent."

And in passing upon such statutes the United States Supreme Court will follow the rule laid down by it in the case of *Henderson v. Mayor of New York,* 92 U. S. 259 (1875), namely, that it will examine the statute and determine its real purpose and effect regardless of the form in which it may be couched. "The contention that securities representing a large part of the world's wealth," says Ruger, C. J., in *People v. O'Brien,* 111 N. Y. 1, at p. 36, "are beyond the reach of the protection which the Constitution gives to property, and are subject to the arbitrary will of successive legislatures, to sanction or destroy at their pleasure or discretion, is a proposition so repugnant to reason and justice as well as the traditions of the Anglo-Saxon race in respect to the security of rights of property, that there is little reason to suppose that it will ever receive the sanction of the judiciary, and we desire in unqualified terms to express our disapprobation of such a doctrine." The policy of the state, so far as the city of New York is concerned, is reflected also in the provisions of the Public Lands Law. Subdivision 5 of §75 of that law provides, first, that "The commissioners of the land office may grant in perpetuity or otherwise, to the owners of the lands adjacent to the lands under waters specified in this section, to promote the commerce of this state or for the purpose of beneficial enjoyment thereof by such owners, or for agricultural purposes, so much of said lands under water as they deem necessary for that purpose. No such grant shall be made to any person other than the proprietor of the adjacent lands, and any such grant made to any other person shall be void." And second: "*No such grant shall be made of any lands belonging to the city of New York, or so as to interfere with the rights of that city* . . . " And in the Act for the construction of the Barge Canal (Chapter 746, Laws of 1911, §6) it is provided that "Lands under water and uplands now belonging to the city of New York *shall not be taken by condemnation for terminal purposes, but by agreement between the city of New York,* acting through its board of estimate and apportionment, and the state, acting through the canal board, with the approval of the governor; and such agreement may fix the compensation to be paid to the city, if any, fix the respective rights of the city and state to income derived from the use of the docks and the rates to be charged for such use, but the state shall have sole title to the terminals, lands under water and uplands and the sole right to the management, regulation, construction and maintenance thereof." The state may, therefore, acquire title to any property owned by the city, but it must do so under terms which recognize the city's obligations to holders of the city's bonds, and recognize the city's interest in the revenue derived from such property. That the views herein expressed with regard to the state's power over the city's waterfront and the rights of private owners acquiring grants from the state or from the city are likely to be sustained by the United States Supreme Court, appears from an examination of both the prevailing and dissenting opinions in the recent case of *Long Sault Development Co. v. Call,* 212 N. Y. 1, affirmed in the United States Supreme Court, 242 U. S. 272. In this case it appeared that by Chapter 355 of the Laws of 1907, the state created a corporation to construct and maintain dams in connection with the St. Lawrence River. The Court of Appeals held that this act was unconstitutional. The prevailing opinion, written by Chief Justice Willard Bartlett, distinguishes the case from the *Langdon, Williams* and other cases cited upon the ground that the Act of 1907 of the legislature " virtually turns over to the corporation entire control of navigation at the Long Sault Rapids." In setting aside the grant from the state as unconstitutional, however, he clearly says, quoting from *Coxe v. State of N. Y.,* 144 N. Y. 396, 407: " ' For every purpose which may be useful, convenient or necessary to the public, *the state has the unquestionable right to make grants in fee or conditionally for the beneficial use of the grantee, or to promote commerce according to their terms. The extensive grant to the city of New York of the lands under water below the shore line around Manhattan Island clearly comes within this principle, since it was a grant to a municipality, constituting a political division of the state, for the promotion of the commercial prosperity of the city, and, consequently, of the people of the state.'"*

Again, at page 8: "The power of the legislature to grant land under navigable waters to private persons or corporations for beneficial enjoyment has been exercised too long and has been affirmed by this court too often to be open to serious question at this late day." The dissenting opinion in the Court of Appeals by Judge Collin is a compendious digest of the law upon the subject, with which the prevailing opinion is in complete accord except with reference to the single matter of the effect of the grant in the case then before it, Judge Bartlett saying (p. 10): "The point that I desire to emphasize is that the legislature cannot authorize the conveyance of a navigable portion of the St. Lawrence to a private company to maintain and control navigation thereon, thereby parting for all time with its own power to improve such navigation. The privilege of the state to control the St. Lawrence as a navigable river (subject to the direction of Congress) cannot be assigned to others in the manner attempted by this legislation." Notwithstanding this, in the United States Supreme Court both Mr. Justice McKenna and Mr. Justice Pitney dissent upon the ground that "chapter 355 of the Laws of 1907 of the state of New York, creating the Long Sault Development Company and conferring upon it certain rights and franchises, when accepted, as it was, by the company, constituted a contract between the state and the company; that the repealing act and accompanying legislation passed in 1913 (chaps. 452 and 453) had the effect of impairing the obligation of that contract, in contravention of §10 of article 1 of the Federal Constitution." The prevailing opinion in the United States Supreme Court, by Mr. Justice Clarke, holds only that the United States Supreme Court will not review the decision of a state court when the claim of contractual rights under a state statute is denied by the state court purely upon the ground that the attempted grant was in conflict with the state Constitution and therefore void *ab initio.* No such question is presented with regard to state grants in and about the Port of New York as was presented in the Long Sault case (above) or in the case of *Illinois Central R. Co. v. People of the State of Illinois,* 146 U. S. 387. In that case, the grant to the Illinois Central Railroad of a substantial part of the waterfront of Lake Michigan was held to be invalid. The title which the States hold to lands under navigable water, says the United States Supreme Court, " is a title held in trust for the people of the state that they may enjoy the navigation of the waters, carry on commerce over them, and have liberty of fishing therein freed from the obstruction or interference of private parties. The interest of the people in the navigation of the waters and in commerce over them may be improved in many instances by the erection of wharves, docks and piers therein, for which purpose the state may grant parcels of the submerged lands; and, so long as their disposition is made for such purposes, no valid objections can be made to the grants." The Court expressly differentiates "grants of parcels of land under navigable waters, that may afford foundation for wharves, piers, docks, and other structures *in aid of commerce,* and grants of parcels which, being occupied, *do not substantially impair the public interest in the lands and water remaining,* that are chiefly considered and sustained in the adjudged cases as a valid exercise of legislative power consistently with the trust to the public upon which such lands are held by the state." But this, says the Court, " is a very different doctrine from the one which would sanction the abdication of the general control of the state over lands under the navigable waters of an entire harbor or bay, or of a sea or lake. Such abdication is not consistent with the exercise of that trust which requires the government of the state to preserve such waters for the use of the public. The trust devolving upon the state for the public, and which can only be discharged by the management and control of property in which the public has an interest, cannot be relinquished by a transfer of the property. The control of the State for the purposes of the trust can never be lost, except as to such parcels as are used in promoting the interests of the public therein, or can be disposed of without any substantial impairment of the public interest in the lands and waters remaining. It is only by observing the distinction between a grant of such parcels for the improvement of the public interest, or which when occupied do not substantially impair the public interest in the lands and waters remaining, and a grant of the whole property in which the public is interested, that the language of the adjudged cases can be reconciled." Accordingly, the Court holds that since the harbor of Chicago is of immense value to the people of the state of Illinois in the facilities it affords to its vast and constantly increasing commerce, and " the area of the submerged lands proposed to be ceded . . . [is] more than a thousand acres . . . more than three times the area of the outer harbor . . . as large as that embraced by all the merchandise docks along the Thames at London . . . much larger than that included in the famous docks and basins at Liverpool . . . twice that of the port of Marseilles, and nearly if not quite equal to the pier area along the waterfront of the city of New York," a grant of such kind " is necessarily revocable, and the exercise of the trust by which the property was held by the state can be resumed at any time." Whether or not the state of New Jersey or the United States Supreme Court would hold that the grants to railroad corporations along the eastern shore of New Jersey were so extensive as to involve an impairment of the navigability of the river and thus come within the two decisions just referred to (the *Chicago* and the *Long Sault* cases) is, of course, difficult to say. Many of these grants were made for the promotion of commerce and the operation of these facilities is, in large measure, necessary for the conduct of the commerce of the port. That they substantially interfere, however, with the further development of the facilities of commerce at the port is clear. It would be rash to assert, however, that there is clear and undoubted authority for the state of New Jersey to resume possession of this waterfront without compensation to the present owners.

The Regulation of Waterfront Franchises

But starting with the assumption that the grants we have been considering are *franchises in aid of commerce,* the reserved power of the States to regulate may in itself be adequate to serve the needs of both States and the Nation. In all of the cases the " trust " relationship of the State to its lands under water is nearly everywhere emphasized, and the grants, when sustained, are sustained upon the basis of the fact that they are in performance and in aid of the execution of the trust.

A Chicago municipal ordinance gave permission to a street railway company to construct a tunnel under the Chicago river, a navigable stream. Later the increased demands of navigation justified the lowering of the tunnel. Accordingly, the city passed an ordinance increasing the channel depth of the river to 21 feet and requiring the lowering of the tunnel under the river of the West Chicago Street Railroad Company. "It is indisputable, on this record," says Harlan, J., (*West Chicago Street R. Co. v. Illinois,* 201 U. S. 506, 522) "that the depth of water over the present tunnel is not sufficient to accommodate many boats and vessels now commonly employed in commerce between Chicago and other cities and towns on the Lakes." The United States Supreme Court held that in a navigable stream the *public right is paramount,* and the owner of the soil under the bed can only use it so far as consistent with the public right. Accordingly, the municipality through which a navigable stream flows cannot grant a right to obstruct navigation thereof nor bind itself to permit the continuance of an obstruction, and this rule is not affected by the fact that the person claiming the right to continue such an obstruction is the owner in fee of the bed of the stream. The duty of not obstructing the navigation is a continuing one; and if the increasing demands of navigation require a deeper channel than when the tunnel was originally constructed, it is within the power of the municipality to compel the railroad company, at the latter's own expense, either to remove the tunnel or lower it to conform with the necessity of commerce. (See also the recent case of *New York Dock Co. v. City of New York,* decided by the New York Court of Appeals July 12, 1918. New York Law Journal, August 8, 1918.) See also *People v. International Bridge Co.,* 223 N. Y. 137.

Thus, too, in *United States v. Mission Rock Co.,* 189 U. S. 391, wherein the Illinois Central Railroad case is referred to with approval, the doctrine and its limitations, as expressed in *Heckman v. Swett,* 99 Cal. 309, is repeated: (p. 407) "'Navigable streams and the shores to ordinary high water mark are held by the State in trust for the public; but qualified rights therein may be granted, so far as they are not inconsistent with, or are in aid of the principal use, viz., for the purposes of navigation.' In other words, the rights granted must be in aid of commerce; and it is recognized, as we have seen, in judicial decisions and established by practical examples that the conveyance by the State of its title to tide lands to be held in private ownership free from any easement of the upland proprietor, is in aid of commerce, and therefore in strict performance of the State's trust." See also *Morris v. United States,* 174 U. S. 196 and *Shively v. Bowlby,* 152 U. S. 1; also *Oakland v. Oakland Water Front Co.,* 118 Cal. 160.

In *People v. N. Y. and Staten Island Ferry Co.,* 68 N. Y. 71, 76, the Court of Appeals held that the soil under navigable waters, being held by the people of the State in trust for the common use and as a portion of their inherent sovereignty, any act of legislation concerning their use affects the public welfare. It is, therefore, appropriately within the exercise of the police power of the State.

In *Union Bridge Co. v. United States,* 204 U. S. 364, the United States Supreme Court held: "Although a bridge erected over a navigable water of the United States under the authority of a state charter may have been lawful *when erected and not an obstruction to commerce as then carried on, the owners erected it with knowledge of the paramount authority of Congress over navigation and subject to the power of Congress to exercise its authority to protect navigation by forbidding maintenance when it became an obstruction thereto.*" So, also, in *New Orleans Gas Light Co. v. Drainage Commissioners,* 197 U. S. 453, 461, where the question related to a franchise to a gas company: "The gas company did not acquire any specific location in the streets; it was content with the general right to use them, and when it located its pipes it was at the risk that they might be, at some future time, disturbed, when the State might require for a necessary public use that changes in location be made . . . We think whatever right the gas company acquired was subject in so far as the location of its pipes was concerned, to such future regulations as might be required in the interest of the public health and welfare." This is the principle recognized also by Judge Cullen in the *New York Central Case,* 202 N. Y. 212. In the *Union Bridge Co. case* the Court quotes with approval the statement of the Indiana court in *Lake Erie & W. R. Co. v. Cluggish,* 143 Ind. 347, which, in turn, is a quotation from *Lake Erie & W. R. Co. v. Smith,* 61 Fed. 885: "'The duty of a railroad to restore a stream or highway which is crossed by the line of its road is a continuing duty; and if, by the increase of population or other causes the crossing becomes inadequate to meet the new and altered conditions of the country, it is the duty of the railroad to make such alterations as will meet the present needs of the public.'" Again, in the same case: "'If by the growth of population or otherwise, the crossing has become inadequate to meet the present needs of the public, it is the duty of the railroad company to remedy the defect by restoring the crossing so that it will not unnecessarily impair the usefulness of the highway.'" (*Indiana ex rel. Muncie v. Lake Erie & W. R. Co.,* 83 Fed. 284, 287, quoted at p. 402 of *Union Bridge Co. case.*) Judge Harlan in the *Union Bridge Co. case* at p. 393 quotes from his own opinion in *Scranton v. Wheeler:* "If the riparian owner cannot enjoy access to navigability because of the improvement of navigation by the construction away from the shore line of works in a public navigable river or water, and if such right of access ceases alone for that reason to be of value, there is not, within the meaning of the Constitution, a taking of private property for public use, but only a consequential injury to a right which must be enjoyed, as was said" in *Yates v. Milwaukee,* 10 Wall. 497, 504, 505, 19 L. ed. 984, 986, 987, "'in due subjection to the rights of the public'—an injury resulting incidentally from the exercise of a governmental power for the benefit of the general public, and from which no duty arises to make or secure compensation to the riparian owner. The riparian owner acquired the right of access to navigability subject to the contingency that such right might become valueless in consequence of the erection under competent authority of structures on the submerged lands in front of his property for the purpose of improving navigation." However, this power must not be exercised arbitrarily. If the means employed have no real substantial relation to public objects which Government may legally accomplish, if they are arbitrary and unreasonable beyond the necessities of the case, the judiciary will disregard mere form and interfere for the protection of rights injuriously affected by such illegal action. The authority of the courts to interfere in such cases is beyond all dispute.

The principle is the same as that applied to railroads crossing public highways. Their franchises are valid, but subject to the superior rights of the public. In *Cooke v. Boston & Lowell R. Corp.*, 133 Mass. 185, (quoted with approval in *Union Bridge Co. v. United States*, 204 U. S. 402) the Court said: "The legislature intended to provide against any obstruction of the safe and convenient use of the highway for all time; and if, by the increase of population in the neighborhood, or by an increasing use of the highway, the crossing which at the outset was adequate is no longer so, it is the duty of the railroad corporation to make such alteration as will meet the present needs of the public who have occasion to use the highway."

In *Erie Railroad Co. v. Public Utility Commissioners*, decided by the New Jersey Supreme Court in 1916 (89 N. J. L. 57), it is held that the orders of the Public Utility Commissioners to abolish grade crossings "constitute a regulation adopted by the legislature for public safety under the police power of the state, and hence are not a taking of private property without just compensation, although conformity to such regulation involves expense."

In *Public Service Railway v. Public Utility Commissioners*, 89 N. J. L. 24 (1916), it is held that the provisions of the Fielder Act, §2, by which ten per cent of the cost of eliminating grade crossings by steam railroads used by a street railway may be imposed upon the street railway, is within the legitimate sphere of legislation under the police power of the State. Judge Garrison, writing the opinion of the Court, said:

"We agree that this imposition of a part of the expense of abolishing dangerous grade crossings is neither a tax nor an assessment for a public improvement, but, we think, that it is a legitimate exercise of the police power. The contention of counsel for the prosecutor is placed squarely upon the proposition that the police power is not legitimately exercised in the present case 'unless the property (of the prosecutor) has become a public nuisance, and so lost its right to protection;' and he then proceeds to demonstrate that a street railway is not a public nuisance. We, of course, agree to this, but we entirely dissent from the narrow definition of the police power which would restrain its exercise to the case of property that had become in a legal sense a nuisance.

"If such a narrow definition has any place in the doctrine of the police power (it is confined to the appropriatory aspect of that power), *i. e.,* to such appropriation as is incidental to the destruction of property as a nuisance and has no place in the vastly wider scope of such power that is regulative of energies that are curbed, not that they may be impaired or destroyed, but, on the contrary, that they may be of greater service and beneficence to the public."

The United States Supreme Court, in the case of *Chicago, Milwaukee & St. Paul Railway Co. v. Minneapolis,* 232 U. S. 430, speaking through Mr. Justice Hughes, said: "It is well settled that railroad corporations may be required, at their own expense, not only to abolish existing grade crossings but also to build and maintain suitable bridges or viaducts to carry highways, newly laid out, over their tracks or to carry their tracks over such highways" (p. 438). And as to other public utilities, the doctrine of their subservience to the police power of the State is held to be the same. See *Jersey City v. City of Hudson,* 13 N. J. Eq. 420; *Stillwater Co. v. Stillwater,* 50 Mo. 498; *Detroit v. Fort Wayne & Elmwood Railway Co.,* 90 Mich. 646; *Columbia Gas & Coke Co. v. Columbus,* 50 Ohio St. 65; *Natick Gas Co. v. Natick,* 175 Mass. 246; *New England Telegraph & Telephone Co. v. Boston Terminal Co.,* 182 Mass. 397; *New Orleans Gas Light Co. v. Drainage Commissioners,* 197 U. S. 453.

The distinction between the regulatory power of Congress and the States and the conscription of a franchise is made clear from a study of the two cases of *Monongahela Navigation Co. v. United States,* 148 U. S. 312, 341, 343, and the recent decision in *Louisville Bridge Co. v. United States,* 242 U. S. 409. In the Louisville Bridge Co. case, the Secretary of War required the alteration of the Ohio Falls Bridge within three years, so as to provide an enlarged horizontal opening for the main navigable channel and to change the swing-span across the canal to a lift-span having a prescribed horizontal clearance and a prescribed vertical clearance when open. The Ohio Falls Bridge was constructed by Act of Congress following the Civil War. In the Monongahela Navigation Co. case there was an actual taking of certain locks and dams which had been constructed and maintained by State authority by a navigation company. The United States Supreme Court held that "the franchise is a vested right. The State has power to grant it. It may retake it, as it may take other private property, for public uses, upon the payment of just compensation. A like, though a superior, power exists in the national government. It may take it for public purposes, and take it even against the will of the State; but it can no more take the franchise which the State has given than it can any private property belonging to an individual" (p. 341). In the Louisville Bridge Co. case, Judge Pitney, speaking for the United States Supreme Court, says (referring to the Monongahela Navigation Co. case): "But it will be observed that this was not a case of removing a structure from the river on the ground that it interfered with navigation, but a taking over of a structure and employing it in the public use as an instrumentality of navigation. In short, there was a clear taking of the property of the company for public use as property, and an attempt at the same time to exclude from consideration an essential element of its value when ascertaining the compensation to be paid" (pp. 422, 423).

We have already considered (see supra, page 29 et seq.) the power of the State to act in the absence of federal action in matters relating to the improvement of navigation and commerce. Mr. Justice Gray, delivering the opinion of the United States Supreme Court in *Chicago, Milwaukee & St. Paul R. Co. v. Solan*, 169 U. S. 133, 137, said: "The rules prescribed for the construction of railroads, and for their management and operations, designed to protect persons and property, otherwise endangered by their use, are strictly within the scope of the local law. They are not, in themselves, regulations of interstate commerce, although they control, in some degree, the conduct and the liability of those engaged in such commerce. So long as Congress has not legislated upon the particular subject, they are rather to be regarded as legislation in aid of such commerce, and as a rightful exercise of the police power of the State to regulate the relative rights and duties of all persons and corporations within its limits."

Broad powers of regulations in the interest of improving the navigability of those waterways which constitute the great public highways of the Port of New York still remain with the two States as part of the police power. In the establishment of such regulations there is no interference either with contract or property rights.

Through What Agencies the State May Act

A: Corporations

Both the State and federal authority may be exercised through the medium of a private corporation. In the Stockton case, the State of New York had granted a franchise to operate a railroad and to construct a bridge across the Arthur Kill (*Stockton v. Baltimore & N. Y. R. Co.,* 32 Fed. 9). Discussing the matter of the grant of power to a private corporation, Judge Bradley said: "At all events, if congress, in the execution of its powers, chooses to employ the intervention of a proper corporation, whether of the state, or out of the state, we see no reason why it should not do so. There is nothing in the constitution to prevent it from making contracts with or conferring powers upon, state corporations, for carrying out its own legitimate purposes. What right of the state would be invaded? The corporation thus employed, or empowered, in executing the will of congress, could do nothing which the state could rightfully oppose or object to. It may be added that no state corporation more suitable than the defendant could be empowered to build the bridge in question in this case, since one-half of the bridge is in the state of New York, and the railroad of the defendant is to connect with it on the New York side.

" In our judgment, if congress itself has the power to construct a bridge across a navigable stream for the furtherance of commerce among the states, it may authorize the same to be done by agents, whether individuals, or a corporation created by itself, or a state corporation already existing and concerned in the enterprise. The objection that congress cannot confer powers on a state corporation is untenable. It has used their agency for carrying on its own purposes from an early period."

In *Wilson v. Shaw,* 204 U. S, 24, the power of Congress to create corporations for the purpose of building interstate highways is considered. Brewer, J., speaking for the Court, said (quoting from *California v. Central Pacific R. R. Co.,* 127 U. S. 1): " The power to construct, or to authorize individuals or corporations to construct, national highways and bridges from State to State, is essential to the complete control and regulation of interstate commerce. Without authority in Congress to establish and maintain such highways and bridges, it would be without authority to regulate one of the most important adjuncts of commerce. This power in former times was exerted to a very limited extent, the Cumberland or National road being the most notable instance. Its exertion was but little called for, as commerce was then mostly conducted by water, and many of our statesmen entertained doubts as to the existence of the power to establish ways of communication by land. But since, in consequence of the expansion of the country, the multiplication of its products, and the invention of railroads and locomotion by steam, land transportation has so vastly increased, a sounder consideration of the subject has prevailed and led to the conclusion that Congress has plenary power over the whole subject." In the creation of the vast system of railroads which connects the East with the Pacific, that traverses States as well as Territories, and which employs the agency of State as well as Federal corporations, wider power was freely exercised, as Judge Brewer points out in *Wilson v. Shaw.* It is in the exercise of this power that Congress created the Panama Railroad Corporation and has created the United States Shipping Board Emergency Fleet Corporation. Mr. Justice Gray, speaking for the Court in *Luxton v. North River Bridge Co.,* 153 U. S. 525, 529, said: "Congress, therefore, may create corporations as appropriate means of executing the powers of government, as, for instance, a bank for the purpose of carrying on the fiscal operations of the United States, or a railroad corporation for the purpose of promoting commerce among the States." Mr. Justice Gray in the same case refers to the power of Congress "exercised early in this century by successive acts in the Cumberland or National road, from the Potomac across the Alleghanies to the Ohio, to authorize the construction of a public highway connecting several States." In short, for the purpose of performing governmental functions either Congress or the States *may create corporations vested with power to perform such functions.*

B: Municipalities

As Judge Dillon has made clear (see Dillon on Municipal Corporations, Vol. I, pp. 25, 26, §15) (9), in general, all of our American cities, towns and counties are public corporations, full or quasi, created by the Legislature and invested with power to decide and control local and subordinate matters pertaining to their respective localities. They are the administrative form of the fundamental American idea of government, namely, that the people are the source of all political power and have the right to exercise it. "This," says Dillon, "is with us no mere rhetorical declamation, but a foundation principle upon which our political institutions rest. As local matters can better be regulated by the people of the locality than by the central power, we provide that each road district, each school district, each city, and each county shall, as to its local concerns, be self-governed. . . . The policy of creating local public and municipal corporations for the management of matters of local concern runs back to the earliest period of our colonial history, is exhibited in all our legislation, and expressly or impliedly guaranteed or assumed in our State Constitutions." Such organizations are, says Dillon, "of course, subject to the legislature of the State."

In the recent case of *People ex rel. Palmer v. Travis,* 223 N. Y. 150, considering the relationship of the governmental function to the franchise granting function, Judge Andrews said: "Clearly, the purely political jurisdiction may at any time be resumed [by the State]."

Chief Judge Denio, in *Darlington v. Mayor, etc., of New York,* 31 N. Y. 164, 196, said the Legislature of the State may modify the charter of the city, may transfer the functions performed by the municipality to other municipalities.

In the *Dartmouth College* case, 4 Wheaton 518, 660, Mr. Justice Washington said that there were two kinds of corporations aggregate, such as were for public government and others of a private character. "The first," he said, "are those for the government of a town, city, or the like; and being for public advantage, are to be governed according to the law of the land." Such corporations, he said, were mere creatures of public institution, created exclusively for public advantage, and therefore it is reasonable that such a corporation may be controlled and its constitution altered and amended by the Government in such manner as the public necessity may require. Such legislative interference cannot be said to *impair the contract* by which the corporation was formed, because there is, in reality, but one party to it; the trustees or governors of the corporation being merely the trustees for the public. "The statutes of this State," said Judge Denio in the Darlington case, "furnish instances, too numerous for citation, of the interference of the legislature with the corporate government of the city of New York. If the charter, like that of Dartmouth College, was private and independent of legislative interposition, these acts would be void upon the principle of the judgment of the case cited, and the regulation of the city government would be confined to the brief prescriptions contained in the charter of the colonial governors."

In the Dartmouth College case Chief Justice Marshall said that "if the act of incorporation be a grant of political power, if it create a civil institution to be employed in the administration of the government, or if the funds of the college be public property, or if the State of New Hampshire, as a government, be alone interested in its transactions, the subject is one in which the legislature of the State may act according to its own judgment, unrestrained by any limitation of its power imposed by the constitution of the United States." See also Dillon on Municipal Corporations, Vol. I, p. 59, §32 (20), Vol. I, pp. 142-3, §92 (54).

Harlan, J., speaking for the United States Supreme Court in *Atkin v. Kansas,* 191 U. S. 207, 220, says: "Municipal corporations . . . are the creatures, mere political subdivisions, of the State for the purpose of exercising a part of its powers. They may exert only such powers as are expressly granted to them, or such as may be necessarily implied from those granted. What they lawfully do of a public character is done under the sanction of the State. They are, in every essential sense, only auxiliaries of the State for the purposes of local government. They may be created, or, having been created, their powers may be restricted or enlarged or altogether withdrawn at the will of the Legislature; the authority of the Legislature, when restricting or withdrawing such powers, being subject only to the fundamental condition that the collective and individual rights of the people of the municipality shall not thereby be destroyed." It is clear that the power now vested in the City of New York or in any of the cities or towns of New Jersey within the Port of New York may be so amended or modified by action of the Legislature of the State in which such city or town is situated as to transfer the regulatory powers over port development to new State agencies. Thus, in New Jersey, the creation of the Passaic Valley Sewerage Commission, which took in as a sewerage district a large number of municipalities and parts of municipalities in the counties of Passaic, Hudson, Bergen and Essex, and constituted the commissioners a "body politic and corporate," was held to be constitutional. See *Van Cleve v. Passaic Valley Sewerage Commissioners,* 71 N. J. L. 183 and 574; 58 Atl. R. 796; 60 Atl. Rep. 214. It is held that the Legislature of New Jersey may establish new political districts by designating and delimiting areas of the State for that purpose. The Supreme Court opinion is written by Judge Pitney and the opinion by the Court of Errors and Appeals is written by Judge Garrison. Judge Pitney says (p. 197): "For all essential purposes, the corporate body created by this act is but an executive and administrative branch of the state government, charged with the duty of carrying out in detail a work that the lawmaking body has determined to establish and maintain for the good and welfare of the citizens of the state, and especially of those residing within the sewerage district." P. 195: "The main purpose of the act is to establish, within and for a designated portion of the area of the state, a great public work for a great public purpose, which work is to be established, maintained and operated through the instrumentality of an administrative branch of the central government of the state, at the cost of the present and future residents of the district particularly affected. . . . In effect, the act declares that the Passaic river and other natural streams within the district are so polluted by sewage and other deleterious matter as to be a menace to the health, not to mention the comfort, of the population. . . . One of the chief objects of this act is to revoke the legislative authority previously given to the municipalities in that behalf." In Judge Garrison's opinion (p. 578), this act did not constitute a regulation of the internal affairs of a town in violation of the constitutional provisions of New Jersey. "Obviously," he said, "the act is local, as from its nature it must be, but it is equally obvious that the purpose of the act is a public enterprise, as distinct from a municipal affair, and that the regulations referred to are purely incidental to such extra-municipal scheme. *It is not, moreover, true that every public utility that exists in whole or in part within the geographical boundaries of a municipality is its internal affair in the same sense that every governmental function that has been committed to it is one of its internal affairs. So that it may well be and often is the case that the special license of municipalities to regulate instruments of public utility within their confines may co-exist with the general legislative power to direct the larger scheme of which such instruments are a part.*"

Again, in *State v. Price,* 71 N. J. L. 249, 58 Atl. 1015, Judge Pitney writing the opinion, held that Paragraph 11 of §11 of Article 4 of the New Jersey Constitution providing that "the legislature shall not pass private, local or special laws in any of the following enumerated cases, that is to say . . . regulating the internal affairs of towns and counties; appointing local offices or commissions to regulate municipal affairs; . . . granting to any corporation, association or individual any exclusive privilege, immunity or franchise whatever . . . the legislature shall pass general laws providing for the case enumerated in this paragraph, and for all other cases which, in its judgment, may be provided for by general laws" is not violated where the purpose of the Act is to deal with lands owned by the State in its sovereign capacity and which it holds in trust for the citizens. "The mere fact," says he, "that a given act of the legislature is limited in its territorial scope to a portion of the state coincident with or less than the bounds of a single county or other municipal division, does not make such act an act regulative of the 'internal affairs' of such county or municipality within the meaning of the constitutional prohibition."

So in New York, Chapter 74 of the Laws of 1866, creating the Metropolitan Sanitary District of the State of New York, was held to be constitutional. *Metropolitan Board of Health v. Heister,*

37 N. Y. 661. This sanitary district took in the counties of New York, Kings, Westchester and Richmond before Greater New York was established. So, too, the Act establishing the Metropolitan Police District of the State of New York, which likewise took in New York, Kings, Westchester and Richmond, was sustained in *People v. Draper,* 15 N. Y. 532. At p. 543, Denio, C. J., said: "Plenary power in the legislature for all purposes of civil government is the rule. A prohibition to exercise a particular power is an exception." Accordingly, the Legislature of each State has undoubted power to create a new district for the purpose of developing the Port of New York, taking in the various municipalities, in order the more effectively to execute the public trust under which the State holds the lands under water in the navigable highways forming the port, and for the State purpose of improving commerce and navigation. In doing so, it may freely transfer power from local municipalities to any new board or commission that it may create for the purpose. In doing so, however, the State may not, as we have already pointed out, destroy the franchise rights of grantees holding waterfront privileges through grants from the State or City, nor impair the obligations of bondholders of such municipalities by taking away the property of such municipalities or the revenue derived therefrom. The distinction is very like the distinction drawn by the Court of Appeals in *People v. O'Brien,* 111 N. Y. 1, in which the right of the State to revoke the charter of a railway corporation is sustained, while the franchise right of the corporation to operate a railroad is at the same time held to be irrevocable.

But though the legal right to take away from cities embraced within the Port of New York all governmental power over the port is clear, the principle of local autonomy to which Ex-Justice Hughes has referred (see supra, p. 42) and which is at the basis (as Dillon tells us) of all municipal government, remains. Nowhere is the demand for "local self-government" so persistent as in the State of New York. In the proposed Constitution adopted at the 1915 Convention and submitted to the voters at the November, 1915, election, Section 3 of New Article XV provided (All new matter): "Every city shall have exclusive power to manage, regulate and control its property, affairs and municipal government subject to the provisions of this constitution and subject further to the provisions of the general laws of the State, of laws applying to all the cities of the State without classification or distinction, and of laws applying to a county not wholly included within a city establishing or affecting the relation between such a county and a city therein.

" Such power shall be deemed to include among others:" The power to organize and manage all departments, fix compensation, etc., to revise or enact amendments to its charter in relation to its property, affairs or municipal government and to enact amendments to any local or special law in relation thereto.

In Section 4 it was provided: " The Legislature may delegate to cities for exercise within their respective local jurisdictions such of its powers of legislation as to matters of state concern as it may from time to time deem expedient.

" The Legislature shall pass no law relating to the property, affairs or municipal government of any city excepting such as is applicable to all the cities of the State without classification or distinction."

Recognizing, however, that there are many functions dual in their nature but primarily of State concern, the following was included:

" The provisions of this article shall not be deemed to restrict the powers of the Legislature to pass laws regulating matters of State concern as distinguished from matters relating to the property, affairs or municipal government of cities.

" Laws affecting cities in relation to boundaries, water supply, sewerage and public improvements, *involving the use of territory outside the boundaries of cities, and in relation to the government of cities in matters of State concern* and applying to less than all the cities of the State without classification or distinction are defined for the purposes of this article as special city laws."

Even had this amended Constitution been adopted by the people, adequate power would have remained, nevertheless, in the State to create a State Commission exercising State functions in the development of the port; and in spite of the provisions for local autonomy existing in the Constitution of the State of New York, adequate power exists, as we have seen, to create commissions exercising a similar State function. The political problem remains still to be solved, namely, to what extent *shall* the power and the initiative of municipalities in the development of the port be preserved? The answer in the proposed plan is this: That there shall be a single Port Authority deriving powers from the two States, covering a district embracing parts of the two States. Within this district the Port Authority shall have veto power upon all port developments and improvements, and in addition shall have power to initiate improvements, and for that purpose shall have power to take and hold property, borrow money, construct and maintain docks, piers and terminals, and collect the revenue therefrom. Subject always to the federal power to regulate commerce and navigation, it shall, additionally, have power to pass rules and regulations governing the port, but *only* after consideration of these rules and regulations by the local communities within the district. In brief, (see Article XVII) before a rule or regulation becomes operative it must be published and the communities affected thereby have the right to register their approval or disapproval. If the regulation affects the entire district, communities embracing one-third of the total population may, through their official bodies, take exception to the regulation. If the Port Authority so desires, it may then apply to the Appellate Division of the First and Second Departments (if the regulation is applicable within the State of New York) or to the Supreme Court of New Jersey (if the regulation is applicable within the State of New Jersey) for a certificate of "reasonableness and public necessity." If such certificate be secured, the regulation becomes binding. If not, it falls. There is thus given full opportunity for hearing, public discussion, careful examination of each regulation upon its merits. Eighty per cent at least of the regulations so adopted, in all probability, will never be questioned, but by this provision every community will be given the opportunity of public discussion and its "day in court." Yet the paramount power of the State will not be thwarted in its exercise by the mere recalcitrance of an unreasonable and dissentient local government.

C: Other Delegated Bodies

In *Erie Railroad Co. v. Public Utility Commissioners,* 89 N. J. L. 57 (1916), it is said that to accomplish the ends of government "it has been found expedient to create various boards and commissions, which are charged with the duty of supervising, directing and controlling particular subjects. It has been held that the granting of such power by the legislature was not a grant of either legislative or judicial power." In the leading case in New York, *Saratoga Springs v. Saratoga Gas Co.,* 191 N. Y. 123, it was held that "the constitutional guaranty does not require or imply that the three great powers of government, legislative, executive and judicial, shall be kept absolutely separate and independent of each other. While legislative powers that are strictly and exclusively legislative cannot be delegated, yet, both before and after the ratification of the Federal Constitution by the state of New York, and under all the constitutions of the state, the legislature has imposed duties, involving the exercise of legislative, as well as administrative or judicial, powers upon administrative and judicial officers. During that time the people have had ample opportunities, in the adoption of four constitutions, or the amendment thereof, to correct any misconception or misconstruction as to their powers, on the part of public officers, whether legislative, executive or judicial, but no constitutional provision restraining the legislature from delegating legislative powers, when necessary for the execution of general laws, has been adopted, and any exercise of power by the legislature which for a long time has passed unchallenged, or, if challenged, has been sustained by the courts, must be deemed to have been approved by the people, unless forbidden by subsequent constitutional provision." (Headnote.)

The United States Supreme Court has repeatedly held that it is not a delegation of legislative or judicial power to charge the Secretary of War or the President or any other administrative officer with the duty of ascertaining, under a general rule, whether, for example, a particular bridge is an unreasonable obstruction to navigation (see *Monongahela Bridge Co. v. United States,* 216 U. S. 177). Thus the President may be authorized to suspend an Act or to put it in operation upon the contingency of the happening of events to be ascertained by him and made known by his proclamation. *Field v. Clark,* 143 U. S. 649, 683. Chief Justice Marshall, in delivering the unanimous judgment of the Supreme Court in *Wayman v. Southard,* 10 Wheaton 1, 43, 45, 46, said that Congress may decide upon a general provision and give powers "to those who are to act under such general provisions to fill up the details." In *Field v. Clark*, the Court said: "As the suspension was absolutely required when the President ascertained the existence of a particular fact, it cannot be said that in ascertaining that fact and in issuing his proclamation, in obedience to the legislative will, he exercised the function of making laws." "The true distinction," as pointed out by Judge Ranney in *Cincinnati, Wilmington R. Co. v. Clinton County Comrs.*, 1 Ohio St. 88, quoted in *Field v. Clark* at pages 693-4, "is between the delegation of power to make the law, which necessarily involves a discretion as to what it shall be, and conferring authority or discretion as to its execution, to be exercised under and in pursuance of the law. The first cannot be done; to the latter no valid objection can be made." "Half the statutes on our books," says the Court in *Moers v. Reading*, 21 Pa. 188, 202, quoted by the United States Supreme Court in *Field v. Clark*, "are in the alternative, depending on the discretion of some person or persons to whom is confided the duty of determining whether the proper occasion exists for executing them. But it cannot be said that the exercise of such discretion is the making of the law." So in *Locke's App.*, 72 Pa. 491, 498: "To assert that a law is less than a law, because it is made to depend on a future event or act, is to rob the legislature of the power to act wisely for the public welfare whenever a law is passed relating to a state of affairs not yet developed, or to things future and impossible to fully know." See also *Buttfield v. Stranahan*, 192 U. S. 470, 496 (giving the Secretary of the Treasury authority to establish uniform standards of purity, quality and fitness of all kinds of teas) and the recent Acts of Congress by which the Secretary of the Treasury, the Commissioner of Internal Revenue, the Secretary of War and the President are authorized to make, by proclamation, general language administratively effective. This principle is also the basis for the power to fix rates by the Interstate Commerce Commission and public service and public utility commissions.

Nor is there any objection to transferring such powers to the judicial department. As Judge Cullen has pointed out in the *Saratoga Springs* case, originally the power to grant divorce was legislative and in this State during Colonial times this power remained purely legislative until 1787, when the State passed an Act which, reciting that it was more advisable for the Legislature to make general provision for such cases than to afford relief to individuals without proper trial, jurisdiction was conferred upon the Court of Chancery to grant divorce for adultery. "This transfer of power to the judiciary," says Judge Cullen (*Saratoga Springs v. Saratoga Gas Co.,* 191 N. Y. 123, 135), "rested solely on legislative enactment until the Constitution of 1846." Likewise, from the earliest times in the history of the State, the power to lay out and construct new roads was with the courts, although as Judge Cullen says: "No student of government would assert that the laying out and construction of roads is properly a judicial function."

In *Citizens' Savings Bank v. Town of Greenburgh* (173 N. Y. 215), the Court considered the validity of the statute providing for the laying out and construction of highways extending through two or more towns upon the presentation of a petition by a freeholder to the Supreme Court, the Supreme Court being directed, after a hearing, to determine *whether the highway was necessary for the public welfare and convenience,* it being urged that the Act conferred non-judicial duties upon the Court. The statute was upheld, Judge Gray saying: "The legislature is unrestricted in its power to provide for the construction of public highways, and, from an early date in this state, there has been legislation devolving functions similar in effect to those imposed in this act, which has never been held to be objectionable by this court." Judge Gray quoted from Judge Nelson's opinion in *Commissioners of Highways of Warwick v. Judges of Orange County,* 13 Wend. 433, wherein Judge Nelson said: "The proceeding by appeal was not intended to be a review of legal questions, or of irregularities that might exist in the preliminary steps, as on a writ of certiorari; but to be an examination of the necessity or propriety of the road, assuming all the previous steps to have been regularly taken." The Legislature in 1797 by Chapter 64 conferred upon the Courts of Common Pleas of the various counties power to grant licenses for the keeping of ferries and to prescribe the tolls to be charged, which power continues to this day, being now vested in County Courts and City Courts (Highway Law, §§170, 171*) and, said Judge Cullen, "a member of this court, when county judge of Erie county, granted such a license and fixed the rates of ferriage." (*Saratoga Springs case,* 191 N. Y. 123, at p. 136.)

In *People v. Babcock,* 11 Wend. 587, the Supreme Court of the State of New York decided that to authorize the conduct of a ferry between that State and Canada over the Niagara river, license must be secured from the Court of Common Pleas of the County in which its terminus within that State was located. In *Canada Northern Railway v. International Bridge Co.,* 7 Fed. Rep. 653 and 8 Fed. Rep. 190, the charter of the International Bridge Co. contained the following provision: "All railway companies desiring to use said bridge shall have and be entitled to equal rights and privileges in the passage of the same, and in the use of the machinery and fixtures thereof, and of all the approaches thereto, under and upon such terms and conditions as shall be prescribed by the district court of the United States for the northern district of New York, upon hearing the allegations and proofs of the parties, in case they shall not agree." Judge Wallace held that this was not a delegation of legislative power, nor was it a conferring upon the court of non-judicial functions. "It devolves upon this court simply the judicial functions of determining the rights of parties when they may be brought into controversy. . . . It is no less the exercise of judicial functions to prescribe a rule of conduct or protect the existence of a right during a future period, than it is to determine whether the right has been invaded in the past. It is one of the common offices of a court of equity to do this."

The duty to grant certificates of "public convenience and necessity" where the consent of property owners has not been secured to the construction of a railroad is now vested in the Supreme Court of the State (see Railroad Law, §174). The power which the States have to regulate commerce and navigation and to remove obstructions to commerce and navigation (subject at all times to the paramount federal power) may, therefore, be exerted by the passage of general laws and the execution of the details either by

*Should read §§ 270, 271.

a municipality, a commission, a board, or a single individual; and the power to determine whether regulation is reasonable and a public necessity may be vested in the courts.

The Legal Basis for Interstate Action

Thus far we have confined ourselves to the consideration of the power of each State in relation to the Federal Government to deal with matters within its own territory and sovereignty. There is still to be considered the extent to which and the manner by which two States may join in the attainment of an object common to both. First of all, as we have seen from the *Stockton* case (32 Fed. Rep. 9), a New York corporation may be granted power by Congress to build a bridge across the waters intersecting New York and New Jersey. But another method which may be employed is the one used for the construction of the international bridge running from New York to Canada. On April 17, 1857 (Chap. 753, Laws of 1857), the State of New York, by Act of the Legislature, authorized the formation of the International Bridge Company to build a bridge across the Niagara River to the American-Canadian line. In the same year the Province of Canada authorized another corporation, the International Bridge Co. (of Canada), to build a bridge across the Niagara River to the Canadian-American line (20 Vict., Chap. 227). On May 4, 1869, by an Act of the New York Legislature (Chap. 550, Laws of 1869), the (New York) International Bridge Company was authorized to consolidate with the (Canadian) International Bridge Company, and a complementary Act was passed by the Dominion of Canada June 22, 1869. These two corporations, one Canadian and one New York, were thus permitted to consolidate and amalgamate by statutes of the State of New York and of Canada, because vested with all of the stock, property and franchises of the two corporations, and were thereafter deemed to be one corporation, to have the name provided in their agreement and to possess all the rights and privileges, and were subject to all the disabilities and duties of each of the corporations so consolidated. The consolidated company became the International Bridge Company. By Chapter 176 of the Second Session of the 41st Congress of the United States (June, 1870), the bridge was authorized to be constructed. The bridge was constructed and is now in operation. The validity of these grants was sustained by Wallace, J., at 7 Fed. Rep. 653 and 8 Fed. Rep. 190, and recently was passed upon by the New York Court of Appeals in *People v. International Bridge Co.*, 223 N. Y. 137.

The Chesapeake and Ohio Canal, as originally planned, required the action of the Legislatures of Virginia, Maryland and Pennsylvania, all of which united in incorporating the "Chesapeake and Ohio Canal Company." The mutual interests of these States could not have been carried out by the action of any one alone. The highest court of Maryland said, "The legislature of neither of the States, could have performed by any separate act of legislation, what was proposed to be accomplished by the concurrent acts of all. One terminus of the canal is proposed to be in the District of Columbia, and the other in the State of Maryland; and Virginia could not of its own authority, by any separate act, authorize a canal to be made through Maryland, nor could Maryland authorize a canal to be made through Virginia, without its consent." Yet all this was accomplished by statutory enactments passed by each of the three States and also by the Congress of the United States in so far as it affected the District of Columbia (Congress in this instance acting as the Legislature for the District of Columbia). This case, one of the earliest in the history of the country (1832), reported in 4 Gil. & J. (Maryland) 1, under the title *Cheasapeake & Ohio Canal Co. v. Baltimore & Ohio Railroad Co.*, is clear authority for the proposition that as a State may contract with an individual, two or more of the States may enter into a compact or agreement *inter se*, and this may be done by the complementary Acts of their respective Legislatures.

The Morris Canal, as is well known, runs from the Delaware River in New Jersey to the Hudson River at a point opposite New York City. In its course it passes the southern border of New York. It required for its supply a reservoir and for that purpose desired to take the basin of Long Pond (or Greenwood Lake), a portion of which was within the State of New York. In the employment of this pond by raising the water, some of the lands around its shore would be appropriated. Could a canal company organized under the laws of the State of New Jersey acquire land within the State of New York for the operation of a canal wholly within the State of New Jersey? This was the question in the *Matter of Townsend,* 39 N. Y. 171. The New York Court of Appeals held, in language appropriate to our situation, Judge Woodruff writing the opinion: "The work promoted belongs to a class long recognized as public in its character; and I think it was for the legislature to say whether the benefit to result to our own citizens, and facilitating internal commerce for the promotion of our trade or otherwise, were sufficient to call for the exercise of the power to take private property therefor; and that the decision of the legislature on that point is not subject to review in this court." There was, of course, no doubt in the case that if the canal had come within our own limits the Legislature could authorize its construction and the taking of lands for that purpose, and, said the Court, "the construction of the reservoir for its supply, would be no less within the power. It does not follow, because the canal is outside the State limits, that its construction and maintenance are not for a public use, within the meaning of our Constitution. If it were within our limits, what are the public benefits to result from its construction? Not merely that our citizens may use it for transportation or travel. Providing transportation to market and facilitating intercommunication are some of the public purposes of such improvements; but communication between our chief cities and the productive regions which lie outside our State, and intercourse with those who dwell there, are as truly objects of public interest and advantage as between two sections of the State itself. Besides, the court cannot say that the Morris canal does not run within the reach of a portion of our own citizens, and directly aid them in the conduct of their intercourse with our eastern border, or the counties along the Hudson river to which it runs." This would seem to be clear authority for the exercise of State power in the development of port facilities, the purpose of which is "providing transportation," "facilitating intercommunication" and "communication between our chief cities and the productive regions which lie outside our State." Especially would this be true if, by solemn treaty, the two States were to engage in the common enterprise.

In the leading case of *State of Virginia v. State of Tennessee,* 148 U. S. 503, at p. 518, the United States Supreme Court observed that "there are many matters upon which different

States may agree that can in no respect concern the United States. If, for instance, Virginia should come into possession and ownership of a small parcel of land in New York which the latter State might desire to acquire as a site for a public building, it would hardly be deemed essential for the latter State to obtain the consent of Congress before it could make a valid agreement with Virginia for the purchase of the land. If Massachusetts, in forwarding its exhibits to the World's Fair at Chicago, should desire to transport them a part of the distance over the Erie Canal, it would hardly be deemed essential for that State to obtain the consent of Congress before it could contract with New York for the transportation of the exhibits through that State in that way. If the bordering line of two States should cross some malarious and disease-producing district, there could be no possible reason, on any conceivable public grounds, to obtain the consent of Congress for the bordering States to agree to unite in draining the district, and thus removing the cause of disease. So in case of threatened invasion of cholera, plague, or other causes of sickness and death, it would be the height of absurdity to hold that the threatened States could not unite in providing means to prevent and repel the invasion of the pestilence, without obtaining the consent of Congress, which might not be at the time in session."

A recent example of the co-operation between two States is to be found in the creation of the Palisades Interstate Park Commission. By Acts of the two legislatures (Chapter 170, Laws of 1900, New York, p. 380, and Chapter 87, Laws of 1900, New Jersey, p. 163), there were created two separate State Commissions, each " a body politic with power to sue and to be sued," each appointing its own officers authorized to acquire, maintain and make available for use as a public park certain lands along the Palisades. Within its State each Commission is supreme, but, like the present Port and Harbor Development Commission, the two Commissions sit in common session and engage in a joint undertaking.

Randolph, in his Law of Eminent Domain, § 29, believes that the observations of the Supreme Court in *Virginia v. Tennessee* contemplate that an undertaking considered as a whole may be of public use common to two States, so that " joint and interdependent grants of the eminent domain may cure deficiences incident to independent grants." In two articles in the *Columbia Law Review* for May and June, 1902, this author expresses the view that two States may combine to secure more equitable enjoyment in a common interest in water than is obtainable by independent action, and for that purpose he suggests, to meet the decision in *Kansas v. Colorado* (which involved an interstate controversy over the diversion of water for irrigation purposes), that the States and Territories interested create, by compact, a public corporation for the promotion of irrigation, which corporation should be charged with the planning, construction and maintenance of a comprehensive system and with the general apportionment of water among the several States parties to the compact, the powers of the corporation to depend upon the compact and upon such ancillary federal and state legislation as might be advisable.

In an opinion by the same author upon the obtaining of a water supply for the State of New York, he urged the making of a compact between the States of New Jersey and New York as a means for securing an interstate water supply. (See his opinion, Randolph Legal Pamphlets, 1888-1915, Library of the Association of the Bar of the City of New York.)

But as we have already seen, the States of New York and New Jersey have already done business with each other. The Treaty of 1834 furnishes at once an historical precedent and a classical example for us to follow. For our present purposes, however, it is defective and inadequate in many respects. Take, for example, so simple a matter as the regulation of the rates of ferriage where, Congress not having acted, the two States are still free to act. In the *New York Central case* (74 N. J. L. 367), Justices Hendrickson, Swayze and Trenchard, Judge Swayze writing the opinion, said (p. 375): " By the treaty between New York and New Jersey (Gen. Stat. p. 3464) New York is given exclusive jurisdiction over the waters of the Hudson river to the low-water mark on the New Jersey shore, subject to the right of property of New Jersey to the land under water west of the middle of the river, and to the exclusive jurisdiction of New Jersey over the wharves, docks and improvements on its shore, and all vessels aground on that shore or fastened to such wharves or docks, and subject to the exclusive right of New Jersey to regulate the fisheries on the westerly side of the river. Even these reserved rights of New Jersey are further qualified by a provision that they shall be subject to the laws of the State of New York in relation to passengers, and that navigation be not obstructed or hindered.

" The limitation of New Jersey's jurisdiction to vessels aground on its shore, or fastened to wharves or docks, and the express reservation by which even those vessels are subject to the laws of New York in relation to passengers, are a plain indication that New Jersey has no control over vessels actually in transit across the river, *and the rates to be charged for transportation of passengers thereon.*" This case went up to the Court of Errors and Appeals of New Jersey and is reported in 76 N. J. L. 664. The opinion of the lower court was there *reversed* and the highest court of New Jersey (Judge Reed writing the opinion) said (p. 682): " It would seem, however, that whether the jurisdiction of the State of New York runs to the middle of the Hudson river or to the New Jersey shore, it would not effect the question now involved. The ferry-house is within the jurisdiction of New Jersey, and it is the right of the state to regulate the charges which the keeper of such ferry-house may impose for transportation to New York that is involved. Now, whether the transportation is partly or wholly over waters of the State of New York seems to be immaterial, for in the one case, as in the other, the transportation would be interstate commerce.

" But apart from this, it is to be observed that the agreement entered into between the commissioners was ratified by the legislature of New Jersey in 1834. It had been in existence, therefore, nearly twenty years when the case of *State v. Chosen Freeholders of Hudson County, supra,* was decided, although this point was not noticed by either counsel or court in that case. We would hardly, on that ground, disturb a decision so well considered which has stood for over half a century upon a new view of the effect of conditions which then existed."

The decision of the Court of Errors and Appeals in this case came up before the United States Supreme Court, and the United

States Supreme Court reversed the Court of Errors and Appeals, sustaining the Supreme Court of New Jersey (see 227 U. S. 248), the United States Supreme Court, however, resting its decision upon the ground that the operation of the ferry (the Weehawken Ferry) constituted interstate commerce. (See supra, p. 102.)

In the *Port Richmond Ferry case,* 234 U. S. 317, as we have already seen (see supra, p. 101), Mr. Justice Hughes held, (distinguishing the Weehawken Ferry case, on the ground that it was not a ferry operated in connection with any railroad), that each State, at the ferry-house situated within its State, could regulate the charges and tolls. " If the State may exercise this power, it necessarily follows that it may not, in its exercise, derogate from the similar authority of another State. The state power can extend only to the transactions within its own territory and the ferriage from its own shore. It follows that the fact that rates were fixed by New York did not preclude New Jersey from establishing reasonable rates with respect to the ferry establishment maintained on its side." In this case, the point with regard to the New York-New Jersey Treaty of 1834 was neither presented nor considered by the Court.

The question, therefore, is either still unsettled and subject to debate (which seems to us to be the better opinion) or each State is still free to make regulations with regard to ferriage tolls on its own side. It may be desirable to construct between the two States many bridges and many tunnels, some of which or some part of the operation of which may be founded upon legal principles identical with those in the Port Richmond Ferry case. Such opportunities for the development of friction should be foreclosed. Problems of this character shauld be committed to a single Port Authority representative of both States and co-operating in the development of the larger port.

The Treaty-Making Power of the States and What May Be Done Under It

The Federal Constitution provides that " no State shall, without the consent of Congress, lay any duty of tonnage, keep troops or ships of war in time of peace, enter into any agreement or compact with another State, or with a foreign power, or engage in

6

war, unless actually invaded, or in such immediate danger as will not admit of delay." We have already seen that the United States Supreme Court held that this provision does not apply to those matters which do not concern the United States. Even the establishment of a boundary line between States — the most familiar and most frequent *raison d'etre* of treaties between States — may not require the approval of Congress. Says the United States Supreme Court in *Virginia v. Tennessee,* 148 U. S. 503, 520: "The compact or agreement will then be within the prohibition of the Constitution or without it, according as the establishment of the boundary line may lead or not to the increase of the political power or influence of the States affected, and thus encroach or not upon the full and free exercise of Federal authority. If the boundary established is so run as to cut off an important and valuable portion of a State, the political power of the State enlarged would be affected by the settlement of the boundary; and to an agreement for the running of such a boundary, or rather for its adoption afterwards, the consent of Congress may well be required. But the running of a boundary may have no effect upon the political influence of either State; it may simply serve to mark and define that which actually existed before, but was undefined and unmarked. In that case the agreement for the running of the line, or its actual survey, would in no respect displace the relation of either of the States to the general government." If the compact or agreement between the States does not affect the political power of either, it would seem, therefore, as though approval by Congress were unnecessary. The treaty between New York and New Jersey of 1834, however, was approved by Congress. That treaty did seriously affect the political relations of the two States, and as we have seen (supra, p. 74 et seq.) settled and disposed of a matter that had been the subject of serious controversy between the two States. It is probable that, in any event, the farsighted lawyers of that day would have recommended the approval of the treaty by Congress in order to avoid any possible question concerning its validity. So in proposing an amendment or supplement to the 1834 treaty, it would seem to be the wiser policy to secure ratification and approval by Congress. The points at which the federal power crosses the State power, the difficulty of always distinguishing between what is a State function and what is a federal function — all of which has been already discussed — would seem to point to the practical wisdom of securing in advance of action ratification of the treaty by Congress. (The time when such a treaty may be ratified and whether by express action or by acquiesence is fully discussed in *Virginia v. Tennessee,* 148 U. S. 503, at p. 521.) Of course, the two States could deal with the port problem as they have dealt with the Palisades Park problem, that is to say, each State could act within its own jurisdiction through a separate commission which would co-operate with a similar commission created by the other State. Each of the two commissions could be a body corporate, as well as politic, and could receive power to hold real estate and to operate port utilities. Such a piece of machinery would be cumbersome, slow in operation, and likely to be ineffective at many points. But plans for port development have been so long delayed and the great war has so imperatively made prompt action necessary, that the most effective agency that can be created should now be devised and put into action as quickly as possible. A single Port Authority, deriving powers from the two States, a body corporate and politic, capable also of performing duties that may be assigned to it by any of the branches of the Federal Government, would seem to be the logical instrumentality. But each State is a sovereign in its own territory and the port lies in the territory of both. Adequate power in such a single Port Authority, similar to the power invested in Port Authorities at London, Liverpool, Hamburg, New Orleans, Montreal, etc., etc., in our situation will involve some yielding upon the part of each State of its supreme and complete sovereignty. To what extent may a State or Nation, retaining its general sovereignty, grant power to another State to deal with property located within the territorial bounds governed by the former? We may assume at the outset that every State, like every nation, will reluctantly yield of its sovereign power, though, in our situation, the fact that the obligations will be equal, mutual and reciprocal may make the problem easier. This branch of the subject is perhaps the most difficult, though at the same time the most interesting of the subjects with which we must deal. It takes us into fields which lawyers do not customarily enter. However, when such a Port Authority comes to take title to property, or conveys title, or borrows money, or issues orders, it will need to rest its action upon firm and well settled principles of law. It will be profitable, therefore, to consider this branch of the problem fully and place where it is accessible the legal theory and the precedents upon which we may rely.

If a State may alienate a part of its territory in perpetuity to an individual, it may, of course, alienate to another State. This is the theory underlying all boundary treaties. Each State grants and conveys to the other — or releases, as the case may be — all its right, title and interest in the property on the other side of the boundary. "It is too late in the history of the United States," says Judge Brewer in *Wilson v. Shaw,* 204 U. S. 24, 32, "to question the right of acquiring territory by treaty." But we are not to change in any respect the boundary lines between New York and New Jersey as settled by the Treaty of 1834. We are simply to vest sovereign authority within a certain portion of territory in both States, and such sovereign authority only to a limited degree, sufficient to accomplish the main purpose. This is already done in the Treaty of 1834. Though, of course, no State in the Union may act beyond the scope of its own Constitution nor infringe any of the provisions of the Federal Constitution, within these limitations it is free and acts with the power of any sovereign State. In *Brien v. West Elliott,* 2 Penrose & Watts (Pa.) 49, 61, Gibson, C. J., speaking for the Court, says: ". . . the power of the two states to regulate questions of title to the soil, even at the expense of rights previously vested under either, [is] not now to be questioned. The compact is necessarily founded in an assumption of it. There was no constitutional limitation on either side; and the parties acting in the capacity of *sovereigns,* were fettered by no rule but their sense of expediency and justice. The consideration was the compromise of an *international dispute.* . . ." Under the Treaty of 1780 between Pennsylvania and Virginia, the title to land conveyed thereby would go one way under the decisions of the Virginia court, while under the decisions of the Pennsylvania court it would go another. In *Marlatt v. Silk,* 36 U. S. (11 Pet.) 1, 9

L. ed. 609, the United States Supreme Court, Barbour, J., writing the prevailing opinion, held that the decisions of the State courts are looked to to ascertain what the law is where the controversy is between private parties arising under a compact made in or by one State, "whereas in the case at bar, the question arises under, and is to be decided by, a compact between two states: where therefore the rule of decision is not to be collected from the decisions of either state, but is one, if we may so speak, of an international character."

So, too, in *Iowa v. Illinois,* 147 U. S. 1, 37 L. ed. 55, 13 Sup. Ct. Rep. 239, where the dispute arose over the boundary line between Illinois and Iowa, the contention of each State was supported by a decision of its court of last resort. The United States Supreme Court recognized these decisions as presenting in the clearest terms the conflicting view as to the line of jurisdiction between two neighboring States bounded by a navigable stream, but proceeded to a determination of the rights of the two States based upon a careful study and review of the authorities on *international law,* in this instance finding that the term "middle of the stream," as established in international law and by the usage of European nations, meant the middle of the channel of such streams.

International law and international precedent, therefore, must be examined for the purpose of determining the effect of such a treaty as we have under consideration.

Servitudes

Two owners of adjoining farm lands require access across both for the full development of the farms of both. To confirm this access they draw a deed or instrument by which the rights are established. The thing created in law is called an "easement," and the burden imposed upon the land which is to serve the easement is called a "servitude;" each piece of property *serves* the other.

In urban real estate there is a very common illustration. Two owners of lots adjoining each other intend to erect separate buildings. Ordinarily, each would erect a separate wall at or near the line of intersection. Where land is expensive, what more natural than for one owner to say to the other: "Let us erect a wall which will serve both buildings and which will be common to us both?" This is what is called a "party wall," and an agreement of this character is called "a party wall agreement." Each piece of property is the beneficiary of a *servitude* assumed by the other. In Roman law "the one piece of land was said to *serve* the other." (Imperatores Justiniani Institutiones, 2 ed., p. 26, note.) Sir Robert Phillimore, in his "International Law," Vol. 1, 3d ed., 1879, says: "In the language of Jurisprudence, when a thing is subject to the exercise of a right by a person who is not the master or proprietor it is said *to serve* (*res servit*) or yield *service* to that other person." This doctrine of *Servitus* plays an important part in Roman law, and in some shape and under some appellation or other is to be found in the jurisprudence of all nations. The obligation to service "constitutes a right in the obligee or the person to whom it is due, and it ranks among the '*jura in re*,' while it operates as a diminution and limitation of the right of the proprietor to the exclusive and full enjoyment (*libertas rei*) of his property." Under Roman law the servitudes consisted either in not doing something (*in non faciendo*) and was negative (*servitus negativa*), or in suffering something to be done (*in patiendo*) and was affirmative (*servitus affirmativa*). Where the owner of a thing assumed the obligation to do something (*in faciendo*) in relation to that thing for the benefit of another, this obligation assumed a technically different character and was not regarded as a *jus in re*. "But (as Bluntschli warns us)," says Sir Edward S. Creasy (Creasy: The First Platform of International Law, 1876, §256), "much caution is requisite in applying to international law the doctrines of the Roman law as to prædial servitudes, urban servitudes, rustic servitudes, and other forensic distinctions." Nevertheless, the principles of "international servitude" are fairly well established and history presents many applications of them.

Probably nowhere in the history of international law has the subject received fuller examination and study than in the North Atlantic Coast Fisheries Arbitration before the Hague Tribunal of Arbitration. In the twelve or thirteen volumes forming the record of this case will be found the expressions upon the subject of nearly every international writer and of all the great international lawyers. English translations of extracts from works of Argentinian, Austrian, Belgian, French, German, Italian, Russian, Spanish and Swiss publicists, together with extracts from the works of British and American publicists, were compiled by James Brown Scott for use before the Hague Tribunal. This volume, called "International Servitudes," printed by the Government Printing Office in 1910, is undoubtedly the most valuable collection of authorities on the subject. (Through the courtesy of Ex-Senator Elihu Root, of counsel for the United States, and Hon. Chandler P. Anderson, the attorney for the United States in the Fisheries Arbitration, a copy of this volume has been made a part of the library of our Commission.)

Sir Robert Phillimore once said (Vol. 9, Proceedings before the Hague Tribunal, North Atlantic Coast Fisheries Arbitration, 569 (338): "In the memorable answer, pronounced by Montesquieu to be *résponse sans réplique,* and framed by Lord Mansfield and Sir George Lee, of the British to the Prussian Government,

"'The law of nations is said to be founded upon justice, equity, convenience, and the reason of the thing, and confirmed by long usage.'

"It is more especially to this usage, as evidencing the consent of nations, that great judges, such, among others, as Lord Stowell and Chancellor Kent, and great jurists of all countries, have continually referred."

From the wealth of learning contained in the volume to which we have referred, we take the following (Vol. 1, Sir Robert Phillimore's "International Law," 3rd ed., 1879, §277): "The property of a state may not only be alienated, but may also be subjected to *obligations* and *services* in favor of another state; as the property of an individual may be burdened and encumbered in favor of another individual."

§279: "States are sometimes placed in such physical relations to each other that some limitations of the abstract rights of each *necessarily* flow from their natural relations, or from the reason of the thing. Thus a state is bound to receive the waters which *naturally* flow within its boundaries from a conterminous State. This obligation belongs to the class of '*servitutes* juris gentium *nat-*

urales,' and here the provisions of the Digest and Institutes may be said to be identical with those of International Law."

§280: "A State may *voluntarily* subject herself to obligations in favor of another state, both with respect to persons and things, which would not *naturally* be binding upon her. These are '*servitutes* juris gentium *voluntariæ*.' "

Hannis Taylor, in "A Treatise on International Public Law," §217, says: "A state may limit or qualify its sovereignty and jurisdiction over its territorial property by permitting a foreign state to perform within its bounds certain acts otherwise prohibited; or by surrendering the right to exercise certain parts of its domestic jurisdiction as a protection to others. Restrictions thus imposed upon the sovereignty of a state are known as servitudes, which may be either positive or negative."

Dr. L. Oppenheim, "International Law," §205: "Since the territory of a state includes not only the land, but also the rivers which water the land, the maritime belt, the territorial subsoil, and the territorial atmosphere, all these can, as well as the service of the land itself, be an object of state servitudes. Thus a state may have a perpetual right of admittance for its subjects to the fishery in the maritime belt of another state, or a right to lay telegraph cables through a foreign maritime belt, or a right to build and use a tunnel through a boundary mountain, and the like. And should ever aerostation become so developed as to be of practical utility, a state servitude might be created through a state acquiring a perpetual right to send military aerial vehicles through the territorial atmosphere of a neighboring state."

Senator Root, in his argument before the Hague Tribunal (see Volume 11, p. 1285), after reading from Bluntschli, Bonfils, Calvo, Chrétien, Clauss, Despagnet, Diena, Fabre, Fiore, Hall, Hartmann, Heffter, Heilborn, Hollatz, Holtzendorff, Klüber, Lomonaco, G. F. de Martens, Neumann, H. B. Oppenheim, L. Oppenheim, Phillimore, Rivier, Ullmann, at p. 1287 (2129) culls as a well-settled principle the following: "Since anybody can grant any right he chooses to a third party concerning his thing, so has each nation a right to grant another nation a certain right in its territory. . . . It belongs even to the mutual duties of nations for the one to create certain rights in his territory for the advantage of the other, in so far as no abuse of the territory takes place."

The North Atlantic Coast Fisheries Case

In the argument before the Hague Tribunal, George Turner, one of the counsel for the United States Vol. 9, North Atlantic Coast Fisheries Arbitration, 564 (335), said: "When one nation grants to another certain rights to be exercised within its territorial limits, rights which possess the attributes and qualities of a servitude by the municipal law, it creates a relation between itself and the other nation which is analogous to the relation which exists between the owners of the dominant estate and the servient estate by the municipal law, in view of the fact that the sovereignty which nations possess, under the conception of to-day, constitutes a species of higher ownership, which the nations may contract about, or may burden or may dispose of, in whole or in part, at their will and their pleasure. When such a grant is made by one nation to another, to be exercised within its territories by the other, a right to resort to the territory and to employ the territory for profit, which right is a perpetual right, and is strictly a national right, we have, in fact, every one of the concepts, every one of the qualities, every one of the attributes of the servitude as it was known to the Roman law."

The controversy before the Hague Tribunal in the Fisheries Arbitration presented a number of interesting questions. The one with which we are concerned, however, called for an interpretation of the fisheries provision of the Treaty of 1818 and arose out of the clause of the treaty which provided that "the inhabitants of the United States shall have forever, in common with the subjects of His Britannic Majesty, the liberty to take fish of every kind" on the so-called treaty coast. "The British contention," says Mr. Anderson (Chandler P. Anderson: The Final Outcome of the Fisheries Arbitration — The American Journal of International Law, January, 1913), "rested on the argument that the words 'in common with the subjects of His Britannic Majesty' ment that American fishermen should be on exactly the same footing as local fishermen in British waters, and therefore subject to the same governmental control exercised by Great Britain and her Colonies over British subjects. The United States, on the other hand, showed by the negotiations resulting in that treaty, as well as by means of the antecedent French fishing treaty rights on the Newfoundland coast, that the words 'in common' were used to negative the implication, which otherwise would have arisen, that American fishermen were to have an exclusive right of fishing. The United States further maintained that, instead of subjecting American fishermen to local regulations, the effect of the treaty was either to establish a fishery common to both nations, in which the United States had an equal interest with Great Britain, thus creating an international servitude depriving Great Britain of a portion of her sovereignty in the treaty waters, or else, in the alternative, that the treaty must be regarded as imposing upon Great Britain a contractual obligation limiting the exercise of British sovereignty in treaty waters, to the extent that the prerequisite of reasonableness must be determined before regulations could be enforced against American fishermen, and that neither Great Britain nor her Colonies could be the sole judge of the question of reasonableness."

In his dispatch to the United States Ambassador in London, Secretary Root said: "The treaty of 1818 either declared or granted a perpetual right to the inhabitants of the United States, which is beyond the sovereign power of England to destroy or change. It is conceded that this right is, and for ever must be, superior to any inconsistent exercise of sovereignty within that territory. *The existence of this right is a qualification of British sovereignty within that territory.*" (Vol. 4, North Atlantic Coast Fisheries Case, Brief for Great Britain, pp. 18, 19.) In the memorable communications between Lord Salisbury and Secretary Evarts (Ibid. 29, 30, 31), Lord Salisbury said: ". . . Her Majesty's Government will readily admit — what is, indeed, self-evident — that British sovereignty, as regards those waters, is limited in its scope by the engagements of the Treaty of Washington, which cannot be modified or affected by any municipal legislation. I cannot anticipate that with regard to these principles any difference will be found to exist between the views of the two Governments." Mr. Evarts replied (1879) that he had nowhere taken any position larger or broader than that stated by Lord Salisbury in the quotation just made. "I have never denied the full authority and jurisdiction either of the Imperial or colonial Governments over their territorial waters, *except so far as by Treaty that authority and jurisdiction have been deliberately limited by these Governments themselves.*"

Sir W. Robson, of counsel for Great Britain before the Tribunal (see discussion, Vol. 11 (1011), 1674 et seq.), in a most enlightening colloquy with Dr. Drago of the Hague Tribunal, stated that " a State may make, for instance, with regard to a railway, a contract with another State, giving that other State any rights it pleases over its own territory, for the purposes of the railway . . . (1674) (1012). It is to the good of mankind, to the good of individual States, and to the good of the whole civilized community, that each State should be encouraged to open its territory to other States, either for economic purposes, or for purposes of general beneficial intercourse. I say they may do it, and I say that the existing international law allows them to do it, without danger. They may do it as sovereigns. They may put their territory, as sovereigns, under all kinds of obligations of the kind which we have heard called real obligations. They may say: "You may come to our territory and fish, or build railways, or build warehouses. You may do all these things.' I say that those are highly meritorious grants to make; that they must be made, and they are made, without any consequence whatever of a character derogating from the sovereignty of the States. That is my case.

" So that I accept the suggestion of the learned arbitrator that such contracts can be made. I say they can be made, and ought to be encouraged. No State ought to be deterred from limiting the exercise of its own sovereignty in any of these respects. It ought not to be deterred from doing it." In other words, the great lawyers representing England did not dispute the power of two states to join in a treaty limiting the exercise of their sovereignty in these respects, but confined the argument to the consideration of whether, *in fact,* they had done so with regard to the fisheries. Sir W. Robson laid stress upon the importance of the Hague Tribunal " in dealing with this great question, so framing its judgment as not to allow of any discouragement to States in making obligations *inter se,* which may open the territory of one to the inhabitants of another without any detriment to the sovereignty of either. That, I think, is the thing we should all aim at. And my own belief is that international law, as it is now constituted, does that. International law, when it is thoroughly considered, as it stands today, does allow a State to open its territory freely, to limit the exercise of its own sovereign rights in certain particulars, without any detriment to its other sovereign rights or its general national sovereignty." Again, in the colloquy with Sir Charles Fitzpatrick: "States may do what they like with regard to their property. In so far as they are owners, they may subject their property to any obligation that they please. I say they may do it without any danger to their sovereignty. That is to say, they put what obligations they like upon themselves as lords of the land. A State may submit its dominium to these rights, without any derogation from its imperium . . ." Sir Charles Fitzpatrick said: "Your contention, briefly, is that a State may part with a share of the public domain, either in favour of a citizen of that State, in favour of the citizen of a foreign country, or in favour of the Government of a foreign country?" Sir W. Robson: "Yes. . . . It is the essential difference between dominium and imperium, which, as one of the learned arbitrators has just pointed out, has to be considered. . . . That general sovereignty is a thing wholly apart and not affected by the grant of particular territorial rights, as the United States say it is affected."

Indeed, we may say that the framers of the treaty between New York and New Jersey of 1834 had clearly in mind this distinction between the preservation of general sovereignty and governmental functions and the grant of title to land, the distinctions between the title to the land under water, which, in the case of New Jersey, extends to the middle of the stream, and the exercise of governmental police power, which is granted to one State even to the shores of the other.

In its decision, the Hague Tribunal did not support the extreme contention of our Government that Great Britain had transferred to the United States sovereign rights in the treaty waters, but "equally to the satisfaction of the United States" (as Mr. Anderson says in his article, "The Final Outcome of the Fisheries

Question"), it decided that though Great Britain retained its sovereignty intact, it had nevertheless imposed a limitation upon the exercise of this sovereignty, that is to say, it was an implied condition of the treaty that whatever regulations were adopted by Great Britain covering the exercise of fishery rights, these regulations must be reasonable. The treaty, said the Tribunal, limited the inherent sovereign rights of Great Britain to regulate the liberty to take fish in and about Newfoundland "in respect of the said liberties therein granted to the inhabitants of the United States in that such regulations must be made bona fide and must not be in violation of the said Treaty." Accordingly, in case of any disputes as to the reasonableness of such regulations, enforcement of them against American fishermen must be suspended until they were passed upon by an impartial tribunal and held by such tribunal to be reasonable. The rules and methods of procedure which should be adopted by the two Governments to carry out this decision were embodied in the award and subsequently took shape in a treaty, adopting with minor modifications the rules and methods of procedure thus recommended. This treaty was signed at Washington on July 20, 1912, and appears in full in the compilation of addresses and papers of Ex-Senator Elihu Root under the title "North Atlantic Coast Fisheries Arbitration" (Harvard Univ. Press, 1917 — Edited by Robert Bacon and James Brown Scott). The method, briefly stated, requires the British Government, when adopting regulations, to publish them in designated newspapers for a certain period of time before they become effective, and provides that they shall not become effective with respect to the inhabitants of the United States "until the Permanent Mixed Fishery Commission has decided that the regulation is reasonable within the meaning of this award." After the publication of these regulations, the United States may convoke the Permanent Mixed Fishery Commission for the purpose of passing upon the regulations. If it shall fail, however, so to do, the regulations become effective. The Permanent Mixed Fishery Commission is made up of experts selected by both nations.

Here, then, is a clear recognition on the part of English and American lawyers, as well as a decision by the highest international court, to the effect that sovereign states may engage in the regulation of commercial privileges in territorial waters without surrendering general sovereignty, and may, for the purpose of administering such regulations or of determining their reasonableness, create a joint tribunal with final and supreme authority in the premises.

The Panama Canal

Recently, the United States Government entered the cities of Panama and Colon for the purpose of maintaining order and preserving health and taking certain necessary sanitary precautions. These two cities are under the sovereignty of the Government of Panama. The authority under which the United States Government acted was the treaty with the Government of Panama. This treaty is in itself but another application of the principles under discussion, not only with reference to our dealings with the Government of Panama, but also with reference to our dealings with England. Again, the repeal of the Panama Canal tolls provision in the Hay-Pauncefote Treaty furnishes a most instructive chapter in the modern history of our Government, considered by many statesmen to be one of the most honorable chapters in the diplomacy of our country. This controversy presented the single question of the obligations that we had assumed towards the governments of other countries, especially that of Great Britain, in the building and operation of the Canal. On the 5th of March, 1914, President Wilson urged the passage by Congress of the bill for the repeal of the tolls exemption in favor of the United States upon the ground that our country had assumed treaty obligations toward Great Britain which made exemption of tolls in our own favor a breach of international duty. Legal title of the United States to the Canal Zone was conceded. The sole issue was whether or not the title was subject to an obligation in the nature of a trust.

In his memorable address to the Senate on January 21, 1913, Senator Root said concerning our obligations to Great Britain: "So, Mr. President, far from our being relieved of the obligations of the treaty with Great Britain by reason of the title that we have obtained to the Canal Zone, we have taken that title impressed with a solemn trust. We have taken it for no purpose except the construction and maintenance of a canal in accordance with all the stipulations of our treaty with Great Britain. We cannot be false to those stipulations without adding to the breach of contract a breach of the trust which we have assumed, according to our own declarations, for the benefit of mankind, as the mandatory of civilization." In other words, absolute sovereignty and control over the Panama territory was vested in the United States, yet was subject to a sacred trust in favor of Great Britain. Senator Root (in the same volume, Addresses on International Subjects), discussing "The Ethics of the Panama Question," traces the history of all the treaties bearing upon the subject and the relations between the various governments. The treaty of December 12, 1846, between the United States and New Granada (p. 182) provided: "The Government of New Granada guarantees to the Government of the United States that the right of way or transit across the Isthmus of Panama upon any modes of communication that now exist, or that may be hereafter constructed, shall be open and free to the Government and citizens of the United States. . . . And in order to secure to themselves the tranquil and constant enjoyment of these advantages, and as an especial compensation for the said advantages and for the favors they have acquired by the fourth, fifth, and sixth articles of this treaty, the United States guarantee positively and efficaciously to New Granada by the present stipulation the perfect neutrality of the before-mentioned Isthmus with the view that the free transit from the one to the other sea may not be interrupted or embarrassed in any future time while this treaty exists, and in consequence the United States also guarantee in the same manner the rights of sovereignty and property which New Granada has and possesses over the said territory." Senator Root, commenting upon this, said (p. 183): "You will perceive that in this transaction New Granada recognized the subordination of her sovereignty to the world's easement of passage by railroad or by canal, and apprehending that other nations might seek to exercise that right through the destruction of her sovereignty and the appropriation of her territory, she procured the United States to assume the responsibility of protecting her against such treatment."

The preamble of the Hay-Pauncefote Treaty of December 16, 1901, recites that the two parties "being desirous to facilitate the construction of a ship canal . . . by whatever route may be considered expedient, and to that end to remove any objection which may arise out of the Convention of the 19th April, 1850, commonly called the Clayton-Bulwer treaty, to the construction of such canal under the auspices of the Government of the United States, without impairing the 'general principle' of neutralization established in Article VIII of that Convention" have for this purpose appointed plenipotentiaries, etc. Article 2 gave our nation the exclusive privilege to buy the right of way and to own it and to build the canal. Article 3 gave rights to protect and govern the great waterway. But Article 4 provided that no change of territorial sovereignty or of international relations of the country or the countries traversed by the canal shall affect the present principle of "neutralization" or the obligations under the present treaty.

Turning now to the international relations between the United States and Panama established by the Hay-Bunau-Varilla treaty of February 23, 1904, we find that the United States secured the grant of lands and the franchise to build and operate a canal across Panama from ocean to ocean. By Article I, "the United States guarantees and will maintain the independence of the Republic of Panama." By Article II, "the Republic of Panama grants to the United States in perpetuity the use, occupation and control of a zone of land and land under water for the construction, maintenance, operation, sanitation and protection of said Canal of the width of ten miles extending to the distance of five miles on each side of the center line of the route of the Canal to be constructed; the said zone beginning in the Caribbean Sea three miles from mean low water mark and extending to and across the Isthmus of Panama into the Pacific Ocean to a distance of three marine miles from mean low water mark with the proviso that the cities of Panama and Colon and the harbors adjacent to said cities, which are included within the boundaries of the zone above described, shall not be included within this grant. The Republic of Panama further grants to the United States in perpetuity the use, occupation and control of any other lands and waters outside of the zone above described which may be necessary and convenient for the construction, maintenance, operation, sanitation and protection of the said Canal or of any auxiliary canals or other works necessary and convenient for the construction, maintenance, operation, sanitation and protection of the said enterprise. . . .

"Article III. The Republic of Panama grants to the United States all the rights, power and authority within the zone mentioned and described in Article II of this agreement and within the limits of all auxiliary lands and waters mentioned and described in said Article II which the United States would possess and exercise if it were the sovereign of the territory within which said lands and waters are located to the entire exclusion of the exercise by the Republic of Panama of any such sovereign rights, power or authority."

"Article VII. The Republic of Panama grants to the United States within the limits of the cities of Panama and Colon and their adjacent harbors and within the territory adjacent thereto the right to acquire by purchase or by the exercise of the right of eminent domain, any lands, buildings, water rights or other properties necessary and convenient for the construction, maintenance, operation and protection of the Canal and of any works of sanitation, such as the collection and disposition of sewage and the distribution of water in the said cities of Panama and Colon, which, in the discretion of the United States may be necessary and convenient for the construction, maintenance, operation, sanitation and protection of the said Canal and railroad. All such works of sanitation, collection and disposition of sewage and distribution of water in the cities of Panama and Colon shall be made at the expense of the United States, and the Government of the United States, its agents or nominees shall be authorized to impose and collect water rates and sewage rates which shall be sufficient to provide for the payment of interest and the amortization of the principal of the cost of said works within a period of fifty years and upon the expiration of said term of fifty years the system of sewers and water works shall revert to and become the properties of the cities of Panama and Colon respectively, and the use of the water shall be free to the inhabitants of Panama and Colon, except to the extent that water rates may be necessary for the operation and maintenance of said system of sewers and water.

"The Republic of Panama agrees that the cities of Panama and Colon shall comply *in perpetuity with the sanitary ordinances whether of a preventive or curative character prescribed by the United States and in case the Government of Panama is unable or fails in its duty to enforce this compliance by the cities of Panama and Colon with the sanitary ordinances of the United States the Republic of Panama grants to the United States the right and authority to enforce the same.*

"*The same right and authority are granted to the United States for the maintenance of public order in the cities of Panama and Colon and the territories and harbors adjacent thereto in case the Republic of Panama should not be, in the judgment of the United States, able to maintain such order.*"

For all of this, it will be recalled, Panama got ten million in gold coin and an annual payment of two hundred and fifty thousand dollars. By Articles VI and XV private land owners are guaranteed against damage, and any damage to private owners is to be appraised and settled by a *joint commission* appointed by the United States and Panama, whose decision shall be final. This commission is to be appointed, two by the President of the United States and two by the President of Panama. In case these disagree by being equally divided, an umpire is to be appointed by the two governments who shall render the decision. By Article XXIII the United States is given the right to employ armed force, if it becomes necessary, for "the safety or protection of the Canal, or of the ships that make use of the same, or the railways and auxiliary works."

While the United States Supreme Court did not pass upon the validity of all of the provisions of this treaty, nevertheless, in the case of *Wilson v. Shaw,* 204 U. S. 24, it refused to interfere with the operation of any of the provisions of the treaty. After reviewing the history preceding the execution of the treaty, Judge Brewer, speaking for the Court, said: "For the courts to interfere . . . would be an exercise of judicial power which, to say the least, is novel and extraordinary" (p. 31). (In the same case the power of the Government to build the Canal, and to authorize the incorporation of a company to operate the railroad, is fully sustained.)

The Suez Canal Convention

The provisions of the Hay-Pauncefote Treaty were taken from the Suez Convention, almost, says Senator Root (Panama Canal Tolls address to the Senate, January 21, 1913), " though not quite — textually." The Suez Convention contained provisions reserving to Turkey and Egypt as sovereigns of the territory through which the canal passed, treating Turkey as the suzerain and Egypt as the sovereign over Egypt, all of the rights that pertained to the sovereigns for the protection of their own territory. (The Suez Canal Convention is given in both French and English in Sen. Doc., 56th Cong., 1st Sess., 1899, Vol. 10, Doc. 151, and in English in Sen. Rep., 56th Congress., 2nd Sess., 1900, Vol. 1, Doc. 1337, pt. 4, p. 318-319, and in House Doc., 62nd Cong., 2nd Sess., 1912, Doc. 680, p. 41-44, and in White's " Expansion of Egypt," p. 339 et seq.)

By the Treaty of Constantinople, Oct. 29, 1888, between Great Britain, Germany, Austria-Hungary, Spain, France, Italy, the Netherlands, Russia and Turkey, providing for the free and open navigation of the Suez Canal " to every vessel of commerce or of war, without distinction of flag," the Powers agreed as follows (Article VIII): " The Agents in Egypt of the Signatory Powers of the Present Treaty shall be charged to watch over its execution. In case of any event threatening the security or the free passage of the Canal, they shall meet on the summons of three of their number under the presidency of their Doyen, in order to proceed to the necessary verifications. They shall inform the Khedivial Government of the danger which they may have perceived, in order that that Government may take proper steps to insure the protection and the free use of the Canal. Under any circumstances, they shall meet once a year to take note of the due excution of the Treaty.

* * * * * *

" They shall especially demand the suppression of any work or the dispersion of any assemblage on either bank of the Canal, the object or effect of which might be to interfere with the liberty and the entire security of the navigation."

The Egyptian Commission of the Public Debt

Lord Cromer in his "Modern Egypt" (Vol. II, p. 304 et seq.) tells the story of the establishment of the Egyptian Commission of the Public Debt, consisting originally of an Englishman, a Frenchman, an Austrian, and an Italian, and later of a German and a Russian. The Powers of Europe having loaned nine million pounds, it was necessary to furnish security for the debt. For this purpose, the revenues of Egypt were pledged to the service of the debt and the Commissioners were authorized to collect these revenues. No loan could be contracted without their consent. The Law of Liquidation passed by Egypt, coupled with the decree of July 27, 1885, gave to the European Powers participation in the judicial system (Cromer: "Modern Egypt," p. 316), all the Powers, without distinction, being represented upon the Courts of First Instance. "The choice of judges rests nominally with the Egyptian Government. In reality, the judges have until quite recently been nominated by their respective Governments" (p. 318). Lord Cromer, commenting upon this system in his chapter on "Internationalism," refers to the wide field for the development of internationalism of which the Egyptian Commission of the Public Debt furnishes an example. For "What can be more natural in cases of this kind," says he (p. 303), "than for the Powers to say — we are agreed as to all that is essential; certain points of detail remain to be settled locally; let us each appoint an expert who will represent our interests and see that they get fair play, but who at the same time will have no very marked political bias, and who will treat the technical questions which come under his consideration on their own merits?"

Sir Robert Phillimore points out that it frequently occurs that a State, having contracted pecuniary obligations toward another State, has mortgaged its revenues, or pledged a portion of its territory, as security for the payment of its debts. Thus, among the instances which he cites, the United Provinces of the Netherlands hypothecated Vlissingen, Rameken and Briel to England, in 1585. Denmark, in 1654, hypothecated the province of Holland to Sweden, as a security for the peace then concluded. Weimar appears to have been pawned, so to speak, to Mecklenburg in 1803, and Corsica by Genoa to France in 1768.

General Provisions of the Congress of Vienna

By the General Treaty of the Congress of Vienna, signed at Vienna, June 9, 1815, Art. XXX (30), the King of Prussia and the King of Hanover agreed:

" 1. The Hanoverian Government engages to cause to be executed, at its expense, in the years 1815 and 1816, the work which a Commission, composed partly of artists, and to be immediately appointed by Prussia and Hanover, shall deem necessary to render navigable that part of the river Ems which extends from the Prussian frontier to its mouth, and to keep it, after the execution of such works, always in the same state in which those works shall have placed it for the benefit of navigation."

Article CVIII provided: " The Powers whose States are separated or crossed by the same navigable River engage to regulate, by common consent, all that regards its navigation. For this purpose they will name Commissioners, who shall assemble, at latest, within six months after the termination of the Congress, and who shall adopt, as the bases of their proceedings, the Principles established by the following articles."

Article CIX: " The navigation of the Rivers, along their whole course, referred to in the preceding Article, from the point where each of them becomes navigable, to its mouth, shall be entirely free, and shall not, in respect to Commerce, be prohibited to any one; it being understood that the Regulations established with regard to the Police of this navigation shall be respected, as they will be framed alike for all, and as favourable as possible to the Commerce of all nations."

Article CX provides that the system for collection of duties and maintenance of the police " shall be, as nearly as possible, the same along the whole course of the River; and shall also extend, unless particular circumstances prevent it, to those of its Branches and Junctions, which, in their navigable course, separate or traverse different States."

The Scheldt

By the Treaty of London, November 15, 1831, between Great Britain, Austria, France, Prussia and Russia and Belgium, relating to the separation of Belgium from Holland, by Article IX it was provided that concerning the River Scheldt, "that the pilotage and the buoying of its channel, as well as the conservation of the channels of the Scheldt below Antwerp, shall be subject *to a joint superintendence; that this joint superintendence shall be exercised by Commissioners, to be appointed on both sides for this purpose; that moderate pilotage dues shall be fixed by mutual agreement; and that such dues shall be the same for the Dutch as for the Belgian commerce."* (British and Foreign State Papers, 1830–31, p. 653 et seq.) By Article X, "The use of the canals which traverse both Countries shall continue to be free and common to the Inhabitants of both."

The Niger and the Congo

The Treaty of Berlin, February 26, 1885 (Vol. 76, British and Foreign State Papers), between Great Britain, Austria-Hungary, Belgium, Denmark, France, Germany, Italy, the Netherlands, Portugal, Russia, Spain, Sweden, Norway, Turkey and the United States, respecting the affairs of Africa, established the freedom of navigation of these rivers, and provided for the creation (Article XVII) of the International Navigation Commission of the Congo, which "shall be charged with supervising the application of the principles proclaimed and perpetuated (consacrés) by this Declaration.

"In all cases of difference arising relative to the application of the principles established by the present Declaration, the Governments concerned may agree to appeal to the good offices of the International Commission, by submitting to it an examination of the facts which shall have occasioned these differences." (Hertslet's "Commercial Treaties," London, 1890, Vol. XVII.)

The Rhine

By the Treaty of Vienna, June 9, 1815 (see Hertslet's "Collection of Treaties and Conventions between Great Britain and Foreign Powers, Vol. 1, 1827), Article X of Annex 16 provided that in order to insure that the navigation of the rivers along their whole course, referred to in the preceding article, "shall be entirely free, and shall not, in respect to Commerce, be prohibited to any one" and ". . . to establish a perfect control over the observance of the general regulation, and to constitute an authority which may serve as a means of communication between the States of the Rhine upon all subjects relating to Navigation, a Central Commission shall be appointed." Each State bordering on the Rhine (Article XI) was authorized to name a commissioner for its formation, which was to assemble regularly at Mentz on the 1st of November in each year. (The Congress was representative of Austria, France, Great Britain, Portugal, Prussia, Russia, Spain and Sweden.) Article XII provided that "in order that a permanent authority may exist, which, in the absence of the Central Commission, may superintend the observance of the regulation, and to which the merchants and boatmen may at all times refer, there shall be named a Chief Inspector and three Deputy Inspectors." Articles XIII, XIV and XV provided in detail for the manner of selection of the Chief Inspector by the Central Commission. It was provided that the Prussian Commissioner should have one-third of a certain number of votes, the French Commissioner one-sixth, the Commissioner of the Netherlands one-sixth and the other German princes, excepting Prussia, one-third. The appointments of the inspectors were to be for life. The Chief Inspector, assisted by the Deputy Inspectors (Article XV), "are to superintend the fulfilment of the regulation, and to arrange everything relating to the police of the navigation. It will, therefore, be his right and his duty to issue orders on this subject to the Offices for collecting duties, and to communicate with the other local authorities of the States bordering on the Rhine." By Article XVI, the Inspectors were to be under the control of the Central Commission, to whom they must report, and were subject in all respects to their superintendence. And by Article XVII, "The decisions of the Central Commission shall be had by an absolute majority of votes, which shall be given in perfect equality; but as its members should be considered as agents of the States of the Rhine, charged with making arrangements for their mutual interests, their decisions shall not be binding upon these States until their consent shall have been given by their Commissioners." By Article XXVII provision is made for the making of detailed regulations, as well as for organizing "judicial authorities of the First and Second Instance, and their mode of proceeding," "the

Police of the ports for shipping, unloading, or shifting cargoes," all of which are to be framed by the Central Commission.

And by additional articles the same principles, it was stipulated, should be applied to the Neck-r, the Mayne, the Moselle, the Meuse and the Scheldt.

The French Fishing Rights at Newfoundland

The ownership of Newfoundland was at one time a matter of dispute between Great Britain and France. By a Treaty of Utrecht in 1713, France ceded all her claims to Great Britain, subject, however, to the provision that "it shall be allowed to the Subjects of France, to catch fish and to dry them on land, in that part only, and in no other besides that, of the said Island of Newfoundland, which stretches from the place called Cape Bonavista, to the northern point of the said Island, and from thence running down by the western side, reaches as far as the place called Point Riche." By the treaty between Great Britain and France in 1783, the territorial limitations were changed, and by the treaty of January 14, 1857, Article I (see U. S. Case, North Atlantic Fisheries Case before the Hague Tribunal, Vol. 2, Appendix, p. 51 et seq.), French subjects were confirmed in the "exclusive right to fish, and to use the strand for fishery purposes, during the season elsewhere specified (Article VIII), on the east coast of Newfoundland, from Cape St. John to the Quirpon Islands. They shall also have the right to fish, and to use the strand for fishery purposes, during the said season, to the exclusion of British subjects, on the north coast of Newfoundland, from the Quirpon Islands to Cape Norman; and on the west coast, in and upon the five fishing-harbours of Port-au-Choix, Small Harbour (or Petit Port), Port au Port, Red Island, and Cod Roy Island. Such exclusive fishing, from the Quirpon Islands to Cape Norman, shall extend to a distance of three marine miles . . . from . . . and as regards the five harbours, shall extend to within a radius of three marine miles in all directions from the centre of each such harbour, but with power to the Commissioners or Umpire elsewhere provided for in this Convention to alter such limits for each harbour in accordance with the existing practice." For the enforcement of these provisions, the naval officers of the

French Government (Article IX) were authorized to enforce "the said French exclusive rights of fishing" by "expulsion of vessels or boats attempting concurrent fishing, in the case of there being no British cruizing-vessel in sight, or made known to be present, within a distance of five marine miles." Article XVIII provided for an arbitration commission, consisting of one commissioner for each Power, with provision for an umpire to settle disputes. These treaty rights remained in force and effect until April 8, 1904, when France limited her advantages in exchange for other rights in Africa, retaining, however, the fishing rights in these territorial waters. (See 2 North Atlantic Coast Fisheries Case, p. 83 et seq.)

Despagnet, a leading French writer, in his work "Cours de Droit International Public," 1899 (see "Coastal Waters," English translations compiled by Borchard, p. 59), says:

"A state may cede to another the right of fishing in territorial seas, even to the exclusion of its own nationals. Such is the case in Newfoundland. Although fishing is free on the Grand Banks of Newfoundland situated in the open sea, and although it belongs exclusively to the French in the territorial waters of her colonies of St. Pierre and Miquelon, it is by exception reserved to France over a part of the territorial waters of Newfoundland, with liberty for French fishermen to establish themselves exclusively on the portion of the shore called, on that account, the French shore, by the Treaty of Utrecht of April 11, 1713, which ceded the island to Great Britain. This reservation has been confirmed in the treaty of Aix-la-Chapelle, 1748, and the treaty of Paris of February 10, 1763, of Versailles of September 30, 1783, of Paris of May 30, 1814, and November 20, 1815, and in the special convention regulating the exercise of fishing of January 14, 1857." (§422.)

Rivier, another French writer (see Borchard: "Coastal Waters," English translation, p. 319), says: "The most well known and important derogations from the exclusive right of fishing in the littoral sea is the servitude constituted in favor of France by Article XIII of the treaty of Utrecht of 1713, ceding Newfoundland to Great Britain and the servitude in favor of the United States in the British waters off Newfoundland and Canada."

The significant fact about the French fishing rights is that they are rights in waters over which Great Britain retains sovereignty, which, during certain periods of the year, may be exercised *exclusively* by Frenchmen.

Other Fishery Cases

By Article XI of the treaty of peace between Russia and Japan, August 23–September 5, 1905, Japanese subjects receive a concession of fishing rights in Russian territorial waters of the Seas of Japan, Okhotsk, and Behring.

United States-Canadian Canals

By the Treaty of 1871 between the United States and Great Britain, the citizens of the United States are given free use "of the Welland, St. Lawrence, and other canals in the Dominion on terms of equality with the inhabitants of the Dominion; and the Government of the United States engages that the subjects of Her Britannic Majesty shall enjoy the use of the St. Clair Flats Canal on terms of equality with the inhabitants of the United States."

In our treaty with Great Britain (the reciprocity treaty) of 1854, "It is agreed that the citizens and inhabitants of The United States shall have the right to navigate the river St. Lawrence and the canals in Canada, used as the means of communicating between the Great Lakes and the Atlantic Ocean, with their vessels, boats, and crafts, as fully and freely as the subjects of Her Britannic Majesty, subject only to the same toll and other assessments as now are or may hereafter be exacted of Her Majesty's said subjects. . . .

"It is further agreed, that British subjects shall have the right freely to navigate Lake Michigan with their vessels, boats and crafts, so long as the privilege of navigating the river St. Lawrence, secured to American citizens by the above clause of the present Article, shall continue; and the Government of The United States further engages to urge upon the State Governments to secure to the subjects of Her Britannic Majesty the use of the several State canals on terms of equality with the inhabitants of The United States."

Nicaragua Canal

By the treaty between the United States and Nicaragua in 1867 it was provided that: "The Republic of Nicaragua hereby grants to The United States, and to their citizens and property, the right of transit between the Atlantic and Pacific Oceans through the territory of that Republic, on any route of communication, natural or artificial, whether by land or water, which may now or hereafter exist or be constructed under the authority of Nicaragua, to be used and enoyed in the same manner and upon equal terms by both Republics and their respective citizens."

United States-Mexico Commission

In 1896 the United States and Mexico referred to "The International (Water) Boundary Commission" the subject of the equitable distribution of the waters of the Rio Grande (see Vol. II, Department of State, Proceedings of the International (Water) Boundary Commission, U. S. and Mexico, Treaties of 1884 and 1889). Among other things, the Commission was to report as to "the best and most feasible mode, whether through a dam to be constructed across the Rio Grande near El Paso, Tex., or otherwise, of so regulating the use of the waters of said river as to secure to each country concerned and to its inhabitants their legal and equitable rights and interests in said waters." On November 25, 1896, after careful study, the Joint Commission thus appointed recommended to the two Governments "that a treaty be entered into, as a final settlement of all questions past and future, regarding the distribution of the waters of the Rio Grande." This treaty was to involve the ceding by the United States to Mexico of a small tract of land, the construction of a dam as designed by joint engineers, the removal of railroads from the bed of the proposed reservoir, and the acquisition of land to be submerged, and required that the further management of the river should be committed to the management of a mixed commission, who, after constructing the dam, should provide for the permanent distribution of the flow, one-half, roughly speaking, for such use as the Mexican Government might see fit to apply it to, and one-half as the United States might see fit to apply it. The treaty between the United States and Mexico of March 1,

1889, provided that all questions arising by reason of the changes which take place in the beds of the Rio Grande and the Colorado Rivers should be submitted "for examination and decision to an International Boundary Commission which shall have exclusive jurisdiction in the case of said differences or questions." Under this power, the construction and limit of works undertaken on the Rio Grande and Colorado along the international boundary line has been freely exercised, notably in the case of the Brownsville and Matamoras jetties in 1895, where the commission recommended the construction of a complete system of defensive and counter-defensive works. (The Rio Grande is a torrential stream. For the greater part of the year it carries no great quantity of water. Then come its flood seasons, which come suddenly, do not last long and pass away quickly. To check these torrential flows "defensive and counter-defensive works" were required.) The International Commission in 1897 settled the matter of the demarcation of the boundary of the two international bridges connecting Eagle Pass, Texas, and Ciudad Porfirio Diaz, Coahuila. It also settled the boundary line in the El Chamizal case.

The International Joint Commission (United States and Canada)

Ex-Senator Root and Ex-Ambassador Bryce negotiated in 1909 the treaty relating to boundary waters between the United States and Canada which is now in full force and operation. This treaty provides (Article I) that "the navigation of all navigable boundary waters shall for ever continue free and open for the purposes of commerce to the inhabitants and to the ships, vessels, and boats of both countries equally, subject, however, to any laws and regulations of either country, within its own territory, not inconsistent with such privilege of free navigation, and applying equally and without discrimination to the inhabitants, ships, vessels and boats of both countries," both parties, however, reserving (Article II) "the exclusive jurisdiction and control over the use and diversion, whether temporary or permanent, of all waters on its own side of the line which in their natural channels would flow across the boundary or into boundary waters; *but it is agreed that any interference with or diversion from their natural channel of such waters on either side of the boundary, resulting in any injury on the other side of the boundary, shall give rise to the same rights and entitle the injured parties to the same legal remedies as if such injury took place in the country where such diversion or interference occurs."*

By Article VII, " The High Contracting Parties agree to establish and maintain an International Joint Commission of the United States and Canada, composed of six commissioners, three on the part of the United States, appointed by the President thereof, and three on the part of the United Kingdom, appointed by His Majesty on the recommendation of the Governor in Council of the Dominion of Canada."

By Article VIII the Commission is given jurisdiction over and is required to pass upon all cases involving the use or obstruction or diversion of the waters with respect to which, under Articles III and IV of the treaty, the approval of the Commission is required. In passing upon such cases the Commission is required to govern itself by the following rules and principles:

" The High Contracting Parties shall have, each on its own side of the boundary, equal and similar rights in the use of the waters hereinbefore defined as boundary waters.

" The following order of precedence shall be observed among the various uses enumerated hereinafter for these waters, and no use shall be permitted which tends materially to conflict with or restrain any other use which is given preference over it in this order of precedence:

"(1) Uses for domestic and sanitary purposes;

"(2) Uses for navigation, including the service of canals for the purposes of navigation;

"(3) Uses for power and for irrigation purposes.

" The foregoing provisions shall not apply to or disturb any existing uses of boundary waters on either side of the boundary."

Furthermore, and this is of very great practical importance and of direct application to our problem, the Commission " may make its approval in any case *conditional upon the construction of remedial or protective works* to compensate, so far as possible, for the particular use or diversion proposed, and in such cases may require that suitable and adequate provision, approved by the Commission, be made for the protection and indemnity against injury of any interests on either side of the boundary."

Pursuant to this treaty, commissioners were appointed on the part of the United States on March 9, 1911, and on the part of Canada, November 10, 1911, organized on the 10th of January, 1912, and adopted rules of procedure (a copy of which is to be found in the library of the Commission). Under this authority, the Commission has acted in many cases, notably the Watrous Island Boom Company application for the approval of plans for a boom in Rainy River, the application of the Receiver of Michigan Lake Superior Power Company for approval of a lease with the United States for diversion of water and the construction of compensating works, the application of the Michigan Northern Power Company for diversion of waters of St. Mary's River at Sault Ste. Marie, Michigan, the application of the Algoma Steel Corporation, Limited, for approval of the construction of compensating works on St. Mary's River. Upon the hearing of the latter application, the Chairman, Hon. James A. Tawney, said: ". . . the people of no two countries in the world, except the people of Canada and the United States, have the opportunity of appearing personally before an international tribunal of any kind with original and final jurisdiction in their respective countries, as they may and are now doing in this case. . . . This tribunal is also unique because composed of citizens of two independent sovereignties. . . . Neither section of the Commission has any authority under the treaty to act in either country independent of the other. *Each section acts in conjunction with the other as a joint international organization.* In cases like the one now before us each member acts as the representative of *both countries,* or as Mr. Commissioner Gore, of Massachusetts, in deciding a case arising under the Jay treaty for the settlement of questions growing out of the War of the Revolution, well said:

" 'Although I am a citizen of but one nation, I am constituted a judge of both. Each nation has the same right and no greater right to demand of me fidelity and diligence in the examination, exactness, and justice of the decision.' "

This is precisely the attitude that we should like a Joint Port Authority to take, though receiving appointment, one-half of its members at the hands of the Governor of New York and one-half at the hands of the Governor of New Jersey. The considerations leading to the information of this International Commission are pertinent to our inquiry. In the opinion of the Joint High Commission in the matter of the compensating works in St. Mary's River, it said:

"Neither Government needed the aid of the Commission to prevent it from acting improvidently in granting persons or corporations authority to use, obstruct, or divert its navigable waters. They were fully capable of taking care of themselves. *But in taking care of themselves on their own side of the line, they did not always consider, or at least did not always adequately provide for taking care of, the interests of their neighbor on the other side of the line.* It was this feature of the situation that led to the establishment of the International Joint Commission. That Commission so long as the treaty remains, *supervises the action of either Government acting singly and alone in the matter of uses, obstructions, or diversions of boundary waters authorized by it, but it does so, not for the protection of the moving government, but for the protection of the passive government, which may be injured by the energy of its neighbor acting within the scope of its municipal authority, if its power be not scrutinized and supervised by an impartial tribunal.*"

The employment of a joint agency to construct "compensating works" finds precedential authority in the opinion of the Joint High Commission in the matter of the application of the Michigan Northern Power Company for approval of diversion and use of the waters of the St. Mary's river on the United States side of the international boundary at Sault Ste. Marie. In its opinion and order, the Joint High Commission directed that compensating works, including power canals, should be built to maintain the level of Lake Superior, but provided that "the operation of all the said works, canals, head gates and by-passes for the above purposes shall be under the direct control of . . . 'the board of control.'" This board of control consists of two members, one appointed by each Government, which board is authorized to formulate the rules under which the compensating works, the power canals, their head gates and by-passes are to be operated, "so as to secure as nearly as may be the regulation of Lake Superior within the range of monthly mean levels recommended and found necessary." In this opinion, the Commission considers its power to create such boards of control and finds that it is not only confirmed by the treaty, "but its existence is a necessary concomitant to the carrying out of the true intent and purpose of the treaty in respect to the prevention and settlement of disputes between the two governments and their people regarding the use of boundary waters. Without this power to approve conditionally, in cases where the proposed obstructions and diversions affect the rights and interests of the people on the other side, the purpose of the treaty would entirely fail." And the Commission adopts the language of Judge Brown in *Tucker v. Alexandorff* (183 U. S. 424) to the effect that "treaties are solemn engagements entered into between independent nations for the common development of their interests and the interests of civilization." Not only are they designed to avoid war and secure a lasting and perpetual peace, but they are designed [as our proposal is designed] to promote a friendly feeling between the people of the two countries [States]. For this reason "they should be interpreted in that broad and liberal spirit which is calculated to make for the existence of a perpetual amity, so far as it can be done without the sacrifice of individual rights or of those principles of personal liberty which lie at the foundation of our jurisprudence." Accordingly, the Joint High Commission, interpreting the treaty in this broad spirit, finds that "there are no limitations whatsoever except the judgment of the Commission" as to what "may be necessary to suitably and adequately protect and indemnify all interests." Thus, to avoid any possible injury to large public and private interests on both sides of the river, it established the joint board of control and finds it "unnecessary to consider the question of whether, under the treaty, the commission has or has not administrative or executive powers." It holds that in exercising the judicial powers given to it by the treaty, it may make the grant of permission conditional upon the construction of works to be supervised by an international board of control. In its order it provides that this board of control is to be made up of the officer of the Corps of Engineers charged with the improvement of the falls of St. Mary's River on the American side, and an officer appointed by the Canadian Government. It is made the duty of these two "to formulate rules under which the compensating works and power canals and their head gates and by-passes shall be operated so as to secure as nearly as may be the regulation of Lake Superior." And by Paragraph 17, in case this board cannot agree, the Commission itself will make the decision. Other applications, involving the construction of compensating works, were treated by the Commission in the same way. Thus the application of the St. Croix Water Power Co., incorporated by C. 203, Acts of 1899, of Maine, and the Sprague's Falls Manufacturing Co. (Ltd.), incorporated 2 Edw. VII, C. 103, Dom. Can., for the construction of a dam across the St. Croix river at Grand Falls, and a power canal to convey water to a power house, was approved on condition that all dams, sluices, by-passes, etc., shall be "under the direct control" of the Board of Control consisting of an officer to be appointed by the Governor-General in Council of Canada and one appointed by the Secretary of War of the United States, with full power to make rules, preserve records, and, in case of disagreement, to refer the matter to the Joint High Commission for final decision. The remarks of Commissioner Magrath in concurring with the decision in this case have value for us. He wishes to point out that "while not strictly pertinent to the matter before the commission, the practice by Governments of making grants of land carrying riparian rights in streams was initiated when these rights were not looked upon as being of much value, and unfortunately the practice has outlived the old condition of things. In recent years, however, owing largely to electrical transmission, power rights have acquired great importance and may properly be regarded as public utilities. It would be well for all Legislatures of both the United States and Canada to consider the desirability of retaining or acquiring these valuable assets for the benefit of the public."

The Lake of the Woods Case

What the Port of New York is to the States of New York and New Jersey, the watershed of the Lake of the Woods is to Minnesota, Manitoba and Ontario. It is 1,485 square miles in area, or about 400 square miles greater than the State of Rhode Island. The entire drainage area of the lake and its tributary waters is 26,750 square miles, an area 5,000 square miles greater than Nova Scotia, and greater than the combined areas of New Hampshire, Massachusetts, Rhode Island, Connecticut and Delaware. The lake on the map appears as only a small water between Lake Winnipeg, Canada, and Lake Superior, United States. It is the westerly point of the water boundary between the United States and Canada. But upon its rise and fall largely depends the commercial and agricultural prosperity of these communities in Canada and in the United States. In 1895, settlers on the south shore of the lake, in Minnesota, began to complain to the Department of the Interior that their lands had been submerged by high levels in Lake of the Woods, caused by the construction of a dam, and these complaints continued down to and including 1905 and 1906. The situation having grown worse, and investigation having been made both by the War Department of our country and a Canadian Government committee, the question was raised, "what rights and remedies the citizens of Minnesota will have" with regard to "diversion of these waters" and what corresponding measures should be taken with a view to the establishment of similar rights and to provide similar remedies for citizens of Canada. Overtures were made by the United States to Canada to submit these questions to the International Joint Commission. It appeared that there was doubt as to whether or not the Commission had jurisdiction, and the rights of the parties were "not rights which either now possess. They are rights which belong to their respective inhabitants and, if not voluntarily granted, can be acquired only for the purposes desired, by and through the exercise of the sovereign power to take private property for a public use." After a most painstaking engineering investigation into the whole problem, covering many volumes, the International Joint High Commission recommends that for the purpose of securing the most advantageous use of the waters of this entire watershed, and also from the standpoint of a sound, comprehensive international policy, . . . the International Joint Commission "be authorized to exercise supervision and control over the operation of all dams and regulating works extending across the international boundary. . . ." And further, that, "as a matter of sound international policy, neither Government should permit the permanent or temporary diversion out of the watershed of any waters within its jurisdiction which are tributary to the boundary waters under consideration," and which would result in any injury on the other side of the boundary, without the approval of the International Joint Commission, and that the decision of the commission in all such cases be made final. The Commission was required to consider "by what means or arrangement can the proper construction and operation of regulating works or a system or method of regulation be best secured and maintained in order to insure the adequate protection and development of all the interests involved on both sides of the boundary, with the least possible damage to all rights and interests, both public and private." In order to accomplish this task, the American Commissioners *recommend acquisition of private property,* and in their report *submit a definite plan of procedure* for the exercise of the powers of eminent domain in each of the two countries by which such private property may be acquired. They examine into the questions of law raised by these recommendations, and say that the use to which the property is to be put "would constitute a public use and authorize the taking of property for this use under the power of eminent domain and expropriation." Their observations upon the value of such a joint undertaking have value to us. "*The interdependent interests, the importance and value to both countries and their people of permanently securing all the material advantages from the use of these waters and preventing such use from hereafter being a disturbing factor between the two Governments, are of such magnitude that the rights acquired in respect thereto should be permanent and irrevocable. If acquired severally and thereafter held by the Government acquiring the same in trust for the benefit of the other the uncertainty of tenure would seriously impair the stability of these rights and probably constitute a barrier in the way of the development of the water powers of this region, because rights thus held could be renounced at will.*" They also consider the question of how the parties "can legally acquire and hold, under the jurisdiction of the other, these necessary vested rights in order to insure the satisfactory maximum water-power development in both countries this region affords, and at the same time safeguard the rights and promote the development of the interests of their respective peoples." They propound the question: "*Can a State in its public capacity hold nonterritorial property in another State or can a sovereign State limit or qualify its proprietary sovereignty by permitting another State to acquire and hold property within its territorial jurisdiction for the use and benefit of such other State within its jurisdiction or for the use and benefit of its inhabitants?*" After a careful review of authorities and the statement that "the doctrine here laid down is supported by all text writers on international law," they say: "The power of a nation to restricts its proprietary sovereignty by granting to another nation the right to acquire and hold title to land or vested rights or easements therein the same as if held by a private individual can not be questioned. Lands, rights, or easements thus acquired are held, however, subject to the political sovereignty of the nation granting the right to hold the same." For this statement they cite *Leavenworth R. R. Co. v. Howe,* 114 U. S. 525, 538. They are of opinion that this doctrine has been "universally recognized and followed by nations 'time out of mind' as appears from their treaties. The granting of this right, however, does not involve or carry *with it any surrender of political sovereignty. That remains unchanged and supreme.*" Further considering the question whether or not the two sovereignties could acquire property and thereafter hold it jointly, the American Commissioners say: "The rights, however, which both parties must have for this purpose are not rights which either now possess. They are rights which belong to their respective inhabitants and, if not voluntarily granted, can be acquired only for the purpose desired, by and through the exercise of the sovereign power to take private property for a public use. Can this power, by agreement, be exercised jointly by the high contracting parties for this purpose?" Recognizing always that whatever procedure is adopted must conform to the fundamental law of each nation, and since the law in Canada and the United States emanates from the same common source and both are protected under the same or similar rules — in the United States under a written Constitution and in Canada under rules perhaps less rigid, and more flexible — therefore, in their belief the recommendation should conform to the requirements of the Constitution of the United States. If it so conforms, " it will not likely be found inconsistent with the laws governing the taking of private property in the Dominion of Canada." " The high contracting parties," say the American Commissioners, " each possess and may exercise the power of eminent domain or expropriation in their respective jurisdictions, for their own or the public good. It follows, therefore, that in their sovereign capacity, they may *by treaty agree to do jointly and for their mutual welfare, in their respective jurisdictions, that which they are authorized to do severally.*" Indeed, they find recognition of this principle in the treaty under which they are acting, by which the two nations have clothed the Joint High Commission with " final jurisdiction in both countries in certain matters which involve the rights, obligations, or interests of either in relation to the other, or to the inhabitants of the other." There is no doubt, therefore, in their opinion, that the two countries may conclude a treaty, providing for the institution of legal proceedings in either or both countries for the taking of private property, provided the purpose of the proposed taking is a public use, and that being so "*it is clearly within the power of the high contracting parties to authorize, by treaty, the making of a special administrative agreement between them for the complete accomplishment of the purposes of that treaty or of any part thereof.*" [These careful observations of the American Commissioners, though contained in a supplemental report, are in accord in the main with the formal recommendations for control made by the Joint Commission.] This determination by an international commission of Canadian and American lawyers, taking full account of the fundamental principles of the English common law and of the limitations of the Federal Constitution, seems to be a most convincing and satisfactory precedent to guide us in the formulation of our treaty.

The European (Danube) Commission

Of all the administrative agencies that have ever been created for the purpose of carrying out the common purpose of several sovereignties, especially in the development of rivers and harbors and the improvement of commerce and navigation, none is so instructive and so valuable in experience as the Danube Commission. Two recent English writers — "The Question of the Bosphorus and Dardanelles" — Phillipson and Buxton, London, 1917 — recommend as the model for the internationalization of the Bosphorus and the Dardanelles the method of internationalization of the Danube. "In many spheres of political and commercial activity," say they (p. 237), "international co-operation has conferred great benefits on all parties concerned." "A system of internationalization means international co-operation. It is, then, manifestly in the interests of the world at large that every opportunity should be seized for internationalizing territories that have given rise to inveterate disputes, as well as waterways that are used for general international commerce and intercourse. To bring about the co-operation of States in this or that undertaking is to promote the habit of association, and to pave the way for a more thorough and comprehensive union, such as is implied in the establishment of a League of Nations subject, in the event of differences, to the arbitration of an International Court." The European Commission for the Danube (p. 241) "has achieved such success that it may be regarded as a remarkable precursor in the art of international government." The Danube played a very important part in European policy and political economy even before the present war. It traverses regions "whose rich agriculture is proverbial" (Le Danube, Baicoianu, Paris, 1917) and its great importance economically and commercially arises from the diversity of the production along its banks. It finds its source in the Grand Duchy of Baden, a distance of thirty to forty kilometers from the approach to the Rhine and about 500 to 600 kilometers "de la Mer du Nord" (North Sea). It travels through Wurtemburg and Bavaria, its branch, the Enns, dividing Lower from Upper Austria. It passes the cities of Linz and Vienna. It then takes a right oblique to the south and goes through the great fields of Hungary, passing Budapest, dividing Slavonia from Hungary. Near the Theiss it changes its direction to the southeast, touching the city of Semlin, at which point commences the front of Servia. The Danube then passes Belgrade between Servia on the south and Hungary on the north and enters

Rumania, nourishing the basin between the Carpathians and the Balkans, separating Dobrudja from Bessarabia. For a distance of four hundred kilometers it is the frontier between Rumania and Bulgaria and enters the Black Sea through three mouths, the Kilia, Sulina and St. George. It travels through nine countries, having a population of 52,783,472. (Baicoianu.)

Of course, the improvement of the navigability of the Danube is of great importance to all of the countries it traverses, but the Associated Chambers of Commerce of the United Kingdom, addressing the Secretary of State for Foreign Affairs, the Right Honorable Earl Granville, K. G., on April 27, 1882, said "it is of great importance to the trade and commerce of this country [Great Britain] that the navigation of the River Danube should be as free as possible, and that British ships, as well as the vessels of other maritime nations, should be allowed to move and carry cargo to and from, and between, all the ports on that river with the same freedom and on the same terms and conditions as vessels belonging to States having territory bordering on the river." (Parlimentary Papers, 1882, Vol. LXXX, London, 1882.) The tonnage leaving Sulina in 1881 amounted to 793,454 tons. The annual receipts in 1881 were Fr. 3,448,190, c. 60. The expenses were Fr. 2,606,095, c. 39. Statistics of the expenditure, debt, sinking fund, etc., are to be found in this volume, as well as in Baicoianu. (See also Encyclopædia Britannica, 11th Edition, title "Danube," p. 819 et seq.)

The history of the various European controversies over the Danube is told by Baicoianu at length, and an excellent map showing in colors the several sovereign States through which the Danube runs and the effect of the several treaties of Paris, 1856, Berlin, 1878, and of London, 1883, is to be found attached to the book of Geffcken (Berlin, 1883), "La Question du Danube."

The European convulsion of 1853, resulting in the Treaty of Paris (1856), afforded an opportunity for the harmonization of the political and economic questions affected by the Danube, and a convenient grouping of a considerable number of States. The principle emphasized by Grotius and expounded more fully by Vattel and other jurists, that navigation of international rivers should be free, was proclaimed in November, 1792, by the provisional Executive Council of France in regard to the Scheldt. This proclamation has been designated "the first charter of contemporary fluvial liberties." (E. Engelhardt: "Du régime conventionnel des fleuves internationaux," Paris, 1879.) In 1814, the Treaty of Paris (Art. V) declared the freedom of navigation on the Scheldt, and on the Rhine from the point at which it becomes navigable to the sea. The following year the final act of the Congress of Vienna stipulated that "the Powers whose States are separated or crossed by the same navigable River engage to regulate, by common consent, all that regards its navigation." And they agreed to the appointment of a commission which should assemble within six months thereafter and which should follow the basic principle established by the Article. Article CIX laid down this fundamental principle and said that "the navigation of the Rivers, along their whole course, referred to in the preceding Article, from the point where each of them becomes navigable, to its mouth, shall be entirely free, and shall not, in respect to Commerce, be prohibited to any one; it being understood that the Regulations established with regard to the Police of this navigation shall be respected, as they will be framed alike for all, and as favourable as possible to the Commerce of all nations." Article CX provides that the system for collection of duties and maintenance of the police "shall be, as nearly as possible, the same along the whole course of the River; and shall also extend, unless particular circumstances prevent it, to those of its Branches and Junctions, which, in their navigable course, separate or traverse different States."

To control the navigation, and as a means of communication between the States of the Rhine, it was agreed that a central commission should be appointed, comprising delegates named by the various bordering States. The Treaty of Paris come to between Great Britain, Austria, France, Prussia, Russia, Sardinia and Turkey (March 30, 1856) provided as follows:

"Art. XV. The Act of the Congress of Vienna having established the principles intended to regulate the Navigation of Rivers which separate or traverse different States, the Contracting Powers stipulate among themselves that those principles shall in future be equally applied to the Danube and its Mouths. They declare that its arrangement henceforth forms a part of the Public Law of Europe, and take it under their Guarantee.

" The navigation of the Danube cannot be subjected to any impediment or charge not expressly provided for by the Stipulations contained in the following Articles: In consequence, there shall not be levied any Toll founded solely upon the fact of the Navigation of the River, nor any Duty upon the Goods which may be on board of Vessels. The Regulations of Police and of Quarantine to be established for the safety of the States separated or traversed by that River, shall be so framed as to facilitate, as much as possible, the passage of Vessels. With the exception of such Regulations, no obstacle whatever shall be opposed to Free Navigation.

"Article XVI. With the view to carry out the arrangements of the preceding Article, a Commission, in which Great Britain, Austria, France, Prussia, Russia, Sardinia, and Turkey, shall each be represented by one delegate, shall be charged to designate and to cause to be executed the Works necessary below Isatcha, to clear the Mouths of the Danube, as well as the neighboring parts of the Sea, from the sands and other impediments which obstruct them, in order to put that part of the River and the said parts of the Sea in the best possible state for Navigation.

" In order to cover the Expenses of such Works, as well as of the establishments intended to secure and to facilitate the Navigation at the Mouths of the Danube, fixed Duties, of a suitable rate, settled by the Commission by a majority of votes, may be levied, on the express condition that, in this respect as in every other, the Flags of all Nations shall be treated on the footing of perfect equality."

By Article XVII a commission is established to be composed of delegates from Austria, Bavaria, the Sublime Porte, and Wurtemburg (one for each of these Powers), to whom are to be added Commissioners from the three Danubian Principalities, which nomination shall have been approved by the Porte. " This Commission, which shall be permanent: 1. Shall prepare Regulations of Navigation and River Police; 2, Shall remove the impediments, of whatever nature they may be, which still prevent the application to the Danube of the Arrangements of the Treaty of

Vienna; 3. Shall order and cause to be executed the necessary Works throughout the whole course of the River; and 4. Shall, after the dissolution of the European Commission, see to maintaining the Mouths of the Danube and the neighboring parts of the Sea in a navigable state."

"Art. XVIII. It is understood that the European Commission shall have completed its task, and that the River Commission shall have finished the Works described in the preceding Article, under Nos. 1 and 2, within the period of two years. The signing Powers assembled in Conference having been informed of that fact, shall, after having placed it on record, pronounce the Dissolution of the European Commission, and from that time the permanent River Commission shall enjoy the same powers as those with which the European Commission shall have until then been vested.

"Art. XIX. In order to insure the execution of the Regulations which shall have been established by common agreement, in conformity with the principles above declared, each of the Contracting Powers shall have the right to station, at all times, Two Light Vessels at the Mouths of the Danube."

In 1865, the European Commission created by the treaties (See Vol. XII, Hertslet's " Treaties," p. 884) having succeeded " after nine years' work in realizing important improvements in the system of navigation — notably, by the construction of two piers at the mouth of the Sulina branch, which have had the effect of admitting into this embouchure vessels of a large draught of water — by the execution of works of correction and cleansing in the course of the same branch — by raising wrecks, and establishing a system of buoys — by the erection of a lighthouse at the mouth of the St. George — by the institution of a regular life boat service, and by the creation of a seaman's hospital at Sulina — lastly, by the provisional regulation of the different services connected with the navigation between Isaktcha and the sea;" the Powers, representing Great Britain, Austria, France, Italy, Prussia, Russia and Turkey, do ratify and establish the rights of the parties by the succeeding articles. Article I provides that all the works and establishments " shall continue to be devoted exclusively to the use of the navigation of the Danube, and can never be turned aside from this object for any motive whatever; *to this end they are placed under the guarantee and protection of international law.*" By the same Article, the European Commission "shall continue charged, to the exclusion of all interference whatever, to administer these works and establishments for the advantage of the navigation, to watch over their maintenance and preservation, and to give to them all the development that the requirements of the navigation may demand." By Article II there is "specially reserved to the European Commission, or to the authority that shall succeed it, the power to design and cause to be carried out all the works that may be deemed necessary, in the event of its being wished to render permanent the improvements, until now of a temporary character, in the branch and at the mouth of the Sulina, and to prolong the piers at this mouth according as the state of the Bar Channel may require it."

By Article VI it is provided "that on neither bank of the river, either in the port of Sulina or St. George, shall there be constructed either by the territorial authorities, by commercial or navigation companies, or by private individuals, any landing jetties, quays, or other establishments of the same nature, of which the plans have not been communicated to the European Commission, and recognized as being in conformity with the general plan of the quays, and as tending in no wise to compromise the effect of the works of improvement."

By Article VIII administrative power is vested in an Inspector General of the Lower Danube and the Captain of the Port of Sulina. Annexed to these articles is a code governing the policing of the Sulina Roads and Port, regulations for vessels crossing and passing one another, towage rules, discharge of ballast, lighterage, etc., etc., with a chapter of penalties resembling a very substantial section of our Penal Code. Phillipson and Buxton ("The Question of the Bosphorus and Dardenelles," p. 245) say that this institution is "unprecedented in international law and usage" and is "a kind of European syndicate, enjoying practically full independence and exercising many functions attaching to sovereignty." Demorgny, a French writer ("La Question du Danube," Paris, 1911, p. 176) also refers to this Commission as a sort of temporary embodiment of sovereignty granted to it in the interest of humanity in general, having administrative, executive, legislative and judicial power. Say Phillipson and Buxton: "Indeed . . . in many respects [it] is in the position of an autonomous State." It is not amenable to the jurisdiction of Rumania, through whose territory it goes. It may negotiate without intermediary with neighboring States. It has a treasury derived from the tolls which it collects for the use of the works which it has built. It publishes its budget in every country that it represents. It possesses a flotilla which flies its own distinctive flag. It may contract loans and dispose of lands. It is both a deliberative and an executive body. It has the power to examine any matter whatever relating to navigation on the Danube and legislates police regulations, shipping rules, tariff scales, plans of necessary works, etc., and its resolutions carried by a majority of votes, become law. As an executive body it carries its own decisions into operation. To accomplish this, it employs a staff of specialists. It punishes violations of its own rules and regulations, and as a supreme tribunal reviews the judgments pronounced by the Navigation Inspector or the Superintendent of the Port of Sulina, who are the judges of first instance. The light vessels of the Powers stationed at the mouth of the Danube are the police force to secure the execution of the legislative, executive and judicial decisions of this Commission.

In 1865, as we have seen, the works and establishments of the Commission were declared to be neutralized so as to be immune from attack in case of war. At the Conference in Paris in 1866, its term was extended for five years. By the Treaty of London, 1871, Russia was allowed to maintain a fleet in the Black Sea, but the neutrality of the European Commission was protected by additional guarantees. Its powers were then extended, also, for twelve years. In the Russo-Turkish War of 1877, the operations of the belligerents interfered with the free navigation of the Danube, and complaints were made against them, but it seems to have been held that the transactions relating to the river did not entirely make of it a neutral zone and imposed upon belligerents merely the duty to respect the works and establishments of the Commission, to impede the navigation as little as possible, and to restore it as quickly as possible in case of any interference with it. Nevertheless, by a Treaty of Berlin of 1878, all fortresses between the Iron Gates and the sea were to be demolished, no new ones were to be constructed, and within these limits no warships other than light vessels used for police and custom purposes were to navigate the river. At this time Rumania, having been made independent, was given representation in the Commission and its sphere of operations was extended to Galatz. By the subsequent treaties of 1883 and 1904, the authority of the Commission was renewed and enlarged. By the Treaty of 1904, provision was made for its continuance for successive periods of three years, but to each of the eight States represented the right was reserved to dissolve the treaty by giving notice a year before the termination of the triennial period.

This great institution of Europe, supported by these several solemn treaties and by international law, has been treated by Germany with a contempt equal only to that which she has paid to similar treaties and institutions. Having subjugated Rumania, she negotiated a "peace" by which she eliminated entirely the Entente Powers from any further participation in the Danube Commission, changed the Commission into the "Danube Mouth Commission," continuing it "as a permanent institution with the powers, privileges, and obligations hitherto appertaining to it," but limiting its organization to "representatives of the States situated on the Danube or the European coasts of the Black Sea." (See Treaty of Bucharest, signed May 7, in "The New Europe," Vol. VII, No. 85, May 30, 1918, at p. 166.) On the 19th of May the Entente Ministers informed the Rumanian Government that they did not recognize that portion of the treaty which dealt with the navigation of the Danube (Idem, p. 166). Nevertheless, even Germany recognizes the principle and effectiveness of internationalization of ports and rivers in this Treaty of Bucharest. The system and method is continued, though the participating Powers are changed.

Sir Charles Hartley, Chief Engineer of the European Danube Commission from 1856 to 1907, in a paper contributed to the Institution of Civil Engineers in 1873 (Vol. XXXVI) (See Encyclopædia Britannica, 11th edition, title "Danube," p. 822) gave a graphic description of the state of the Sulina mouth when the Commission began its work in 1856. "The entrance to the Sulina branch," said he, "was a wild open seaboard strewn with wrecks, the hulls and masts of which, sticking out of the submerged sandbanks, gave to mariners the only guide where the deepest channel was to be found. The depth of the channel varied from 7 to 11 feet, and was rarely more than 9 feet.

"The site now occupied by wide quays extending several miles in length was then entirely covered with water when the sea rose a few inches above ordinary level, and that even in a perfect calm; the banks of the river near the mouth were only indicated by clusters of wretched hovels built on piles and by narrow patches of sand skirted by tall weeds, the only vegetable product of the vast swamps beyond."

Prior to the time when the great improvements were made an average of only 2,000 vessels, with a tonnage capacity of 400,000 tons, visited the Danube, and of this number more than three-fourths loaded either the whole or part of their cargoes from lighters in the Sulina roadstead, where, "lying off a lee shore, they were frequently exposed to the greatest danger." "Shipwrecks," says Sir Charles Hartley, "were of common occurrence, and occasionally the number of disasters was appalling. One dark winter night in 1855, during a terrific gale, 24 sailing ships and 60 lighters went ashore off the mouth and upwards of 300 persons perished." The method by which all of the improvements have been made was by levying tolls upon the vessels entering the Danube. By the Treaty of Galatz, April 30, 1868, Great Britain, Austria, France, Italy, Prussia and Turkey agreed to contract a loan for the completion of the works at Galatz. This loan was not to exceed £135,000. This loan was made September 29, 1868, through Messrs. Bischoffsheim and Goldschmidt, and was paid off in full prior to January 15, 1884, all the nations interested in guaranteeing the loan being thus relieved of further liability. (See Declaration by Percy Sanderson, Her Majesty's Commissioner for the Danube, Vol. XVII, Hertslet's "Commercial Treaties," p. 1039.) The Commission now has an average annual income of about £80,000 derived from taxes paid by ships when leaving the river. The normal annual expenditure amounts to £56,000, while £24,000 is generally allotted to extraordinary works, such as new cuttings. (See Encyclopaeedia Britannica, 11th edition, title "Danube," p. 823.) Between 1857 and 1905 over one and three-quarter million pounds sterling were spent on engineering works, including the construction of quays, lighthouses, workshops and buildings, and from being a collection of mud hovels Sulina has grown into a town of 5,000 inhabitants, has a well organized hospital where all merchant sailors receive gratuitous treatment, and has lighthouses, quays, floating elevators and an efficient pilot service, which all combine to make Sulina "a first-class port." (See Encyclopædia Britannica, 11th edition, title "Danube," p. 823.)

Other Examples of International Government

Reinsch, in his "Public International Unions" (Ginn & Co., 1911), says: ". . . the realm of international organization is an accomplished fact." (Introduction, p. 4.) At that time (1911) there were already in existence over forty-five public international unions composed of States, of which thirty are provided with bureaus or commissions. These include unions for postal and telegraphic communications, and for improvement in the means and methods employed by them. "International co-operation," says Reinsch, "has become an absolute necessity to States, along all the various lines of national enterprise." Again (p. 137), Reinsch says: "International co-operation may, in the present state of our civilization, *be represented as an ethical duty.* No State has the right, by stubborn aloofness, . . . to exclude its citizens from the advantages of civilization. But this ethical duty is reenforced by a very practical necessity, which is plain to any common-sense administration."

"*International Government*" (1916), a recent book written for the purpose of establishing the practicability of an international authority to settle points of difference among nations, consists of a study made by L. S. Woolf and a committee of the Fabian Society, with an introduction by Bernard Shaw. Part II gives many examples of the internationalization of administration, reviewing the theory and experience of the *Universal Postal Union, the Telegraphic Union, the international control of wireless, of railways, of other means of communication, the international regulation of public health and the prevention of epidemic diseases, of international monetary unions, sugar commissions, etc., etc.*

It would unduly lengthen this report to discuss in detail the various legal phases of the instrumentalities that have been devised by governments, legislative, executive and judicial, to effect a common purpose. It has not been the purpose to make a complete resumé of all precedents upon the subject, but to make clear the legal theory and to cull those special precedents that have value in the framing of our interstate treaty and, in addition, perhaps fix guideposts for the determination of legal controversies that may hereafter arise.

The Enforcement of an Interstate Treaty

The private client about to enter into an agreement asks his lawyer how it may be enforced. The sovereign States in this situation may properly ask: "If we enter into such a treaty, how is it enforcible?" So far as immediate pecuniary obligation is assumed, it is confined (Article XIV) to equal annual appropriation of such sum as the Commission and the two Governors may recommend to the Legislatures. But in the future, it is reasonably certain that the Legislatures will desire to vest the Port Authority with power to incur obligations mutually binding upon each State. Happily, neither State need resort to war to enforce the obligations of a compact between them. The treaties between two States who are members of the Federal Union are not mere "scraps of paper."

By the compact between Virginia and West Virginia for the purpose of constituting the area of the State of West Virginia, the new State, coincident with its existence, became bound for and assumed to pay its just proportion of the previous public debt of Virginia. A compact was made with the approval of Congress. In 1906, West Virginia having failed to pay its share of this debt, suit was brought in equity in the United States Supreme Court and judgment rendered in 1915 for $12,393,929.50, with interest. (See 234 U. S. 117, 58 L. ed. 1243, 34 Sup. Ct. Rep. 889.) West Virginia having failed to pay this judgment, a petition was presented by the State of Virginia to the United States Supreme Court for a writ of mandamus to compel the levy of a tax by the Legislature of West Virginia to meet the amount thus adjudicated.

The United States Supreme Court in its recent decision in *Virginia v. West Virginia* (246 U. S. 565) holds that the Federal Supreme Court has power to enforce by appropriate proceedings a judgment rendered against a State by that Court in the exercise of its original jurisdiction of controversies, and that, notwithstanding the rights reserved to the States by the Federal Constitution, the United States Supreme Court may exert authority over the governmental powers and agencies possessed by the State to the extent necessary to discharge the State's obligation. In this case, Chief Justice White reviews the early history of the formation of the Constitution of the United States and the reasons for delegation of power to the United States Supreme Court to settle controversies between the States. He considers two questions: (a) The power of Congress to legislate to secure the enforcement of a contract between two States; and (b) the appropriate remedy which may, by the judicial power, be exerted to enforce the judgment. He says: "The vesting in Congress of complete power to control agreements between states, that is, to authorize them when deemed advisable and to refuse to sanction them when disapproved, clearly rested upon the conception that Congress, as the repository not only of legislative power but of primary authority to maintain armies and declare war, speaking for all the states and for their protection, was concerned with such agreements, and therefore was virtually endowed with the ultimate power of final agreement which was withdrawn from state authority and brought within the Federal power. It follows as a necessary implication that the power of Congress to refuse or to assent to a contract between states carried *with it the right, if the contract was assented to and hence became operative by the will of Congress, to see to its enforcement.* . . .

"Having thus the power to provide for the execution of the contract, it must follow that the power is plenary and complete; limited, of course, as we have just said, by the general rule that the acts done for its exertion must be relevant and appropriate to the power. This being true, it further follows, as we have already seen, that by the very fact that the national power is paramount in the area over which it extends, the lawful exertion of its authority by Congress to compel compliance with the obligation resulting from the contract between the two states which it approved is not circumscribed by the powers reserved to the states." "Indeed," says Judge White, "the argument that the recognition of such a power in Congress is subversive of our constitutional institutions from its mere statement proves to the contrary, since at last it comes to insisting that any one state may, by violating its obligations under the Constitution, take away the rights of another, and thus destroy constitutional government. Obviously if it be conceded that no power obtains to enforce as against a state its duty under the Constitution in one respect, and to prevent it from doing wrong to another state, it would follow that the same principle would have to be applied to wrongs done by other states, and thus the government under the Constitution would be not an indissoluble union of indestructible states, but a government composed of states each having the potency with impunity to wrong or degrade another,— a result which would inevitably lead to a destruction of the union between them." And Judge White reminds West Virginia that to maintain the proposition which it now urges "would compel a disregard of the very principles which led to the carving out of that state from the territory of Virginia; in other words, to disregard and overthrow the doctrines irrevocably settled by the great controversy of the Civil War, which, in their ultimate aspect, find their consecration in the Amendments to the Constitution which followed." Which statement, coming from a Civil War veteran who wore the gray, is pregnant with meaning. The Court decides that whether Congress shall go first in providing for the enforcement of the compact, or whether the Supreme Court shall act in the first instance, it reserves for further consideration, and that branch of the subject it sets down for discussion at the next term (the one just past). Nevertheless, it gives what may be regarded as a very broad hint to West Virginia that the Court is "fain to believe," having determined "the right judicially to enforce by appropriate proceedings as against a state and its governmental agencies" and "the constitutional power of Congress to legislate in a twofold way" — "that if we refrain now from passing upon the questions stated, *we may be spared in the future the necessity of exerting compulsory power against one of the states of the Union to compel it to discharge a plain duty resting upon it under the Constitution.*" Besides, says Judge White, even assuming " that both the requirements of duty and the suggestions of self-interest may fail to bring about the result stated," the Court nevertheless thinks, because of " the character of the parties and the nature of the controversy,— a contract approved by Congress and subject to be by it enforced, — we should reserve further action in order that full opportunity may be afforded to Congress to exercise the power which it undoubtedly possesses."

This would seem to be a full and adequate indication of what Congress or the United States Supreme Court or both may do to a State which refractorily refuses to meet its solemn obligation to another, and in this respect it is always important to bear in mind that, by the Constitution itself, there is a grant of judicial power to the United States Supreme Court by the respective States, which power is one of original jurisdiction. The States waive their exemption from judicial power as sovereigns of original inherent right by their own grant of its exercise over themselves in such cases, a power which they would not grant to any inferior tribunal. By this grant, the United States Supreme Court acquired jurisdiction over the parties by their own consent and delegated authority *as their agent* for exercising the judicial power of the United States in the cases specified. (See *Rhode Island v. Massachusetts,* 12 Peters 725, 9 L. ed. 1233.) (In footnote 3 to the decision in *Virginia v. West Virginia* is a list of litigations between States which have come before the Supreme Court of the United States.)

State Limitations Upon Borrowing Capacity

The Constitution of the State of New York limits the borrowing capacity of the City of New York, and the Constitution of the State of New Jersey limits the borrowing capacity of the State: By Article 4, Section 6, paragraph 4, of the New Jersey Constitution, the Legislature may not in any manner create any debt or liability of the State exceeding $100,000 without the previous approval of the people at a general election. This provision the courts of New Jersey have held has no application to local or municipal indebtedness. *Van Cleve v. Passaic Valley Sewerage*

Commissioners, 71 N. J. L. 183 and 574, 58 Atl. R. 796, 60 Atl. R. 214. See also *People v. Flagg,* 46 N. Y. 401, 406; *Cass v. Dillon,* 2 *Ohio St.* 607, 613; *Clark v. City of Janesville,* 10 *Wis.* 136; *Bushnell v. Belvit,* Id. 195, 211; *Pattison v. Board of Supervisors,* 13 Cal. 175, 182; Cooley on Constitutional Limitations (7th ed.) 325.

The capacity of the new Port authority, as a body corporate or politic, to borrow money is not limited, therefore, by the constitutional limitations on the borrowing capacity of the State of New Jersey or the City of New York. The argument that this is to create a power which the State itself does not possess is completely disposed of by Paine, J., in *Clark v. City of Janesville,* 10 Wis. 136, at pp. 172, 173: "The State may have power to grant a power, and at the same time not have power to execute it. This is clearly shown by reference to this very prohibition [constitutional debt limitation] against its being a party in carrying on internal improvements. No one doubts that it may authorize a railroad company to build a railroad. But it could not build one itself. And is that deriving power from a source where it does not exist? Clearly not. Because the State has the power to grant the authority, and is prohibited only from being itself a party in its execution. The difficulty with this objection is, that it confounds the power of granting a right, with the power of being a party to its exercise; whereas the two are essentially distinct."

Conclusions

From all of which it would appear that the States of New Jersey and New York may join in the consummation either of an original treaty, or, preferably, one amendatory of and supplementary to the Treaty of 1834, preserving in full the sovereignty of each State, but pledging each to the other perpetual co-operation in the development of the port which is common to both. For the purpose of carrying out the comprehensive development of the port, they may create an agency vested with as little or as great power as it shall please the States to grant. Included in this power is the power to take and hold real estate, to construct, maintain and operate every conceivable kind of terminal facility, and to regulate, within the limitations arising from the paramount power of

Congress, and to govern the operation of such facilities. Such a body may be authorized to borrow money upon the credit of the States, to the extent that each State is willing to pledge its credit or to borrow upon its own credit. Upon its acquisition of property, it may itself hold and operate it or lease it to private enterprise upon satisfactory terms. It can receive grants of the power of eminent domain which each State possesses. It can receive power from Congress to the extent that it pleases Congress to grant power, and like the United States towards the Panama Canal, the two States may declare that they create and hold all of these powers and properties under *a sacred trust — for the benefit of the nation as a whole.*

It is clearly feasible to leave municipal power where it now resides, and is essential, as we have seen, not to disturb those property and contractual rights which are protected by the Federal Constitution. Without disturbing private grants or the rights of municipalities, the great power of the States to *regulate* may be exercised in the interest of promoting navigation and commerce. In short, the underlying principles governing such action on the part of the two States may be regarded as fairly well settled, and the problem largely one of details and form. The time has come — indeed, is already here — when the need for constructive planning is imperative.

It would be a mistake, however, to take for granted that the public generally — that even members of the legal profession generally — in both States will be prepared to aid in the formulation of such a treaty without the assistance of a preliminary survey of legal theory and precedents bearing upon the problem.

Dated, New York, December 2, 1918.

JULIUS HENRY COHEN,
Counsel.

APPENDIX C

LEGISLATION ESTABLISHING THE COMMISSION

Laws of 1917 of the State of New York

CHAPTER 426.

An Act to establish a commission to act jointly with a similar Commission of the State of New Jersey in the investigation of Port conditions at the Port of New York and to submit a comprehensive report recommending the proper policy that shall be pursued for the best interests of the entire Port of New York, and the legislation, State and Federal, that will be necessary to make such recommendations effective, and making an appropriation for the expenses of said Commission.

Became a law May 8, 1917, with the approval of the Governor. Passed, three-fifths being present.

The People of the State of New York, represented in Senate and Assembly, do enact as follows:

Commission created; duties.

Section 1. The Governor shall appoint three Commissioners who shall have power on the part of the State of New York to meet Commissioners appointed, or who may be appointed, under or by virtue of a law of the Legislature of the State of New Jersey, to negotiate or agree upon a joint report, recommending a policy to be pursued by the State of New York, the State of New Jersey and the United States by legislative enactment or treaty or otherwise, to the end that said Port shall be efficiently and constructively organized and furnished with modern methods of piers, rail and water and freight facilities and adequately protected in the event of war. Before making such report, such Commission shall make a thorough investigation of Port conditions in this country and shall take and employ such engineering, legal or other professional skill and assistance as it may need for the effective working out of a comprehensive and adequate interstate and Federal Port policy, to meet commercial needs in times of peace and the protection of the harbor and adjacent localities in times of war.

§ 2. The Commissioners appointed pursuant to the provisions of this act shall be paid the necessary expenses incurred in the performance of their duties, but shall serve without compensation. They shall select one of their number as Chairman and may employ a Secretary and such other assistants as are needed in the performance of their duties. The sum of twenty-five thousand dollars ($25,000), or so much thereof as may be necessary, shall be hereby appropriated out of any moneys in the State treasury not otherwise appropriated, for the expenses of the Commission. The moneys hereby appropriated shall be paid out by the State treasurer on the warrant of the comptroller upon vouchers audited by the Chairman of the said Commission.

Expenses; no compensation.

Chairman and employees.

Appropriations.

§ 3. This act shall take effect immediately.

Laws of 1917 of the State of New Jersey

CHAPTER 130.

An Act to establish a Commission to act jointly with a similar Commission of the State of New York in the investigation of Port conditions at the Port of New York, and to submit a comprehensive report recommending the proper policy that shall be pursued for the best interests of the entire Port of New York; and the legislation, State and Federal, that will be necessary to make such recommendations effective; and making an appropriation for the expenses of said Commission.

BE IT ENACTED *by the Senate and General Assembly of the State of New Jersey:*

1. The Governor shall appoint three Commissioners who shall have power on the part of the State of New Jersey to meet commissioners appointed, or who may be appointed, under or by virtue of a law of the Legis-

Commission to investigate Port conditions.

lature of the State of New York, to negotiate or agree upon a joint report recommending a policy to be pursued by the State of New Jersey, the State of New York and the United States by legislative enactment or treaty or otherwise, to the end that said Port shall be efficiently and constructively organized and furnished with modern methods of piers, rail and water and freight facilities, and adequately protected in the event of war.

Duties.

Before making such report such Commission shall make a thorough study of Port conditions in this country, and shall take and employ such engineering, legal or other professional skill and assistance as it may need for the effective working out of a comprehensive and adequate interstate and Federal Port policy, to meet commercial needs in times of peace and the protection of the harbor and adjacent localities in times of war.

Expenses met.

2. The commissioners appointed pursuant to the provisions of this act shall be paid the necessary expenses incurred in the performance of their duties, but shall serve without compensation.

Officers and assistants.

They shall select one of their number as Chairman, and may employ a Secretary and such other assistants as are needed in the performance of their duties.

Appropriations.

The sum of seven thousand five hundred dollars ($7,500), or so much thereof as may be necessary, is hereby appropriated out of any moneys in the State treasury not otherwise appropriated, when included in any supplemental appropriation bill; and the sum of ten thousand dollars ($10,000), or so much thereof as may be necessary, is hereby appropriated out of any moneys in the State treasury not otherwise appropriated, when included in any annual appropriation bill, for the expenses of the Commission. The moneys hereby appropriated shall be paid out of the State Treasurer upon warrant of the Comptroller, upon vouchers signed by the Chairman of the said Commission.

3. This act shall take effect immediately.

Approved March 26, 1917.

New York, New Jersey port and harbor development commission.
...Progress report 1919.

www.ingramcontent.com/pod-product-compliance
Lightning Source LLC
LaVergne TN
LVHW011203110826
845150LV00006B/1300